Father Thaddeus

The Franciscans in England, 1600-1850 : being an authentic account of the second English province of Friars Minor

I0741048

Father Thaddeus

The Franciscans in England, 1600-1850 : being an authentic account of the second English province of Friars Minor

ISBN/EAN: 9783743462724

Manufactured in Europe, USA, Canada, Australia, Japa

Cover: Foto ©Lupo / pixelio.de

Manufactured and distributed by brebook publishing software (www.brebook.com)

Father Thaddeus

The Franciscans in England, 1600-1850 : being an authentic account of the second English province of Friars Minor

FATHER JOHN GENNINGS.

(From the Portrait at West Gorton, Manchester.)

THE FRANCISCANS IN ENGLAND

1600–1850

BEING AN AUTHENTIC ACCOUNT OF THE SECOND ENGLISH PROVINCE OF FRIARS MINOR

BY THE

REV. FATHER THADDEUS, O.F.M.

Author of "THE PILGRIM'S MAY WREATH," "MARY FORESHADOWED,"
"GLITTERING STARS ON OUR LADY'S MANTLE," "LIFE OF
BLESSED JOHN FOREST," ETC.

Generatio præterit, et generatio advenit. Tu autem, Domine,
in æternum permanes. *Eccles.* i. *Ps.* ci.

One generation passeth away, and another generation cometh;
Thou, O Lord, endurest for ever.

LONDON AND LEAMINGTON
ART AND BOOK COMPANY
1898

Nibil obstat :

> Fr. Alfredus Mc Laughlin,
>> Minister Provincialis.

Londini, 1 Maji, 1897.

Imprimatur :

> ✠ Herbertus Cardinalis Vaughan,
>> Archiepiscopus Westmonasteriensis.

1 Maji, 1897.

PREFACE.

Two considerations have chiefly induced me to write the following pages.

The first is that inquiries are not unfrequently made, both by priests and lay people, concerning our brethren of the Second Province. The desired information is not forthcoming without much reading and study. When tracing one individual, you fall in with others, for whom you may again have to look ere long. It appears therefore desirable to collect all the evidence, from which inquirers may be able to glean what they seek.

In the second place I feel convinced that the subject matter of this work is in itself edifying. The various details of the history of the illustrious Order of St. Francis, which is bound up with the history of the Catholic Church, and the incidents connected with the English Franciscan Province, which has supplied many labourers for the English missions, are well worthy of our attention. And those who peruse this book will, I trust, not spend their time unprofitably.

As I wish to be understood by all, and some of my readers are perhaps not well acquainted with the Franciscan Order, I have thought it necessary to give, as briefly as possible, a general idea of the Order, and also of the first English Franciscan Province. This will be found in Chapters II. and III.

In a few cases where useful information could be gathered from existing authors, I have thought it but right to avail myself of it, and reference to these sources will be found in the proper places. With these few exceptions all the materials for this work have been collected from the writings of the old Franciscans.

CONTENTS.

List of Illustrations.

CHAPTER I.

FATHER ANTHONY PARKINSON, in his remarkable work on the *Antiquities of the English Franciscans*, in which he gives the history of the first Province of the Order in England, also makes mention of the foundation of the second by Father Gennings, and then adds : " But I will not go beyond my prefixed bounds of the old Province. So I leave the history of the new one for a better head and pen than mine are."

It is to be regretted that a man of his learning and ability did not bring down the history to his own day ; he would have covered a century full of interesting events, then, in a manner, still fresh in men's minds, and consequently easier to chronicle ; and he would thus have lightened the task of whosoever should carry on his work. But we must also admit that it is not always safe or prudent to narrate events that are still in a manner present, or the effects of which have not passed away. Now, however, we can confidently take up the pen, and treat the subject before us without fear of giving offence to anyone.

The English Franciscan Recollects have undoubtedly deserved well of Religion and of their country. They had generally about forty fathers on the English mission, when times were bad and priests were scarce, whilst others, on the other side of the Channel, almost within sight of our shores, were engaged in training future missionaries, or endeavouring by every means in their power to promote both the spiritual and temporal welfare of English nuns. No one can gainsay Father Parkinson's statement: "One truth," he says, "I dare venture to assert, which is that, considering the time of its date, and slender number of its members, this second Province is as holy and as learned as the former, and may vie with any community of English religious men." Let it not be thought that these words are mere idle boasting: the second Province counted men of talent, learning and piety. It had its glorious band of martyrs and confessors of the faith. It possessed men filled with zeal and charity: they worked well, and worked with fruit. From among many instances, we take by way of illustration Father Hall's list of converts, taken from a letter dated May 8, 1737.

John Cotterill, from the village of Solihull.
Mary Barton, from same.
Thomas Fenton, from same.
Richard Dawler, from same.
Anne Back, from same.
Ursula Overton, from same.
Anne Vaux, from same.
Bridget Roach, from same.
Jane Gleaves, from same.
Michael Brooks, from same.
Mary Brooks, from same.
Jane Joyce, from same.
Thomas Millard, from same.
Elizabeth Smith, from same.
Jane Smith, from same.
Elizabeth Roach, from same.
Elizabeth Madew, from same.
Jane Joseph, from same.
Mary Ross, from Wakegreen.
Jane Clark, from Ansley.
Thomas Cotton, from Uttoxeter.
Jane Wilde, from Tamworth.
Sarah Wilde, from same.
Catherine Pidgeon, from same.
Mary Platt, from Birmingham.
William Clare, from same.
Mary O'Brian, from same.

Richard Wheel, from same.
Francis Renshaw, from same.
Daniel Francis, from same.
Lydia Hichcote, from Edgbaston.
Samuel Jefferies, from same.
Anne Kempster, from same.
William Grafton, from Baddesley.
Anne Burton, from same.

Susan Silvester, from same.
Anne Newey, from same.
Charles Potter, from Wootten.
James Howard, from same.
Elizabeth Alport, from Bellemore.
Elizabeth Heveningham, from Piphall.
Edward Moore, from same.
Elizabeth Smith, from Yardley.

At that time Father Hall had probably been about a dozen years on the mission.

Does not a shadow of sadness pass across our minds when we reflect that this glorious second Province dwindled away and is no more! But Divine Providence cannot be mistaken in its wise dispositions: God knows how His glory can best be promoted. When the second Province was as it were at the last gasp, and the Franciscan Order was all but extinct in England, it suddenly seemed to rise to a new life, like the phenix from its ashes. And as the seal of the first Province had been handed to Father Gennings by one who was its last representative, so once again the seal of the second was delivered by the old Franciscans to their brethren, who have long used it.

A very interesting and rather complex question presents itself here, which we shall try to answer. What caused the decline of this once flourishing English Franciscan Province? To attribute it solely to the violent suppression of the establishment at Douai would seem to be a mistake. The loss of St. Bonaventure's College was indeed one of the causes; but let us consider other facts which, if less striking, are none the less real. Father Gennings and his companions proposed to themselves, as their primary object, self-sanctification and perfection by means of religious observance; then afterwards the mission, the salvation of souls, the conversion of England. Young men were trained and moulded at Douai, but when ordained, only those who were judged fit were allowed to come to England; the others were kept in Flanders. Those that came were apostolic men, real missionaries, filled with a desire for martyrdom. But as time went on, residences were multiplied, and for these fathers had to be found. The secondary object was taking the place of the primary end. Moreover, circumstances had changed here in England: there was no longer any fear of being cast into prison, hanged, drawn and quartered for being a priest; religion was reviving and spreading; the Church was resuming by degrees its normal condition. It is questionable whether the Religious Orders were worth preserving as they then were; or had the time not rather come for putting them on their proper footing? A regular must live in community, in the observance of his rule; otherwise he will by degrees lose the religious spirit.

Scarcely had the eighteenth century reached the middle of its course when we begin to perceive a diminution in the number of vocations for the Franciscan Province. It looked as if the cessation of the persecution, and the peace and security which English Catholics began to enjoy, had lessened their religious fervour, and the charity of many seemed to be growing cold. The scarcity steadily increased, and made itself more felt as time went on, causing no small amount of apprehension and inconvenience.

But, it may be urged, there were fathers enough left after the French Revolution to form communities. I answer first that for some years the Franciscans hoped against hope that they would ultimately recover their house at Douai. Besides, the formation of regular communities is not the work of a day : places and means must be found. The fact is, that the fathers wished to form communities here in England, and did all they could for this object. But by the time it became possible, a quarter of a century had elapsed. Then, to bring the old fathers together, and make a properly conducted community of them, was next to impossible. It is necessary to begin with the young, and fashion them after the proper pattern : old trees do not bear transplanting. And how can men teach others what they have never learned themselves ?

The Franciscan Order in England was, however, not to die, but to be renewed. The work was done in an almost imperceptible manner; everything took, as it were, its natural course. But the end was obtained : God had directed men's efforts.

The closing years of the second Province had a lustre of their own. We cannot but be filled with admiration at the sight of a handful of veterans and jubilarians, protesting their undying love for the Order of St. Francis, and vowing to do all in their power to continue the work. Unsuccessful yet noble efforts in God's cause, mingled with such names as those of

Bishops Collingridge and Hendren, Fathers Richards and McDonnell, and last but not least, Father O'Farrell, whose memory is still cherished in the places where he laboured, spread a halo of glory around its tomb. *Sepulchrum ejus gloriosum.*

—

BLESSED AGNELLUS OF PISA,

FIRST PROVINCIAL OF THE FRANCISCANS IN ENGLAND, DIED MARCH 13, 1236.

(From the ancient Portrait on Mount Alverna.)

To face p. 7.

CHAPTER II.

THE FRANCISCAN SPIRIT.

THE Franciscan Order possesses a peculiar attraction which has captivated many souls generously disposed towards God from the very beginning of its institution. The striking character of the founder, no doubt, largely contributed to its success. But besides this it has a prominent feature, a distinctive mark, which consists in the manner in which the children of the seraphic patriarch observe the Gospel counsel of holy poverty.

For although the three solemn vows of obedience, chastity and poverty are common to all religious, there is in the manner in which these vows are observed, according to the nature of the rule and constitutions of each Order, almost as great a variety as there is in the different habits worn by the members.

As regards the observance of the vow of evangelical poverty in particular, it is scarcely possible to describe it more clearly and accurately than Father John Baptist Weston in his explanation of the rule of the Friars Minor. In this work he embodies the doctrine of the Fathers and saints. And as he was a prominent member of the Seraphic Order when the second Province of the English Franciscans was in full life and vigour, it is almost a duty for us to let him speak on this subject. Here are his words.

" Behold here a perfect disinheriting of ourselves, forsaking all worldly goods for God's sake, purely with the intention of serving Him with greater freedom. And this is holy and meritorious, as Pope Nicholas says, in his declaration on the rule. This Christ Jesus our Lord and Master, showing to mankind the way of perfection, has taught by word and example. This his apostles and first disciples have likewise practised, according to the counsel He gave to the young man in the Gospel, when He said, 'If thou wilt be perfect, go sell what thou hast, and give to the poor, and thou shalt have treasure in heaven: and come, follow me.'

" But to give my reader a more clear and exact notion of our Franciscan poverty, and distinguish it from that of other Orders, it will be necessary to take notice, that there are three sorts of renunciations of temporal goods, which are more or less perfect according to their different degree.

" The first degree is of those who, living in the world, retain to themselves the property and dominion of all they possess, as money, lands, houses, goods, cattle, yet are free from all covetousness, and without setting their affections upon their treasures, but using them according to religion and justice ; and out of devotion giving part of them to supply the wants of the poor, as occasion requires. And these are the poor in spirit, though rich in substance, who follow the counsel of the royal prophet : 'If riches abound, set not your heart upon them ' (*Ps.* lxi.) ; and of whom it is said in another psalm : 'He hath distributed, he hath given to the poor : his justice remaineth for ever and ever : his horn shall be exalted in glory ' (*Ps.* cxi.)

" The second degree belongs to those who, in particular and as to their own persons, renounce all temporal goods for God's sake, but retain the dominion and property thereof in common, and as to what relates to the body of which they are members, having one common stock out of which all their wants are supplied, according to the need of each one, after the example of the first Christians, of whom the Acts of the Apostles make mention in these words : ' And all they that believed, were together, and had all things common. Their possessions and goods they sold, and divided them to all, according as every one had need ' (*Acts* ii. 44). And again : ' Neither was there any one needy among them. For as many as were owners of lands or houses sold them, and brought the price of the things they sold and laid it down before the feet of the apostles. And distribution was made to every one according as he had need ' (*Acts* iv. 34). And this is the poverty of all those Religious Orders that now-a-days possess anything in common ; whose first founders, in imitation of those Christians of the primitive times, have introduced and caused to revive again in the Church this second degree of abdication ; obliging their followers to a personal renunciation of all temporal goods, retaining the property thereof in common, or in the body of their Orders. Which, though it be meritorious and holy, and withdraws in part those that embrace these institutes from the care and solicitude of worldly goods, yet as to the common, they are still entangled with them, and exposed to all those disquiets and dangers which attend earthly possessions.

" The third and most perfect degree is that of Christ and His apostles, which we Friars Minor make profession of. And it differs from the former principally in three things—first, that this community of primitive Christians did not properly abandon and give away from themselves what they possessed, but only transferred the dominion thereof to their body. But the apostles sold all they had, and gave it to the poor, renouncing all manner of right and title thereto, without retaining any the least thing to themselves, so much as in common; second, those that incorporated themselves in this first society of Christians sold what they had, and brought their money with them, to be put into the common stock, out of which their needs were afterwards supplied by means of the said money, to which they had recourse to procure what they stood in need of. But as for the apostles all use and administration of money whatsoever was forbidden them; neither was it lawful for them so much as in their journeys to carry in their purses any coin or money, to supply their daily wants; third, the members of this first Christian community were not obliged to any strait or penurious use of things, either in clothes, victuals, or lodging; but freely enjoyed all their conveniences, without restraint. But the apostles were denied several things commodious for the use and civil life of man, as shoes or multiplicity of garments.

" Behold here all the conditions of the most sublime poverty of the Seraphic Order of St. Francis, styled therefore by a special title, and most deservedly, ' the Patriarch of the Poor of the Crucified.' From whence it is easy to gather its perfection and excellence beyond that of other religious, it being an absolute and complete renunciation of money and all things of this world, both in particular and in common, purely depending upon the providential care of the heavenly Father, and the charity of the people, for their support, in imitation of our Saviour."

To this beautiful description of Franciscan poverty by Father Weston not much need be added to complete the portrait of a Franciscan. We expect indeed to find in a true Friar Minor many other qualities ; but these spring from that apostolic poverty which Francis loved so much, as from their source : they rest on it, as on their foundation. When men beheld the Franciscans travelling along the highways "two and two" and "shod with sandles" and possessing "neither silver nor gold, nor money in their purses," little wonder if there came vividly to their minds the words of our Lord in sending forth His disciples. So they waited not to hear the name of the newcomers, but with the intuitive accuracy of " Catholic instinct," proceeded themselves to give them a name : " the Order of the Holy Apostles."*

The Franciscans were popular with all classes, from the king who employed them as ghostly fathers or trusty messengers, to the poor wayfarer who received from them, with a kind word and cheerful countenance, a crust of the loaf given them by a charitable benefactor.

* Mgr. J. Moyes, *The Franciscan Movement in the Thirteenth Century.*

CHAPTER III.

BRIEF RETROSPECT.

THE rapid growth of the Seraphic Order was not to be confined to Italy. One day St. Francis, having been favoured with a vision, said : " My dear children, for your sakes I must needs tell you what I have seen, though I would rather have kept it a secret, if charity did not prompt me to speak. I saw a great multitude of men coming to us, wishing to put on our holy habit, and join in our manner of life : and the sound of their steps, guided by the command of holy obedience, is still in my ears. I saw the roads crowded with a multitude from every nation : the French come, the Spaniards hasten, the English and Teutons run, and vast numbers from other lands are approaching with all speed."

Scarcely had Blessed Agnellus * with his eight companions landed on our shores when pious souls began to flock around them, and friaries began to spring up. They were founded in the true spirit of St. Francis, as one instance, chosen from among many, will suffice to show.

The Franciscan Friary of Reading dates from the year 1233. By a deed of July 14 of that year the

* The English Franciscans keep his feast with Office and Mass on March 13, the anniversary of his death.

Benedictine abbot granted to the Friars Minor a certain piece of waste ground near the king's highway leading to Caversham bridge, with permission to build and dwell there, so long as they should continue without acquiring any property of their own. But if at any time, by any accident, or by any means, it should come to pass that the Friars Minor should have any property, or anything of their own, they agreed for themselves, and their successors for ever, that it should be lawful for the abbot and his successors by their own authority to expel them from every part of their land, without the hindrance of any contradiction or appeal.*

St. Francis had received an assurance from God that the Order would never lack holy brethren who would observe the rule in its purity. Already in the fourteenth century efforts were made to purge the Order from whatever abuses might have crept in. This movement began to spread rapidly in the fifteenth century, under the title of " Regular Observance." Its chief promoters were St. Bernardine of Siena, St. John Capistran and St. James della Marcha. Their followers were called " Observants." The movement reached England about the middle of the fifteenth century, as we learn from a letter written by St. John Capistran to King Henry VI., in which he says : " As I know your holy intention to raise new establishments to the honour of God and St. Bernardine, I have only to add that faith without works is dead. Hence, if you should

* Charles Coates, LL.B., *History and Antiquities of Reading*, 1802.

build such friaries, let it not be to please me or others, but only with the object of securing for yourself as many mansions in heaven. If your Majesty for your conscience sake should erect houses of the Observance, I shall write to the Father Vicar of France and the nearest Guardian, who will give you every assistance.

" Dated October 24, 1454." *

Although we do not hear of any immediate step being taken by the king, the Regular Observance must have obtained a footing, for in 1470 the General Chapter of Palencia numbered England amongst the Provinces of the Observants.

At length about the year 1480 King Edward IV. gave the friars the Chapel of the Holy Cross at Greenwich, where later Henry VII. erected a new building for the Observants.

This new movement caused no division among the English Franciscans, for in 1498 the Provincial Chapter of the Observants, at which the Regular Observance was, by the king's command and letters, introduced at Newcastle, Canterbury and Southampton, was held at the Grey Friars in London, which was not a house of the Observants.

From a note written by Cromwell on the back of a letter dated September 13, 1532, it is evident that at that time the Regular Observance counted six friaries in England. In this note, made immediately after the Franciscan Chapter, we read :

* Fr. Francis a S. Clara, *Historia minor.*

Minister Father Peyton.
Warden of Greenwich, Freer Henry Elston.
Warden of Richmond, Freer Ryche.
Warden of Canterbury, Gabriel Pekoke.
Warden of Newarke, Father Rykys.
Warden of Newcastle, Father Baker.
Warden of Southampton, Father Scryvener.

It may be safely assumed that in this note the names of all the houses of the Regular Observance are mentioned.*

The chapter had been held at Richmond, for we find, September 26, 1532, a "Warrant under the sign manual to Cromwell as master of the jewels, to deliver to the Friars Observants, now at their Chapter at Richmond, to be employed as alms, £6 13s. 4d.

At the time of the Dissolution the total number of friaries belonging to the English Franciscan Province was 73. A few of these were situated in Scotland; but there was a Scotch Province besides. We give them here in alphabetical order:

Aylesbury; Bedford; Berwick; Beverley; Bodmin; Boston; Bridgenorth; Bridgewater; Bristol; Brougham in Westmoreland;† Bury Saint Edmunds; Cambridge; Canterbury; Cardiff; Carlisle; Carmarthen; Chester; Chichester; Colchester; Coventry; Doncaster; Dorchester in Dorsetshire; Dumfries; Dundee; Dunwich; Exeter; Gloucester; Grantham; Greenwich; Grimsby; Haddington; Hartlepool; Hereford; Ipswich; Lancaster; Leicester; Lewes in Sussex; Lichfield;

---

* Chapuis speaks of seven houses of the Observants, but does not mention their names. Cf. *Calendar of State Papers, Henry VIII.,* vii. 1057.   † Leland's *Itinerary.*

Lincoln; Llanfaes near Beaumaris; London; Ludlow; Lynn; Maidstone; Newark; Newcastle; Northampton; Norwich; Nottingham; Oxford; Penrith; Plymouth; Pontefract; Preston; Reading; Richmond in Surrey; Richmond in Yorkshire; Roxburgh; Salisbury; Scarborough; Shrewsbury; Southampton; Stafford; Stamford; Stoke-under-Ham in Somersetshire; Walsingham; Ware; Winchelsea; Winchester; Worcester; Yarmouth; York.

To these must be added Becmachen or Bewmaken, in Kirk Harberry parish, Isle of Man, founded in 1373.*

The Scottish Province, according to Gonzaga,† counted at that time nine houses : Aberdeen; Ayr; Edinburgh; Elgin; Glasgow; Jedburg; Perth; St. Andrews; Stirling. They had all adopted the Regular Observance in the year 1517.

The English Franciscans have left us noble examples of fortitude in days of danger and persecution.

About the year 1534 Fathers Peto and Elstow, having preached against the divorce at Greenwich, were brought before the Privy Council, and reprimanded there. The Earl of Essex told them they deserved to be put into a sack and thrown into the Thames. The reply was: "My Lord, be pleased to frighten your court-epicures with such sentences : such threats make no impression upon us. And as for your Thames, the road to heaven lies as near by water as by land."

In the same year, on April 20, Father Hugh Rich

* Tanner, *Notit. Monast.*, and Dugdale's *Monast.*

† *De Origine Seraphicæ Religionis*, 1587, by Fr. Francis Gonzaga, Minister General, afterwards Bishop of Mantua.

and Richard Risby suffered martyrdom, together with Elizabeth Barton, two Benedictines and two secular priests.

In 1537 the Venerable Fathers Anthony Brookby, Thomas Cort and Thomas Belchiam laid down their lives for the Faith.

Four Franciscans, Thomas Packington, Bonaventure Roe, John Tuit and Richard Carter, who had been cast into prison, were set free in 1537. But they had suffered such hardships in their confinement that they died soon after their release.

On May 22, 1538, Blessed John Forest was burnt in Smithfield.

In the same year, August 9, Father Anthony Browne was burnt at Norwich.

In that year also thirty-two Franciscans died in prison in various parts of the country.

On July 8, 1539, the Venerable Father John Waire, or Maire,* was executed at St. Thomas' Waterings, together with the vicar of Wandsworth, his curate and his servant.

Some of the Observants made good their escape into Belgium and other parts of the Continent. A few fled to the south of Ireland, and were hospitably received by the people of Kinsale.

With Mary's accession came a short respite. The surviving Observants began to re-assemble at Greenwich in 1553. The queen restored their friary

* I hope that this will meet the eye of those who wish to mention this venerable martyr's name, and that we shall not hear again of N. Waire, or Francis Waire, or Nicholas Waire.

and church, which was solemnly reopened in 1555. Among those who received the Franciscan habit in those days was Father Thomas Bourchier, the well-known author of the work *De Martyrio Fratrum Minorum*, printed at Ingolstadt in 1583.

Later, in 1634, when the Franciscans assembled in chapter at Greenwich, they chronicled that the conventual buildings still existed in a perfectly regular form, with the church, cloisters, dormitory and community rooms, and a large garden.

In 1559 Queen Elizabeth utterly suppressed and expelled the Franciscans. Some again took the road into exile, others hid themselves and remained at home in seclusion and oblivion.

Among this remnant of the Order, three names stand prominent, and are deserving of more than a bare mention.

Father John Gray, a Scotch Franciscan, born of a noble family, some say English, others Scotch, after his expulsion went to the house of his Order at Brussels, where he was kindly received and lived in great repute for sanctity. But at length the Geuzian heretics broke into the church; and as Father Gray was kneeling in prayer before the high altar, they inflicted mortal wounds upon him. He said, "Lord, forgive them, and receive my soul;" and so expired on June 5, 1579. The Catholics afterwards came to the friary to see the body; and one of them who was suffering from an incurable disease, kissing a cloth dipped in the martyr's blood, was instantly cured.

Father Lawrence Collier was arrested for his

religion, and thrown into prison, where he died after two years' confinement. This occurred probably at Stafford, in 1590.

Venerable John Buckley, *alias* Jones, was a secular priest, and lay confined in Wisbeach Castle in 1587. After that he either escaped or was released. He then went abroad, and was received into the Order of St. Francis, probably at Pontoise. Returning to England in 1593, he laboured for three years with great fruit, and then fell again into the hands of the persecutors. He was hanged, drawn and quartered at St. Thomas' Waterings on July 12, 1598. It was he who handed the seal of the English Province to Father William Staney.

Among the other surviving Franciscans of this period were the following: Father Thomas Ackrick, who was a prisoner in Hull Castle in the year 1583; Father Henry More, a relative of Blessed Thomas More, who received the habit abroad on September 22, 1584; Father Thomas Langton; Father George Dennis, who died in the friary of the Order at Liége in 1585; Father Thomas Bourchier, who died at Ara-Cœli, Rome, in 1586; Father Stephen Fox, who died at Lisbon in 1588; Father John, commonly known as "the Old Beggar," who died at Leyland about the year 1590; Father John Richel, who died at the Franciscan friary, Louvain, in 1599; Father Richard, who died in Spain in 1619; Father Nelson, who died in 1628 in England, where he had remained hidden all his life.

But not the least remarkable among the few

scattered English Franciscans was Father William Staney, or Stanney, who forms as it were the connecting link between the first and the second Province. He was made the first Commissary of his English brethren since the suppression, as the continuator of Wadding says, in 1601. It was he who admitted Father John Gennings to the Order, and afterwards gave him the seal of the English Province. He was the author of a treatise "On the Third Order of St. Francis, commonly called the Order of Penance, for the use of those who desire to lead a holy life, and do penance in their own houses." It was printed at Douai in 1617. *

We do not hear much of him subsequently, probably because he acted independently of the other English Franciscans. But it is recorded that in 1620 he summoned a nun of the Third Order, Petronilla Kemp, from Brussels to England. Shortly afterwards she returned to Brussels with one postulant, and, visiting her native country again the following year, she brought six more.

After this year no further mention occurs of Father Staney. It must only be added that in the annals of the Order he is praised for his integrity and holiness of life.

* The continuator of Wadding says at Mechlin, but this is a mistake; the work does not appear to have passed through more than one edition.

SIGILLV . MAIVS . COLL . D . BONNAV . FF . MINOR . RECOL .
ANGLORVM . DVACI.

Seal of St. Bonaventure's, Douai.

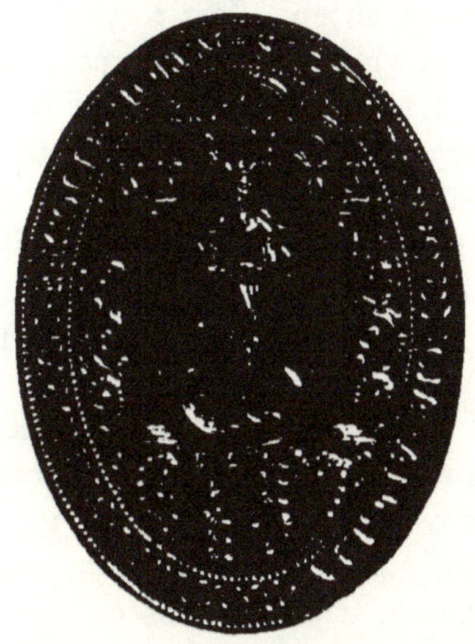

SIGILLVM   PROVINCIÆ . ANGLIÆ . FRATRUM . MINORVM.
RECOLLECTORVM.

Seal of the Second English Province.

To face p. 21.

CHAPTER IV.

FATHER JOHN GENNINGS AND HIS PIOUS PROJECT.

EDMUND GENNINGS, a convert to the Catholic faith, having been ordained priest at Soissons in 1590, returned to England to labour on the mission. He went to Lichfield, his native town; but found that most of his friends and kindred were dead, except one brother, who, he heard, was in London, but in what part of the town he could not learn. Understanding that the state of his soul at that time was very bad, his charity determined him to go up to London to seek after this stray sheep. For a whole month he left no place untried where he could suspect his brother might be; but still not finding him, and having now no hopes of meeting with him, he resolved to leave the town for a time. Then, however, God Almighty unexpectedly brought him to the sight of his brother, though at first without knowing him, and that in a strange manner, as Father John Gennings relates in his life.

"Having, as I have said, a determination to leave London for a while, he walked forth of his inn one morning, a few days before he proposed to travel, to visit a friend on the other side of the city; and passing by St. Paul's Church, when he was on the east side thereof, he suddenly felt a strange sensation in his body, so much that his face glowed, and, as he thought, his hair stood on end ; and all his joints trembling for fear, his whole body seemed to be bathed in a cold sweat.

" This strange accident causing him to fear some evil to threaten him, or danger of being taken up, he looked back to see if he could perceive any one pursuing him ; but seeing nobody near, but only a youth in a brown-coloured cloak, making no reflection who it should be, he went forward to his intended place to say Mass that day.

" Not long after, on the very morning he proposed to depart out of the town, the blessed man, recollecting himself in his devotions, earnestly prayed that his departure without finding his desired brother might increase his patience ; and though it afflicted him very much, yet he cried out, ' *Fiat, voluntas tua !* My will is Thy will; sweet Lord, Thy will be done ! '   His devotions being finished, he went abroad to another place where he had promised to celebrate Mass before his departure.   Which done, as he was returning homewards towards his inn upon Ludgate Hill, suddenly he felt the same sensations as he had done before ; his joints trembled as dreading some great trouble or misfortune to ensue ; and as the lamb naturally fears the ravening wolves, so his innocency fearing the malice of his persecutors, he looked back to see who followed him.   And behold, no man of mark, only a youth in a brown cloak.   At the same instant, reflecting on the time past, when he had suffered the like agitation, and steadfastly looking at the young man (he had left his brother a little boy in the the country, and had not seen him for eight or nine years), presently he was struck with the thought, ' This may be my brother.'

"Upon this he approached the youth, and courteously saluting him, he inquired what countryman he was; and hearing that he was a Staffordshire man, civilly demanded his name. The stranger made answer that his name was Gennings; by which he knew him certainly to be his brother, so long sought after. Then casting his eyes towards heaven, by way of love and thanks, smiling upon the party, he told him he was his kinsman, and was called ' Ironmonger,' which was the name he had assumed on his return to England, and that he was very glad to see him well; and thus they walked down Ludgate Hill, he questioning of all his friends, and asked him what had become of his brother Edmund.

"The youth not suspecting him to be the man, told him he had heard that he had gone to Rome to the Pope, and was become a notable Papist, and a traitor both to God and his country; and that if he did return, he would infallibly be hanged.

" Our sweet martyr, hearing this, and smiling at the boy's folly, told him that he had heard his brother was a very honest man, and loved both the queen and his country, but God above all. ' But tell me,' said he, 'good cousin John, do you not know him if you see him?' To which John answered, ' No ; ' but beginning to suspect that he was his brother, and a priest, told him he could not tell him where he was ; that he greatly feared he had a brother a Papist priest, and that he was the man; swearing withal that, if it was so, he would discredit himself and all his friends, and protesting that in this he would never follow him, although in other matters he would greatly respect him; which words Edmund hearing, could no longer conceal himself from his brother, but told him truly he was his brother indeed, and for his love had taken great pains to seek him, and begged of him to keep secret the knowledge of his arrival.

"To which the youth answered, he would not for a world disclose his return; but yet he desired him to come no more unto him, for that he feared greatly the danger of the law, and to incur the penalty of the new-made statute in concealing him. The good man, hearing this, thought it neither time nor place convenient (being then in a tavern) to talk of religion. They had, however, much conversation about divers things, by which he well perceived his poor brother to be far from any good affection towards the Catholic religion, but rather wilfully given to persist in Protestantism, without any hope of a present recovery; and therefore declaring unto him his intended departure out of town, took his leave, assuring him that, within one month or little more, he intended to return, at which time he would see him again, and confer with him more at large about some necessary affairs which concerned him very much. And thus the two brothers parted, the one to his function of converting souls, the other to meditate how to corrupt his own; the one to spend his time in studying how to persuade, the other how to withstand; the one purposed to make haste back again, hoping to save a soul, brotherly love thereunto provoking him; the other wishing his brother never to return, through fear of being converted, licentious liberty perverting in him brotherly love."

The conversion of John Gennings was not to be brought about by discussion: it was to be the fruit of his brother's death, which, after labouring for some time in preaching, catechising, and performing other priestly functions in the country, he suffered in London on Friday, December 10, 1591.

Miraculous signs were not wanting at his martyrdom; but the most wonderful event that followed was the sudden conversion of this same brother, which he, speaking of himself in the third person, thus relates:

" This much loved brother, this John Gennings, being in London at the very time of his execution, hearing of the same, rather rejoiced than any way bewailed the untimely and bloody end of his nearest kinsman, hoping thereby to be rid of all persuasions which he suspected he should receive from him touching the Catholic Religion. But about ten days after his execution, towards night, having spent all that day in sport and jollity, being weary with play, he returned home, where to repose himself he went into a secret chamber. He was no sooner there set down, but forthwith his heart began to be heavy and his head melancholy, and he began to weigh how idly he had spent that day. Amidst these thoughts, there was presently represented to his mind a strange imagination and apprehension of the death of his brother; and amongst other things, how he had, not long before, forsaken all worldly pleasures, and, for his religion only, endured intolerable torments. Then within himself he made long discourses concerning his religion and his brother's, comparing the Catholic manner of living with his, and finding the one to embrace pain and mortification, and the other to seek pleasure; the one to live strictly, and the other licentiously; the one to fear sin, and the other to run into all kinds of sin; he was struck with exceeding terror and remorse. He wept bitterly, desiring God, after his fashion, to illuminate his understanding, that he might see and perceive the truth.

"Oh, what great joy and consolation did he feel at that instant! What reverence on the sudden did he begin to bear to the Blessed Virgin, and to the Saints of God, which before he had never scarcely so much as heard of! What strange emotions, as it were inspirations, with exceeding readiness of will to change his religion, took possession of his soul! And what a heavenly conception had he now of his dear brother's felicity! He imagined he saw him; he thought he heard him. In this ecstasy of mind, he made a vow upon the spot, as he lay prostrate on the ground, to forsake kindred and country, to find out the true knowledge of his brother's faith; which vow he soon after performed, and departed from England without giving notice to any of his friends, and went beyond the seas to execute his promise."

He became a Catholic without persuasion or conference with any one; then he was enrolled an alumnus of Douai College, where he was ordained priest in 1607, and was from thence sent upon the English mission in 1608.

It was here that in 1610 he met Father William Staney, who had been made Commissary of the English Franciscans in 1601, and had in virtue of this commission power to receive novices. This zealous missioner had been imprisoned in the Marshalsea for the faith before the year 1599.

Father Anthony Parkinson in an unedited manuscript states that John Gennings received the habit of St. Francis in England about the year 1610; others say in 1614.* Father Staney, observing his great fervour and desire of restoring the English Franciscans, and conceiving good hopes of success from such promising beginnings, four years later delivered into his hands the seal of the province, which he had held for some years, having received it from Venerable Father Jones, or Buckley, the martyr.

This seal, which bears the inscription, *Sigillum Provinciæ Angliæ Fratrum Minorum Regularis Observantiæ,* may date from about the year 1500, when the Observance began to flourish here. Father Gonzaga appears to have been unable to find it; for in his work, edited in 1587, the space allotted to it in the collection of seals is blank, as well as that intended for the seal of the Scotch Province. But he accurately describes the English seal in these words:

---

* It does not appear quite certain in what year Father Gennings joined the Franciscan Order. The dates given in his mortuary bill and his epitaph do not agree.

"It represents our Blessed Lady with the Child Jesus in her arms, having the moon under her feet; beneath is the coat of arms of the kingdom."

It is now kept at Forest Gate.

Of the Scotch seal there is an impression extant, carefully preserved as a precious relic, at the Franciscan Friary, Glasgow. It is inscribed: *Sigillum Ministri Provincialis Fratrum Minorum Regularis Observantiæ Provinciæ Scotiæ*, and represents St. Bernardine with the monogram of the Holy Name in his hand.

After his admission Father Gennings went for a time to the friary of Ypres in Flanders, there to be trained in the Franciscan manner of life, and to make himself thoroughly familiar with the rule and constitution of the Order. It was in this religious establishment also that some of his first companions received the habit.

We shall give the sequel of this history from the unpublished manuscript of Father Parkinson.

Father John Gennings, understanding that some of the priests and students of the English College at Douai were much affected to the Order of St. Francis, conceived that it was possible to restore the Province of England, which in former times had been famous throughout the whole Christian world for both virtue and learning. With this view he addressed himself to Father Andrew a Soto, Commissary General of the Order on this side the Alps, from whom he obtained the admission of some priests and other students of the said seminary; and then for the present procured a residence of nine religious, six fathers and three novices, at Gravelines, where, as Father Angelus Mason says, the first fathers of Douai made their religious profession.

Some also of those who were received into the Order for the Province of England, by the Commissary General Andrew a Soto, were by the same authority admitted to make their noviceship in the Franciscan friary at Ypres; amongst which number was Christopher Davenport, *alias* Francis a Sancta Clara, who with two others was there clothed on October 7, 1617.

CHAPTER V.

DOUAI.

PERCEIVING his pious design in a hopeful way, Father Gennings proposed to himself the getting of a fixed settlement for his friars in the town and university of Douai. He set to work with great foresight and prudence, and prevailed with one Father William Thompson, a doctor of laws and Franciscan Conventual, to go as his agent and procurator to Spain, to the General Chapter of the Observant Franciscans, held at Salamanca in 1618; and there he so effectually represented the pious wishes of Father Gennings that he obtained letters patent from Father Benignus of Genoa, Minister General of the whole Order, and from his Definitory, not only for the carrying on of the work of the restoration of the English Franciscan Province, but also to give authority for its first settlement in the university town of Douai. In order to enforce this concession of the General of the Order and his Definitors, a grant was likewise procured from the king of Spain himself for the said setttlement, provided the Archduchess of the Low Countries and the magistrates of Douai consented.

About the same time the English Poor Clares of Gravelines had petitioned to be transferred from the

jurisdiction of the Bishop of St. Omers to that of the
English Franciscans. Leave was granted them by the
same letters of the General, which we take from the
authentic records.

BROTHER BENIGNUS OF GENOA,

*Minister General and Servant of the whole Order of
Friars Minor, and the Definitors of the Family
this side of the Alps.*

We have thought well to receive, and we accept the
place intended for a seminary, for our brethren of the
English nation, in the university town of Douai, to
begin the restoration of the English Province, formerly
famous among us. And we approve and confirm the
conditions upon which our Commissary General of the
Belgian provinces, the Very Reverend Father Andrew
a Soto, has thereto obtained permission from the said
town. And we grant to that place, to its superior and
brethren, the same graces, privileges, immunities and
exemptions which the other houses and colleges of our
Order enjoy.

Moreover, for the comfort of our noble and devout
daughters, the Poor Clares of the Convent of Gravelines, of the same English nation, in the province of
Flanders, of whose piety, austere life, and zeal for the
restoration of our Order in the said kingdom we have
been informed, we grant that their vicar, or confessor,
shall have the jurisdiction of a Guardian over the
the brethren living there, whose number may be nine

or ten, and among whom three or four may be novices, so as to facilitate the beginning of the restoration of this once celebrated Province. And we doubt not, from the information we have received, that the friends, parents and benefactors of the said sisters will sufficiently provide for the support of the brethren. We desire that the place be not called a convent, but a vicariate of nuns. Further, in order to ensure the efficacy of these Letters, it is our will that all the English and Scotch fathers who are in Belgium, England and Scotland, shall be subject to our Commissary General of the Belgian nation, Father Andrew a Soto, who may call to him any of the English or Scotch fathers whom he may think suitable for the English Province, in whatever place or office they may be engaged.

To the same Commissary also we give power to dispose and ordain what he thinks proper for the dress and life of Tertiaries, with the advice of our English and Scotch brethren, who will suggest what they think expedient in the present state of the country, and the danger of Catholics among heretics.

We recommend our English and Scotch brethren to the said Commissary and to all the ministers and prelates of our Belgian provinces, beseeching them to favour and promote the restoration of the English Province. And if any English or Scotch youths present themselves, to charitably admit them to the holy habit, and piously educate them.

Given at Salamanca, in the friary of our Holy

Father St. Francis, at the General Chapter, June 8, 1618.

F. BENIGNUS, of Genoa, *Minister General.*
F. JOHN VENIDO, *Commissary General.*
F. DIDACUS A BARRASA, *Definitor General.*
F. JOSEPH BERGAIGNE, *Definitor General.*
F. FUANTIN SHINO, *Commissary of Rome.*
F. FRANCIS LE RUE, *Definitor General.*
F. BONAVENTURE DE MON ROY, *Definitor General.*
F. JOHN CLERQ, *Definitor General.*
F. HENRY SEDULIUS, *Definitor General.*

Being thus encouraged, Father Gennings addressed himself to their Highnesses Albert and Isabella, then Governors of the Spanish Netherlands; and by the intervention of Father Andrew a Soto, who was not only commissary general of the Order in those provinces, but also confessor to the Archduchess Isabella, a free and full consent was obtained. Then Father Gennings made his application to the authorities of the town and university of Douai, who with great charity and humanity granted his request, the magistrates giving him in addition a piece of waste ground in the town, whereon to build a friary and college.

Thereupon the zealous founder began to collect alms in England, chiefly in his own part of the country. Among the benefactors were the Countess of Castlehaven, Sir William, a citizen of London, and many noblemen; and in Flanders Philip Gavarel, Benedictine Abbot of St. Vedast, and John Jonquay, Abbot of Marchienne of the same Order. Many hands were soon at work in constructing a suitable building for the Friars ; and in the meantime a charitable townsman of Douai lent them a private house to dwell in, till they could take possession of the new friary.

In this same year, 1618, on October 30, the English Franciscans first assembled at Douai in community, under the presidency of Father Bonaventure Jackson, who had been called thither by the commissary from the friary of Malines or Mechlin, in Belgium, and was made the first Preses. He was appointed to this post by the following letter.

BROTHER ANDREW A SOTO,

Commissary General of the Order of Friars Minor of the Regular Observance, with fulness of power over the Provinces of Belgium, Britain, Strasburg, Cologne, and Scotland, to the Reverend Father Bonaventure Jackson, Priest and Confessor of the same Order, eternal salvation in the Lord.

Whereas, with the consent of our Most Serene Governors, of the Bishop of Arras, and of the Magistrates of Douai, we have lately obtained a place for a College in that town for our English Fathers ; and this foundation has been approved by the Most Reverend Father General with his Definitors at the General Chapter held last year at Salamanca, upon the conditions required by the said Magistrates ; and the said General has granted to this place, and to the superior and brethren, all the graces, privileges, immunities and exemptions which the other Houses and Colleges of our Order enjoy.

Hence we, knowing both by our own experience and the testimony of the other brethren, thy edifying life and zeal for Holy Religion, and trusting in thy prudence and ability to give an impulse to this pious undertaking; we appoint thee Preses of the friary to be founded in the said town of Douai, with all the authority belonging to the superiors of our Houses And in virtue of Holy Obedience we command all the Fathers and Brothers, who shall be sent to that place, to revere and obey thee as their legitimate superior.

Farewell in the Lord, and pray for us.

Given at Brussels, under our signature and seal of office, October 13, 1618.

FR. ANDREW A SOTO, *Commissary General.*

The first members of this community were, according to the Annals,* Fathers Anthony Clercke and Francis Davenport. About the month of December they were joined by Jerome Pickford, a learned priest, and George Perrot. Father John Jennings was also a member of this religious family. Before the end of the following year Fathers Nicholas Day and Francis Bel were called hither out of Spain, from whence Father John Bullaker afterwards also came.

The English Franciscans, as Father Parkinson continues, in their first poor house at Douai had not as yet the convenience of teaching; and therefore such of them as had not finished their higher studies,

* The official relation sent to Rome for the continuation of L. Wadding's Annals of the Order.

went daily to school to St. Vedast's College, particularly Francis Bel, who, having studied Divinity for only two years, went with others to the lessons of the English monks, Reverend Fathers Rudisind Barlo, and Leander Jones, Doctors of Divinity, and Thomas Torquatus Latham, by whom they were carefully and charitably taught, until such time as their little college at Douai was habitable.

The long-desired time came at last; and in 1621 the English Franciscans removed from the borrowed private house to their new Friary of St. Bonaventure. Here Father Francis Davenport immediately opened schools, and was the first professor that taught the brethren in this place, from whence, in due time came out many learned Franciscans.

The community continued to be governed by a Preses until the year 1624, when it was made a Guardianate by the Commissary General, who, at the same time, appointed Father Bonaventure Jackson the first Guardian. But he, being wanted in England, was called thither the same year, and Father Francis Davenport was appointed to succeed him in that office.

The following year, Father Francis Davenport was sent by Father John Gennings to Rome, to the General Chapter of the Order, to solicit there a further enhancement of the English Province. And this he effected by procuring letters patent from Father Bernardine de Senis, Minister General of the Order, who, with the consent of the whole chapter, restored to it its ancient rights and privileges of a Province, and appointed Father John Gennings Custos, until such time as the number of brethren would be sufficiently increased to have a Provincial. In the meantime, he granted him the right of voting in the General Chapters of the Order, and of having both an active and passive voice in all elections of that venerable assembly.

For the text of this document the Annals refer us to the "Certamen," where we read as follows:

BROTHER BERNARDINE DE SENIS,

Minister General and Servant of the whole Order of Friars Minor, to our beloved Brother in Christ, Father John Gennings, Vicar of England, greeting.

By our authority, and with the consent of the general Definitory, held at the general Chapter in Rome in the year of the great Jubilee, 1625, our Province of England has been restored, and all the privileges enjoyed by other Provinces of the Order have been granted it, with this only restriction—that until such time as the number of brethren shall have increased, the Superior shall not be called Provincial, but Custos: he shall, however, have the full power of a Provincial, with the right of sitting in the General Chapters, where he shall have both an active and passive vote, like other Provincials.

We therefore, by virtue of our office, institute and declare thee by these our letters Custos of the said Province.

Given at Ara-coeli, Rome, May 27, 1625.

Having thus far followed the successful course of the English Franciscans, it will not be amiss to cast a glance at the doings of their Scotch brethren.

CHAPTER VI.

EFFORTS TO RESTORE THE SCOTCH PROVINCE.

AT the sight of the success which crowned every move of their English brethren, the Scotch Franciscans felt desirous of obtaining a footing in the same university-town of Douai. They set to work with a good will, and before long a pious friend and benefactor turned up in the person of the parish priest of Marny, or Masny.

This venerable ecclesiastic gave them three houses in the town for a foundation in the year 1624; and Father Jackson, then Guardian of the English Franciscans, was requested by the Commissary General, Andrew a Soto, to see that the kind gift was accepted by our Syndic according to the benefactor's intention. The following is a translation of the letter which the Commissary wrote to Father Jackson.

BROTHER ANDREW A SOTO,

Of the Order of Friars Minor of the Regular Observance, Commissary General with plenitude of power, to the Reverend Father Bonaventure Jackson, priest, of the Province of England, and Guardian of the college of English Franciscans at Douai, greeting.

Whereas Anthony Chemin, the worthy parish priest of Masny, has, from pure charity and the desire of assisting the Scotch Franciscans, given them three houses with gardens and outhouses, on certain conditions: we, gratefully accepting the gift, upon the same conditions, command thy Paternity with the merit of holy obedience, to see that the aforesaid houses be accepted by the Syndic of thy friary, in witness of which we have given these letters, signed with our hand and sealed with the greater seal of our office, at Brussels, this 30th of August, 1624.

BROTHER ANDREW A SOTO, *Commissary General.*

But after mature consideration the Scotch fathers did not find it possible to comply with the conditions laid down by the magistrates of Douai as to sufficient means of support. The negotiations broke down, and the houses, as it appears, reverted to the former owner.

A few years later, in 1632, Father Bel, who had then finished but half the term of his office of guardian at Douai, to which he had been appointed in 1630, was sent to Scotland as first provincial of the Scotch province, which he was called upon to restore. This step was taken in consequence of a resolution recently passed by the General Chapter of the Order held in Spain. It was certainly not Father Bel's fault that his efforts were not crowned with success. But the time was not opportune for the restoration of the Order in Scotland, and after a few years stay there, Father Bel returned to England. He was back before the middle of June, 1637, for he was then made Titular Guardian of London.*

* In November 1635, Father Cornelius Ward, O.S.F. (an Irish

In the year 1687, in consequence of the zeal of
a Scotch Franciscan, Father Francis Macdonnell, for
the spread of the Order in that country, a fresh effort
was made for the restoration of the ancient province
of Scotland. He addressed himself to the ecclesiastical
authorities in Rome on the subject. But before
coming to a decision, the general of the Order desired
to have the opinion of the English provincial, to whom
he sent the following letter.

To the Very Reverend Father Provincial of England.

Father Francis Macdonnell, who has for many years
been Prefect of the missions in Scotland, and has rendered himself very deserving in that capacity, has lately
been sent back thither by order of His Britannic
Majesty. It now appears agreeable to the Sacred
Congregation of Propaganda that for the good of
religion he should restore our Province there, with
.the assistance of some of our brethren ; that for this
object more authority should be granted him than
he had before ; that he should have the title of
Provincial of Scotland, with power of receiving brethren,
founding houses, and act as Provincial Minister.
But in order to proceed with due caution in this
matter, I have thought it well first to consult your
Paternity ; and I desire that, putting aside all prejudice

Franciscan) arrived as Prefect (of Scotland) ; and on his retirement from the Scottish Mission in 1640, he was succeeded by
Father Patrick Hogarty, O.S.F., who, after five years imprisonment, was forced to return to Ireland, in August, 1648.—*Catholic
Directory.*

and private interests, you should tell me zealously, fraternally and confidentially what you think best for the service of God, the good of the Church, and the spread of the Faith in England, under the government of the pious King whom heaven has granted us. Pray to God for these intentions and farewell.

Given at Rome, April 12, 1687.

Of your Paternity the devoted servant in the Lord,

BR. PETER MARINUS, *Minister General.*

The Provincial, Father John Cross, sent the following reply.

MOST REVEREND FATHER GENERAL,

It is only now that I have, with due humility, obedience and joy, received your Paternity's kind letter, dated Rome, April 12. For I have just returned from the visitation of the northern and eastern parts of the country, North and South Wales, and the neighbouring counties in this your Province of England. In this work I have spent several months, erecting public chapels, and appointing missionaries and rectors for them, for the exercise of religion and the increase of our Seraphic Order in this kingdom. I have been encouraged by the special devotion and kindness of our most pious king, whose only desire is that, with the help of zealous labourers, our Holy Faith may spread, and strike deep root in every part of his dominions. I have still to visit the western parts of the Province, then our places across the sea in Belgium, before the celebration of our intermediary Chapter in London, about the middle of September. Then I shall begin to prepare for my departure to the General Chapter, where, at your Paternity's feet, I shall explain at greater length and to our common joy the progress of the Catholic Religion and of our Province in England. I shall then also repeat the prayer of our brethren that this ancient and once famous Province may be restored to its former place in the Order, from which it has long since been removed for no other reason than its fidelity to the Holy See, and the part it took in defending the matrimonial rights of Catherine of Aragon against Henry VIII. For as this king and his daughter Elizabeth slew the brethren and suppressed their houses, the Province became extinct; nor had it an advocate to defend its rights at the General Chapters, either among its own fathers or elsewhere, until the restoration of the Province in the beginning of this century.*

With regard to the subject of your Paternity's letter, I beg to say that I well know the Reverend Father Francis Macdonnell. He is a prudent, peaceful and zealous man; and, under the protection of the illustrious Baron Macdonnell, he has worked for many years, together with two companions, for the spread and preservation of the Catholic faith. But his two assistants having died, and he being taken ill, and deprived of all help, was forced to discontinue the

---

* This is a reference to the fact that a promise had more than once been made that the English Province should be restored to the place of precedence on the list of Provinces of the Order which it occupied before the Reformation. This promise remained as yet unfulfilled.

undertakiug. He is, however, willing to resume his duties, under the protection of our most pious Sovereign. Thus it is evident that he well deserves the esteem and favour of the Sacred Congregation and of your Paternity.

Now I shall state my mind plainly aud with all submission concerning the erection or restoration of the Scotch Province. In order to satisfy the wishes of the Sacred Congregation, and to promote the welfare of the new Province, we should safeguard the rights of the English Province, from which it would depend and obtain assistance in its beginnings, as well on account of the proximity and union of the districts, as because the King's Majesty resides in the capital of Great Britain. Hence Scotland was formerly as it were dependent on the English Province, having been founded and governed by the English fathers, as appears from the records of the Order and the Province. And although it was afterwards erected into a separate Province, it nevertheless frequently had Provincial Ministers from England. There was also the Custody of Newcastle, one of the seven old Custodies of England, which possessed several friaries in Scotland, until the extinction of the English Province. Under the pious, martyred Queen Mary, great-grandmother of our King, the Scotch Province survived for a few years, and tried with other rival Provinces to supplant us in the order of precedence.

I wish to point out with all deference that, in order to safeguard our rights, it would be better to erect Scotland first into a Custody annexed to the English

Province, from which it could obtain helpers ; and Father Macdonnell might be appointed Custos. We could also by this means exclude restless spirits, who will not fail to turn up and impede the good work, as I already foresee. Let us first have a sufficient number of members and houses, and then erect a Province not in name only, but in deed. I am convinced that this would also be more in accordance with the political views of our pious Sovereign.

For my own part, I promise Father Macdonnell every assistance and friendship, if your Paternity should appoint him Custos for Scotland. And, provided the rights of our English Province be respected and restored, let your Paternity in wisdom and piety do what seems best.

May the most merciful God long preserve your Paternity for the good of our Order and of this Province.

Your most obedient son and servant in Christ,

BR. JOHN CROSS,
Provincial Minister of England.

London, June 3, 1687.

The English Provincial had, no doubt, taken a practical view of the matter, and it was well that his counsel prevailed.

Although no further attempt was made for the restoration of the Scotch Province, some of the English Franciscans were occasionally sent to labour there. Thus we find Fathers Peter Gordon and Clement Hyslop on the mission in Scotland in the beginning of the eighteenth century.

VENERABLE ARTHUR BEL, O.S.F.

(From the Portrait at Lanherne.)

To face p. 45.

CHAPTER VII.

FOUNDATION OF CONVENTS OF THE SECOND AND THIRD ORDER. FORMAL ERECTION OF THE ENGLISH PROVINCE.

WHILST devoting his attention and energy to the consolidation of the English Province of Friars Minor, Father Gennings had not forgotten the interests of those of the other sex who might be called to a life of greater perfection under the Rule of St. Francis. With the co-operation of other superiors, he succeeded in establishing two convents of English nuns, one of the Second, the other of the Third Order.

Already towards the end of the sixteenth century some English ladies had been admitted among the Poor Clares at St. Omers. In 1607 they settled at Gravelines, and from this place a colony went out in 1627 to make a new foundation. The following year they settled in the town of Aire, and flourished there under the jurisdiction and patronage of the English Franciscans until the French Revolution. The sisters then came to England, where they first settled at Britwell, Nettlebed, Oxon, and later, in 1813, at Coxside near Plymouth. Eleven of the nuns died there, and the community rapidly dwindled. In 1834 two of the sisters joined the community at Scorton (now at Darlington). The remaining sisters went to Gravelines to help in bringing back better times to the dying mother house. Finding their efforts useless after two years, they returned to England and joined the community at Scorton in 1836. Thus ended the Aire foundation.

The foundation of the English Convent of the Third Order was started in 1619 at Brussels, where two English ladies received the habit in the Church of the Friars Minor. They were soon joined by six others, and in 1626 they had increased to thirty-four, whilst more continued to arrive. After sixteen years' residence at Brussels they removed to Nieuport, from whence a colony went afterwards to Paris. In the year 1662 the nuns finally settled at Bruges, where they remained until the storm of the French Revolution forced them to seek shelter in their native country. They were eleven years at Winchester, but removed in 1805 to Taunton.

After this brief reference to the convents of nuns, we resume our narrative in the words of Father Parkinson.

" The English Franciscans being now sufficiently numerous, and having a noviceship and schools of both philosophy and divinity, and also two convents of nuns under their obedience and direction, their case was again represented to the General of the Order Father Bernardine de Senis, who, at the instance of the said friars and of several of their chief patrons in England, did enforce the decree of the General Chapter held at Rome in 1625, in pursuance whereof he constituted and declared them a Province of the Order,

and restored to them their ancient place and privileges
by letters patent, whereby Father John Gennings,
hitherto Custos, was constituted Provincial, Father
Francis a S. Clara Davenport Custos, and Fathers
Bonaventure Jackson, Nicholas Day, Francis Bel and
Jerome Pickford Definitors." Thus far Father Parkinson. The charge of expediting and concluding this
business was committed to Fathers Joseph Bergaigne,
then Commissary General for the northern parts
of Europe, who afterwards became Archbishop of
Cambrai.

This official signified to Father Bel, in his letter
dated Brussels, September 24, 1630, that he had just
returned from Ratisbon, and found the letters of the
Minister General awaiting him; that he had been
directed to summon the above-said Father Provincial,
Custos and Definitors, as also the six senior Fathers in
England, to assemble at Douai on the first Sunday of
Advent; that there and then he might declare the
wishes of the General, and make all necessary arrangements in that Provincial Chapter. Circumstances,
however, intervened which induced the Commissary
to alter the place of meeting; and on November 12,
following he addressed another letter from Alost to
Father Bel, in which he stated his belief that very
few could attend from England, and that he antici-
pated no great inconvenience would result to the
nuns of St. Elizabeth if the first Chapter were celebrated in their Convent at Brussels, instead of meeting
at Douai, on the first Sunday of Advent. And he
begged Father Bel, the director of those nuns, to

despatch immediately intelligence of this altered arrangement to those whom it might concern.

On November 24 Fathers Gennings and Davenport arrived at Brussels; Father Heath joined them on the 29th. On the day appointed the Chapter was opened in due form, and the following decree of the General was published.

BROTHER BERNARDINE DE SENIS,

Minister General and Servant of the whole Order of our Seraphic Father St. Francis, to our beloved Fathers and Brothers of the English Province, health and peace in the Lord.

Whereas at the last General Chapter of the whole Order, celebrated in Rome in the year 1625, the Province of England, which had become extinct through the persecution of heretics, was restored to its former rank and place, with this only restriction that it should be called a Custody until the number of brethren should have sufficiently increased: now, understanding that it continues to flourish more and more, that it possesses a novitiate and schools of Philosophy and Theology, and that the Religious are becoming more numerous; having moreover been requested to restore the Province more fully by giving it a Provincial and Definitors, and this not only by our fathers but also by leading Catholics, who know the state of affairs in England, and the good which may result from this step: hence we have resolved to give the English Province a regular existence, as we do by virtue of this decree, and we institute the Very

Reverend Father John Gennings, heretofore Custos, Provincial Minister; we appoint the Very Reverend Father Francis a S. Clara Custos, and the Very Reverend Fathers Bonaventure Jackson, Nicholas Day, Francis Bel and Jerome Pickford Definitors, granting them at the same time all the faculties, rights and privileges which by our Rule and Constitutions belong to the Provincial, Custos and Definitors of the Province. And in order that these appointments may speedily come to the knowledge of the Fathers and Brothers of the said Province, we charge the Very Reverend Father Joseph Bergaigne, Commissary General over the Provinces of Belgium and Great Britain, to promulgate them as soon as possible, and to do all he deems expedient, according to God, for the welfare and increase of the English Province.

Given at Madrid, under our signature and seal of office, August 6, 1629.

BROTHER BERNARDINE DE SENIS,
Minister General.

It will be interesting to our readers to see the document relating to this first Chapter meeting, wherein we are made acquainted with the offices which the fathers held in early times, and with some regulations then made.

TABLE OF THE FIRST CHAPTER OF THE ENGLISH
PROVINCE,

restored to its rights and rank by the authority of the General Chapter celebrated in Rome in 1625, and of the Most Reverend Father Bernardine de Senis, Minister General of the whole Order of Friars Minor, held at the Convent of St. Elizabeth, of the Sisters of the Third Order of our holy Father St. Francis in the city of Brussels, on the first Sunday of Advent, 1630, under the presidency of the Very Reverend Father Joseph Bergaigne, Definitor General of the same Order, and Commissary General with fulness of power over the Provinces of Germany, Belgium, Ireland England and Scotland.

In the first place, by the authority of the Most Reverend Father General, the Very Reverend Father John Gennings, for many years Vicar and Custos, is instituted and declared Provincial.

Custos, the Very Reverend Father Francis a S. Clara, professor of theology, and for some years Guardian of the College of the English Province at Douai. Definitors: Very Reverend Father Bonaventure Jackson, formerly first Preses and Guardian of the said College at Douai; Very Reverend Father Nicholas Day, preacher and professor of theology; Very Reverend Father Francis Bel, preacher and Confessor in the said Convent of St. Elizabeth of Sisters of the Third Order; Very Reverend Father Jerome Pickford, preacher, and formerly Preses of the College at Douai.

The Very Reverend Father Francis Bel, Definitor, is instituted Guardian of the College at Douai. Vicar, Very Reverend Father Paul a S. Magdalena.

Guardian of London, Very Reverend Father

Bonaventure Jackson, Definitor. Guardian of Berkshire, Very Reverend Father George Perrot.

In St. Bonaventure's College at Douai, theology and philosophy shall be taught. Head professor of theology, Very Reverend Father Francis a S. Clara; second professor, Reverend Father William a S. Augustino. Professor of philosophy, Father Lawrence a S. Edmundo. The Very Reverend Father Guardian will teach the Hebrew language.

Confessor of the Convent of Gravelines, for the nuns who reside at Aire, Father Peter of Alcantara.

Confessor of the Convent of St. Elizabeth, of nuns of the Third Order at Brussels, Father Egidius a S. Ambrosio.

It is moreover decreed, by the authority of the Most Reverend Father General, that, for the better and easier direction of the brethren and despatch of business, the Provincial, when residing in England, may appoint a Commissary, invested with his authority, for our brethren in Belgium; and, when residing in Belgium, he may in like manner provide for England. But the said Commissary shall not have power to admit ladies to the convents of nuns, unless they provide a dower of at least three thousand florins, besides the necessary expenses for their clothing and profession. Nor shall the Commissary, when residing in Belgium, admit novices to our Order without the consent of the Discreets of Douai, which is the noviciate of the Province. Father Lawrence a S. Edmundo is appointed master of novices.

We also exhort all the fathers and brothers of the

Province, in the name and by the authority of the Most Reverend Father General, that they work unanimously for the preservation and increase of the Province now restored by God's grace; and that they observe the Rule and Statutes of the Order as far as the circumstances of times, places and persecutions will allow.

Finally, leave is granted to the Very Reverend Father Provincial to admit priests of edifying life to the noviceship in England, as had already been granted heretofore by the General Chapter, and by letters patent of the Most Reverend Father Andrew a Soto of happy memory, on the feast of St. Michael the Archangel, 1620. But this must only be done for a grave reason, and after the manner agreed upon by the Commissary and some of the fathers who were present at the National Congregation held at Brussels. By the same authority he may admit sisters to their clothing and profession at Aire for the Convent of Gravelines, the Convent of Aire being now incorporated in the English Province. To this end the consent of the Provincial of Flanders has also been obtained, to whose jurisdiction the Convent was formerly subject.

Suffrages.

For the Most Reverend Father General of the whole Order, by whose authority and favour this Province has been restored to its rights and rank; for His Excellency Prince Emanuel of Portugal and others who have procured and promoted by their kindness the restoration of this Province; for the prosperity of the same Province, and for the spiritual and temporal welfare of the kingdom of England, each priest shall say three Masses; the clerics three times the seven penitential psalms with the litanies; the lay brothers three hundred Our Fathers and Hail Marys.

F. JOSEPH BERGAIGNE, *Commissary General.*

F. JOHN GENNINGS, *Provincial Minister of England.*

F. FRANCIS A S. CLARA, *Custos of the Province.*

F. FRANCIS BEL, *Definitor.*

In the name of the absent Definitors and others, who have been unable to come, on account of the dangers of the road and other obstacles, and who have excused themselves by letters addressed to the Most Reverend Father Commissary General, and have promised to concur in all that should be enacted, I have signed.

F. PETER LOMBAERTS,
Secretary to this Chapter meeting.

CHAPTER VIII.

NAMES AND OFFICES IN THE ORDER. GOVERNMENT OF THE PROVINCE.

WHEN candidates enter religion, it is customary to give them along with the habit of the Order also a new name. Among the members of the second English Franciscan Province we find some, like Francis a S. Clara, Lewis a S. Maria and others, called after two Saints. This custom must be traced to Spain, and found its way into the English Province through some of the early Fathers of the Second Province having been admitted to the Order there. In Italy the religious are called after their birthplace, as Benignus of Genoa, Bernardine de Senis. In England and Belgium the Fathers retained their surname, as John Gennings, Joseph Bergaigne. This had also been the practice before the Reformation, as we see by such names as John Forest and Henry Elston. In the second Province we also meet with peculiar names, such as Lawrence Lawrence, Masseus Massey. These names had the advantage of preventing confusion; for as at Douai the Fathers were known by their name in religion, and on the English mission by their surname, it must have been convenient if both were the same, or had a similar sound.

At the time of the formation of the second English

Province, the Franciscan Order had marvellously increased, and it was found impossible for the Minister General with his staff in Rome to efficiently govern 100,000 brethren. It had been deemed expedient to appoint a Commissary General for the north-western parts of Europe, comprising the Provinces of Germany, Belgium, and the British Isles. There were at that time four or five Provinces in Belgium and at least four in Germany. This Commissary General was dependent from the General of the Order, but had full delegated powers. The Fathers of these Provinces also assembled from time to time in Council, which was called a National Congregation of the Order, and had power to make regulations similar to that of the General Chapter, but, of course, subject to the approval of the General of the Order. The English Franciscans, like the others, sent delegates to these Congregations.

It has already been mentioned in the decree of erection that the English Franciscans had, besides the Provincial, also a Commissary for either of the two portions of the Province, England or Belgium, as the case might be, where the Provincial did not reside. His powers were regulated by the Chapter or by the General Minister.

The name of Guardian, or Warden as he was called before the Reformation, is given to the local superior of a regular House of the Order with a sufficient number of inmates. The Second English Province possessed but one such establishment, which was at Douai. This might have caused a serious inconvenience in connection with the election of the officials of the Province, in which the Guardians have a vote. But a way was found out of this difficulty by appointing titular Guardians, who should not indeed rule over a friary, but have jurisdiction over a District, with the right of voting. Two such Guardians were appointed at the first Provincial Chapter in 1630, one of London, the other of Reading or Berkshire. The District of London comprised the counties in which the city and suburbs were situated; the Reading District extended to Berkshire, Hampshire, and Sussex. This points to the fact that the missionary labours of the Franciscans at that time were limited to those parts.

Two new Districts with their respective Guardians were created in 1632: Dorset and York.

In 1634 a Guardian of Greenwich was appointed, with jurisdiction over Kent and Essex.

In 1637 it was resolved that " as some of our Fathers labour in the District of Leicester, a Guardian of Leicester be appointed." Two new Districts were formed in 1640: Oxford and Chichester. In 1647 all the Districts were re-arranged and classed in the following order:

London, comprising Middlesex, Kent, Wiltshire and Hertfordshire.

York, comprising Yorkshire, Lincolnshire, Lancashire and Rutlandshire.

Cambridge, comprising Cambridgeshire, Norfolk, Suffolk, Essex, Huntingdonshire and the Isle of Ely.

Bristol, comprising Somersetshire, Gloucestershire, Herefordshire, Dorsetshire, Devonshire, Cornwall and South Wales.

Oxford, comprising Oxfordshire, Berkshire, Bedford-shire, Northamptonshire, Derbyshire and Buckingham-shire.

Newcastle, comprising Northumberland, Westmore-land, Cumberland, Durham and Richmondshire.

Worcester, comprising Worcestershire, Warwickshire, Shropshire, Cheshire, Staffordshire and North Wales.

Greenwich, to have a Guardian of its own, because it was the first house of the Regular Observance in England, and after the restoration the first Chapter in England was held there.

To these Guardianates that of Canterbury was added in 1662; then Coventry in 1668, with Warwickshire for district; finally, in 1675, at the request of Lord Henry Howard, Earl Marshal of England and Duke of Norfolk, a titular Guardian of Norwich was appointed.

The following titles of the Guardianates or Districts are given in the "Statutes for the Mission," 1713. *

Greenwich, The Most Holy Name of Jesus.†

London, Our Holy Father St. Francis.

York, St. Thomas the Martyr.

Cambridge, The Stigmata of St. Francis.

Bristol, St. Anthony of Padua.

Oxford, Blessed Agnellus.

Newcastle, St. Francis with a Cross in his hand.

Worcester, St. Bernardine.

The titular Guardians did not always reside in their respective districts.   This was indeed generally the

* See Chapter XIII.

† This is the only Guardianate of which there is a seal : it represents the Holy Name.

case with some, such as London, Greenwich, York and Coventry. But on the other hand we find titular Guardians living at Douai or Bruges.

However, a regulation was made in 1659 that the Guardians shonld visit their respective districts once a year. This was afterwards found inconvenient on account of the difficulty of travelling and the troubles of the times; and in 1692 it was considered sufficient for the Guardians to visit their subjects once during their term of office.

In order to ensure the success of the twofold object they had in view, namely, the preservation of the Faith and the conversion of England, the fathers made two wise regulations. The first was, that none should be allowed to go on the English mission unless they were judged fit for the work; the others should be employed on the continent, either at Douai, or at Aire or Bruges, in each of which places the fathers had a residence attached to the convent for two priests and two or three lay brothers. The other was, that those who did not give satisfaction on the mission could be immediately recalled; and in order to make sure of this, the missionaries had on their departure to swear before the community "that whenever they should be recalled, or sent back by their superiors, they would obey and conform to the command, circumstances notwithstanding." This oath they had to sign with their own hand.

The English Franciscans of the second Province first styled themselves " of the Regular Observance;" afterwards they assumed the name of " Recollects," and the street where their old church at Douai stands is called to this day " Rue des Récollets Anglais." They were induced to make the change chiefly by two considerations. One was that probably all the Provinces over which the Commissary General presided were termed "of Recollects;" the other that there was already an establishment of Recollects at Douai. The Franciscans had settled in that town in the thirteenth century, and had erected their friary in the Rue Notre-Dame, now called de Valenciennes. Their house and church were burned in 1553, but soon afterwards rebuilt. They had changed their old name of " Cordeliers " for that of " Recollects ; " and the people, seeing that the English fathers were of the same Order, gave them also the same name. A citizen of Douai, in his notes on Church matters,* says of the English Franciscans that their dress was the same as that of the Walloon Recollects, but their tonsure appeared larger, as only the top of their head was shaved. He also tells us that the English Recollects joined their brethren, the Walloon Recollects, at public processions, walking under the same cross, from the year 1670. The English Recollects were also allowed to make the quest in and around Douai, as well as their Walloon brethren. From the year 1676 the term Recollects is inserted in all their documents, and they had also the inscription of the old seal, " Regularis Observantiæ," changed on a new one then made into " Recollectorum."†

---

* Douai, État Ecclesiastique, Notes recueillies par Mr. Plouvain. No. 1021.

† The term *Regularis Observantiæ* applied to the Observants, *Strictioris Observantiæ* to the Discalced, Reformed and Recollects.

We may quite safely endorse the explanation of the term " Recollects " given by Father Anthony Parkinson under the year 1503.

" This is the first year," he says, " wherein I find the Observants called Recollects ; which name was given them on account of a statute made amongst them obliging every Province of the Regular Observance to have some Houses of Recollection, particularly appointed for such as were desirous to give themselves up wholly to Divine contemplation, most rigorous mortification, and the strictest observance of their Founder's Rule. These Recollects were no separate body distinct from the rest of the Observants, but made up a part of it, giving themselves first to the contemplative life, as the most proper preparation for the better discharging the duties of the active ; as also for recovering their spirit when dissipated by preaching, teaching, ruling as superiors, or other similar exercises of obedience and charity."

We will give the words of one more historian of the Order : " Discalceati, Recollecti et Reformati non sunt nisi Observantes strictius viventes."*

Now, however, the term " Recollects " has a purely historical interest, since all distinctions in the Franciscan Order have been abrogated by Pope Leo XIII. in his bull *Felicitate*, October 4, 1897. †

The English Franciscans were not only strict in name, but from the beginning of the Province they

---

* Fr. Van den Haute, *Brevis Hist. Ord. Min.*

† Extinctis nominibus Observantium, Reformatorum, Excalceatorum seu Alcantarinorum, Recollectorum, Ordo Fratrum Minorum sine ullo apposito, ex instituto Francisci patris appelletur.

were also strict observers of their Rule, especially in the matter of Holy Poverty, as the following regulations, made in 1637, will show:

For the essential observance of Holy Poverty, inasmuch as our circumstances on the mission allow we declare:

1. No one shall have a sum of money by him, or deposit it with another person, or cause it to be deposited, or keep it, without the Provincial's leave in writing. He that acts otherwise, incurs the transgression of the vow of poverty and the punishment of a proprietor.

2. The same guilt and punishment is incurred by him who assigns an annual rent for himself, the Province or the College, from alms given him.

3. Also he who accepts an alms given by way of rent, temporarily or for life, except with due stipulations and the Provincial's permission.

4. Also he who, without Superiors' leave, presumes to dispose of alms, or to send or give them away at will.

5. Also he who makes use of money received as alms for things curious, precious or superfluous, in food, clothing, and the rest which may be called extravagant considering the condition of the mission, according to the judgment of the Provincial Minister.

The faithful observance of these regulations was undoubtedly a great safeguard for the Franciscans on the English mission.

CHAPTER IX.

SERAPHIC CONFLICT OF THE SECOND PROVINCE FOR THE FAITH.[*]

DEATH did not tarry in coming to thin the slender ranks of the English Franciscans.

In 1634 five had died, including Father William a S. Augustino, head professor of theology at Douai. It must have been with mixed feelings that the fathers followed to the grave the mortal remains of their beloved brethren, whom they could as yet ill spare.

But others were ere long to wing their flight to the Heavenly Jerusalem; no tears would be shed over their graves, but the religious would unite in a joyous "Te Deum." Their death would not be considered a loss, but a most desirable gain, as it won for the English Province a crown of immortal glory.

Five fathers were put to death for the Catholic religion : Thomas Bullaker, Henry Heath, Arthur Bel, John Woodcock and John Wall. To these must be added Charles Mahony, an Irish Franciscan.

Four died in prison: Walter Colman, Francis Levison, Paul Atkinson and Germanus Holmes.

---

[*] What is said in this chapter must merely be taken as historical evidence; and as these sufferers for the Faith are not yet canonized, we have no intention of anticipating the judgment of the Church.

Others suffered imprisonment, some of them for many years.

We shall give a brief account of the sufferings of these Franciscan heroes.

Venerable Thomas Bullaker.

Scarcely had Father Bullaker landed at Plymouth, whither he had travelled from his friary of the Province of the Immaculate Conception in Spain, when he was apprehended and thrown into prison. But not long after he was liberated, and worked on the mission, where for about twelve years he longed and sighed unceasingly that he might lay down his life for Christ.

The long desired day came at last. On hearing the death sentence pronounced upon him, Father Bullaker could not contain his joy. He fell on his knees, and, with hands and eyes lifted up towards heaven, sang the " Te Deum " in thanksgiving to God. Then rising, he made a profound reverence to the court, thanking them for the great favour they had done him.

On Wednesday, October 12, 1642, he was brought out of Newgate prison, laid on a hurdle, and so drawn to Tyburn, showing all the way a wonderful cheerfulness in his countenance. At the place of execution he spoke to the people upon the text, " Thou art a priest for ever, according to the order of Melchisedech " (Ps. 109), and began to instruct them on the Sacrament of Christ's Body and Blood, until he was silenced by the officers, who ordered him to make an end. He readily obeyed, giving them hearty thanks for bringing him thither to die for his faith, a happiness which, he said, he had always longed for, though he acknowledged himself unworthy of it. He then received absolution from one of his brethren in the throng, on giving the sign agreed upon before, which was to hold his hands up to his face. He stood a short time in silent prayer, as it were in contemplation, till the cart was drawn away. He was cut down still breathing ; his palpitating heart was torn from his bosom and held up aloft, that the crowd might see it. " Behold," cried the executioner, " the heart of a traitor."

His head was set upon London bridge, and his quarters upon the gates of the city. His heart, which had been thrown into the fire, was saved from the flames by the same Franciscan who had given him absolution. Among the relics at the Franciscan Convent at Taunton is an arm-bone of the martyr.

Venerable Henry Heath.

From his entrance into religion Father Heath had led a life of extraordinary perfection. In 1641 he determined to seek the consent of his superiors to enter upon the English mission, hoping to meet there with the crown of martyrdom : his desire was soon fulfilled.

On the very day of his arrival in London he was apprehended on suspicion and committed to the Compter prison. The next day he had to appear before the Lord Mayor, and, owning himself to be a priest, was sent to Newgate.

Soon after this he was brought to the bar, accused of being a priest and returning to England, and therefore guilty of high treason. The trial was soon over, for as

he had acknowledged himself a priest, he was brought
in guilty of the indictment, and sentence was passed
accordingly. Father Heath, making a low reverence
to the bench, said : " My lords, I give you thanks for
the singular honour you have done me; for now I shall
die for Christ." This occurred on April 11, 1643.

The 17th of the same month was the day of his
triumph. Being asked how he could look so cheerful
at such a time, he said that, though he always was
convinced that the martyrs experienced much joy and
consolation when they were to suffer for Christ, yet he
never could have imagined this delight to be so exceeding great, as he now found by his own experience.

On seeing the hurdle with the horses standing ready
to take him to Tyburn, he offered to lay himself down
on the ground to be drawn in that manner over the
stones and through the mire ; but this was not allowed,
and he was laid on the sledge. Arrived at the place
of execution, he readily and cheerfully got up into the
cart under the gallows, saying with an audible voice,
" Into thy hands, O Lord, I commend my spirit." In
that very cart he reconciled one of the malefactors who
were to be executed with him. He prayed some time
silently with joined hands and closed eyes. Then he
recited aloud the hymn of Lauds for a martyr, "Martyr
Dei, qui unicum," it being the feast of St. Anicetus,
Pope and Martyr. This was followed by short aspira-
tions, " Jesus, pardon me my sins ! Jesus, convert
England ! Jesus, have mercy on this country ! O
England, be converted to the Lord thy God." He
raised his hands above his head, possibly for absolution;

the cart was drawn away, and he was left hanging even as he had stood before, with his hands lifted up towards heaven and his eyes cast down; and thus he calmly expired.

After his death he was cut down, disembowelled and quartered. His head was fixed upon London bridge, his quarters on four of the city gates. The Franciscan nuns at Taunton possess a bone of his about three inches long.

VENERABLE ARTHUR BEL.*

After returning from Scotland, Father Bel laboured most zealously on the English mission for the space of nine years, at the end of which it pleased God to grant him the martyr's crown, which during twenty years he had earnestly prayed for.

On Monday, November 6, 1643, he set out from Brigstock in Northamptonshire for London, but the next day he was apprehended by the Parliament soldiers at Stevenedge in Hertfordshire. On the Thursday he was taken to London and committed to Newgate prison. He had not been there full twenty-four hours, when he received a letter from the Provincial, requiring him to fill up the vacancy in the office of Guardian at Douai, caused by Father Heath's martyrdom. To this he sent the following reply.

REVEREND FATHER,

I received your command with humility and readiness in putting it into execution. Twenty hours

* His own signature is " Bel," not " Bell."

before it reached me I had taken possession of Father Heath's place in Newgate. It only remains for me to ask your prayers, that I may persevere to the end ; and I beg of all Christians, with St. Andrew, not to hinder my passion. Your poor brother,

F. BEL.

The death sentence was pronounced upon him on December 7. Father Bel entoned the " Te Deum," and returned hearty thanks to the court.

The 11th of December was the day fixed for his execution. He was laid upon a hurdle, and drawn by four horses to Tyburn. When he came to the place of execution, he said: "Now I see verified in me what was foretold by happy Thomas Bullaker." For, when Father Bel was complaining to him in prison that as he was the elder brother in religious profession, he ought rather to have gone before him, he replied: "God will have me to go first, but you shall soon follow."

Being put on a cart, he addressed a few words to the people, finishing thus : " I forgive with my whole heart those who have contributed to my death, even as I desire to be forgiven ; and I die joyfully for the Faith of Christ." Many a heart was moved, especially that of a parliamentary officer, who was about to suffer death for stealing. With tears in his eyes he turned to Father Bel, saying, " I wish to die in your religion." It was observed that the martyr spoke to him for some time in a whisper, probably suggesting acts of contrition and giving absolution.

As the cart was being drawn away, Father Bel raised his hands, and the prior of St. Magdalen's gave him absolution. He was allowed to hang for a short space of time, then cut down, drawn and quartered. In stripping him they found under his secular dress the habit of his Order, which he was accustomed to wear. Seeing this, the people cried out with astonishment, "See what mortified men these are, who thus despise the pleasures of the world!" Guards were appointed to prevent the Catholics from carrying off anything by way of relics. Some of these, however, were secured; and portions are kept by the nuns of the Third Order at Taunton.

Among the portraits of ten of the English Martyrs, commonly called "the miraculous portraits," at Lanherne in Cornwall, are those of the Franciscan Fathers Bullaker, Heath and Bel. The history of these portraits is thus told by the Carmelite nuns of Lanherne:

"Our community at Antwerp being distressed for novices, they determined to have recourse to the English Martyrs, and therefore made a novena in their honour. Shortly after, Miss Mary Gifford, of Staffordshire, presented herself and made her profession on April 8, 1681, aged forty-two, taking for her religious name Sister Mary of the Martyrs. She brought with her the portraits of these ten martyrs, with whom her own father had been a prisoner for some time, for the Faith. They were about to give their lives for it, and he was exceedingly anxious to obtain their portraits beforehand. Therefore he tried to take them; and although entirely unacquainted with the art of painting, he succeeded almost in a miraculous manner. These portraits have ever since been preserved with the utmost respect and veneration by our community."

Venerable John Woodcock.

Thirsting for martyrdom, Father Woodcock landed at the end of the year 1643 at Newcastle-on-Tyne, with the intention of spending a short time in his native county of Lancashire, in the hope of converting some of his relations. Having made his way thither, he was apprehended the very first night after his arrival; and the next day a justice of the peace committed him to Lancaster gaol, where he was left two years before being tried. During this time he acted the part of a missionary among his fellow-prisoners.

His trial at length came on, August 6, 1646, when he was placed at the bar with two secular priests, the Venerable Edward Bamber and the Venerable Thomas Whitaker. He confessed himself a priest and a Franciscan; indeed his zeal during the time of his imprisonment was sufficient proof, and the questions were put to him merely as a matter of form. Upon this confession he was condemned to die, as in cases of high treason. It is scarcely possible to imagine the joy with which he received the sentence, exclaiming, " Praise be to God! God be thanked!"

He passed his last night in prayer and meditation, and the next day, being August 7, 1646, he was drawn together with his two companions to the place of execution. The sight of these three champions of the Faith filled the Catholics with sentiments of wonder and edification, whereas the Protestants were amazed, seeing the courage and joy with which these servants of God went to meet a barbarous and ignominious death.

At the place of execution, Father Woodcock, being ordered up the ladder, after a short prayer, offered to speak to the people to explain the cause of his death and the truth of the Catholic Faith ; but he was quickly interrupted by the sheriff, and flung off the ladder by the executioner. It is said that the rope broke immediately, and he was ordered up the ladder again, to be hanged a second time ; then cut down more than half alive and barbarously butchered.

His head was kept in the cloister of St. Bonaventure's at Douai before the French Revolution. The Franciscan nuns at Taunton possess an arm-bone of the venerable martyr.

We have his portrait, as well as those of the three preceding Martyrs, in the " Certamen. "

Venerable John Wall.

Father Wall was zealously labouring on the mission in Worcestershire, when he was apprehended at Rushock Court, not long after the first breaking-out of Oates's plot, by the sheriff's deputy and others, who were making search for another man. He was taken before Sir John Packington, justice of the peace, and refusing to take the oaths of allegiance and supremacy, was committed to Worcester gaol in the beginning of December, 1678.

The sentence of death was pronounced upon him in the usual form on April 25, 1679, at Worcester. The confessor made a bow and said, " Thanks be to God ! God save the king ! I beseech God to bless your lordship and all this honourable bench ! " The judge replied, " You have spoken very well : I do not intend you shall die, at least not for the present, until I know the king's further pleasure."

Father Wall was taken back to prison, and after some time was sent up to London, as were also several other priests, who lay under condemnation for their sacerdotal character. There he was examined and then brought back to Worcester. Four months had elapsed since his condemnation, when he was ordered to be executed. A priest named William Levison, brother to the Franciscan, Venerable Francis Levison, visited him in prison, heard his confession and gave him Holy Communion. He again gave him absolution at his execution, which took place at Red Hill, near Worcester, on August 22, 1679. His head was cut off, and his body permitted to be buried in St. Oswald's churchyard, where it was afterwards remarked that his grave remained green when the rest of the place was all bare.

His head was secretly conveyed by the said priest, William Levison, to Father Leo Randolph, to be taken to St. Bonaventure's, Douai, where it was respectfully preserved until the French Revolution. A tooth and also a bone of the martyr are among the relics at Taunton.

VENERABLE CHARLES MAHONY.

Returning from abroad to his native country, this Irish Franciscan was driven by stress of weather upon the coast of Wales, in the heat of the persecution. When he was discovered to be a priest, he was committed to prison, and tried at Denbigh, upon an indictment of high treason, for taking orders in the Church of Rome and being found in this kingdom. He confessed himself to be a priest and was thereupon condemned, and sent to Ruthin to be executed. On August 12, 1679, he was drawn to the place where he had to suffer, in the habit of his order. Arrived there, he said: " Now God Almighty is pleased I should suffer martyrdom, His Holy Name be praised, since I die for my religion ! "

He suffered with great constancy, being cut down alive and butchered according to sentence. His age was under forty.

WALTER COLMAN.

He was condemned, with six other priests, on December 8, 1641, in the sessions at the Old Bailey, to be hanged, drawn and quartered on the 13th following. They were, however, reprieved ; but ultimately no further steps were taken in the matter, and, one of the number having died, the others were allowed to linger away their lives at Newgate.

Refined and cultivated, belonging to one of England's oldest families, brought up in the midst of plenty, Father Colman must have suffered a hundred martyrdoms in his loathsome prison cell, where he lingered three or four years. So obscure was his fate that not even his own brethren knew exactly when his imprisonment was terminated by a precious death, which occurred in the year 1645.

His portrait is in Father Mason's work, " Certamen Seraphicum."

VENERABLE FRANCIS LEVISON.

William Levison, the priest who visited Father Wall in prison, in his letter dated August 25, 1679, writes of his brother, Venerable Francis Levison, as follows: " My poor brother continues still a close prisoner, and complains much of want. The justice who committed him has endeavoured to bribe witnesses to swear against him, but as yet cannot prevail with any. What will be the event of these proceedings, only God knows."

After fourteen months close confinement he died in prison a confessor of Christ, February 11, 1680.

His precious death is thus recorded in the Register, in the necrology of the Chapter held on June 16 of the same year: " V. A. P. F. Ignatius a S. Clara, qui in carcere post 14 mensium inclusionem ibi obiit in Anglia."

FATHER PAUL ATKINSON.

This glorious confessor of the faith had been duly summoned on his mission to attend the twenty-third Chapter, to be celebrated in London on July 9, 1698, but did not appear, nor was any excuse received for his absence. This was shortly after accounted for. He had been apprehended and hurried off to gaol, and condemned to perpetual imprisonment for priesthood. His brethren employed every effort, but in vain, to procure his liberation from Hurst Castle, the place of his strict confinement. They did not, however, forget him, and a sympathetic mention of him was made at every Chapter meeting, that is thirteen times, until 1731, when his happy death is thus recorded :

"In Hurst prison, Hants, died the venerable Confessor of the Faith and of Christ's priesthood, Father Paul Atkinson, formerly professor of theology, Definitor of the Province, and a jubilarian in the Order, who, during a continual martyrdom of thirty years, reflected honour on his prison, on our Province and on the English mission ; who, though not cut off by the persecutor's sword, still, as we piously trust, did not forego the palm of martyrdom. Wherefore we do not so much recommend him to the prayers of our brethren as propose him as a model for their imitation."

He departed this life on October 15, 1729.

We have his engraved portrait, made in the year 1728.

Father Germanus Holmes.

This is the last Franciscan who died in prison for the faith. After the Stuart rising of 1745 Father Holmes was seized during the revival of persecution consequent on that event, thrown into the Castle of Lancaster for being a priest, and there died a prisoner in 1746. At the Chapter held in London on October 19 of that year, his death is thus recorded in the necrology :

"The venerable confessor of Jesus Christ, Germanus Holmes, at one time professor of philosophy in our college at Douai, who, after suffering various insults from the insolent dregs of the populace on account of his priestly character, was consigned by the magistrates to Lancaster Castle and loaded with iron chains, where for four months he fought the good fight, and happily, as we hope, finished the course of his mortal life, having contracted the fever through the filthiness of the place ; but not without suspicion of poison administered to him by the wicked woman who brought him his food."

FRANCISCANS WHO SUFFERED IMPRISONMENT.

Probably the first father of the second Province who suffered imprisonment was BONAVENTURE JACKSON.

In a letter from a London secular priest, named Clark, to the Rev. Mr. Fitton, the clergy agent at Rome, dated December 18, 1633, there is this passage : " Within this fortnight I heare there are four prisoners released upon bond, videlicet, Mr. Henry More, a Jesuit, out of the New prison, and Mr. Tresame, agent for the Benedictines, out of the said prison, Father Bonaventure, a Franciscan, out of Newgate, and a fourth, whose name I know not." *

Father Jackson is described in the " Certamen " as "having been called to England by Father Gennings, laboured with great fruit of salvation, earning praise and gratitude, and having suffered persecution, affliction and imprisonment, died an eminent confessor."

During the troubled period subsequent upon the tragical end of Charles I., it is recorded in the Register, in the year 1653, that "three fathers have suffered imprisonment, and have with danger of their lives undergone their trial, showing great constancy."

* *Records of the English Province S.J.*

In 1656 we read: "Since the last Chapter three fathers have suffered imprisonment."

In 1679 and 1680 Fathers BERNARDINE LANGWORTH and FRANCIS OSBALDESTON were under a "Præmunire" for refusing to take the oaths of allegiance and supremacy.

Father MARIANUS NAPIER was tried and condemned for Oates's plot, but was not executed. In 1684 his death sentence was commuted into one of exile, whereupon he returned to Douai.

Father GERVASE CARTWRIGHT was arrested at the Revolution, and thrown into Leicester gaol. Having been in prison for twenty-eight months, he was sentenced to death. But this sentence was commuted by the Prince of Orange into that of exile. His brethren looked upon him as a confessor of Christ, which is shown by the fact that his head was enshrined in the cloister of the English Convent at Bruges.

Fathers FRANCIS HARDWICK and WILLIAM LOCKIER were consigned to Newgate prison, London, in the beginning of December, 1688.

Fathers DANIEL SELBY and LEWIS GRIMBALSON were imprisoned in York Castle; and Father BERNARDINE BARRAS in the dungeon of the Kidcote prison, at the end of York bridge, for several months at the period of the Revolution.

Thus did the English Franciscans of the second Province prove by deeds better than by words that the Seraphic spirit flourished among them.

VENERABLE JOHN WOODCOCK, O.S.F.

(From the " Certamen Seraphicum.")

To face p. 77.

CHAPTER X.

VOCATIONS. ZEAL AND DEVOTION. MARYLAND. DEATH OF FATHER GENNINGS.

FATHER GENNINGS, himself an old student of the English College at Douai, had recruited his early companions from among the alumni there; thus this famous institution had contributed its share at the beginning of the Province. Some of those who entered the Order afterwards had also made their early studies there.

From time to time also natives of Douai or the neighbourhood, moved by the eminently self-sacrificing spirit they saw in the English Franciscans, preferred to join them rather than their native brethren at Douai, either as clerics or as lay brothers. We can distinguish them among the other members of the English Province by their names.

A secular priest, John Talbot, who was labouring on the English mission, petitioned to be admitted to the Order. The Provincial, as we have seen, had the power of receiving such candidates in England, and he applied it in this case. At the Intermediate Chapter of 1638 it was resolved after mature deliberation not to send him to Douai for his noviceship, but to give him the habit of the Order, and let him pass his year of probation in England, in a place where he could most of the time wear the habit and be under the direction of a novice master to be appointed by the Provincial.

In the year 1650 another extraordinary vocation is chronicled.   One of the Benedictine fathers of Douai, Francis Tresham, a man of irreproachable life, was desirous of exchanging the habit of St. Benedict for that of St. Francis.   When the application had been duly considered, it was thought that his vocation came from God, as had been the case with St. Anthony of Padua before.   Shortly after his admission he was sent on the English mission, where during the ten remaining years of his life he zealously laboured for the good · of souls.

The English Franciscans secured a useful helper in 1663.   The Very Reverend Father Augustine Niffo had been delegated by the Commissary, Father James de Riddere, to make the visitation of the Province and preside at the Chapter in London, in 1662.   No doubt he thoroughly understood the nature of the work in which our fathers were engaged, for he was Superior of the missionaries * of the Order in Flanders.   He must have been favourably impressed with what he saw in England, for he joined the English Province with little delay, and was straightway made Custos.

The fathers did not leave undone anything they thought conducive to the good of religion in England. Thus it was resolved in 1632 to set up a printing press at Douai for the greater facility of publishing works

* His title in the Acts of the Chapter of 1662 is " Provinciæ S. Josephi in Comitatu Flandriæ Missionariorum Superior, olim Custos Custodum."

against our sectaries. Father Bonaventure a S. Thoma was appointed manager of this press.

A regulation was made in 1638 that the missionaries were bound frequently to catechise children and others, either in their own homes or at the priest's residence. The inculcation of the necessity of catechising was often afterwards repeated.

Devotion to our Blessed Lady, which the Franciscans have inherited from their Founder, was not forgotten by the fathers of the second Province. So early as 1632 it was enacted that daily after Compline the antiphon " Tota pulchra " should be recited in honour of the Immaculate Conception. Also that before the principal Mass the litany of our Blessed Lady should be said every day for the conversion of England. Among the regulations made in 1648 for the College of St. Bonaventure at Douai are the following:

" Every Saturday the Mass of the Immaculate Conception shall be sung for the conversion of England.

" On the feasts of the Visitation and Presentation of the Blessed Virgin, High Mass shall be sung, as well as the ' Tota Pulchra ' after Compline, both at first and second Vespers."

There was also a Confraternity of the Immaculate Conception erected in our church at Douai.

The English Franciscans, while giving so many proofs of devotion to the Mother of God, were not unmindful of St. Francis, the sure guide to perfection for persons in the world. They admitted candidates to the Third Order both at Douai and on the mission, but not until they had obtained sufficient information, and convinced themselves in each individual case that the step was not rashly taken.

They also had some pictures printed, representing St. Francis descending into purgatory, as he is piously believed to do every year on his feast, according to Bartholomew of Pisa and other historians, to deliver the souls of the members of the three Orders which he has founded. They distributed these pictures among their friends and others, so that in the end a great number of them were circulated among the people. This gave rise to some controversy, and Father Peter Marchant, of the Province of Flanders, who presided as Commissary Visitor at the Chapter held in London in 1637, thought it well to intervene. He decided, first, that the said tradition and picture contained no error, but was conformable to piety, as it was handed down by pious authors; secondly, that it was not expedient to spread them promiscuously in England, which was a heretical country, as it might give offence to some who did not understand the nature of this devotion among Catholics; thirdly, if the Fathers wished to give them to pious people who were devout to our Holy Father St. Francis, they should do so privately, explaining at the same time the nature of the subject, in order to avoid all occasion of misapprehension or contradiction.

The labours of the English Franciscans were not confined to the territory of their native country : they were ready to go where they could serve the spiritual interests of their countrymen ; and this they showed by accepting a share in the missionary work in Maryland, where the Fathers of the Society of Jesus had settled about forty years before, four of them with one lay brother having accompanied the colonists when they sailed for the New World in 1633.

Maryland was granted in 1632 by King Charles I. to the second Lord Baltimore, whose father, for whom it was intended, had died before the Charter was issued. His brother, Leonard Calvert, was the first Governor of the colony, which received from Charles the name of Maryland in honour of his queen, Henrietta Maria. The Baltimores were Catholics, but all religious denominations were tolerated in Maryland from the beginning. The words, "The harvest indeed is great, but the labourers are few," could be applied with truth to the colony, for in the "Maryland Annual Letters" of the Society of Jesus we read in 1671 as follows: "In the mission of Maryland this year are two priests and two temporal coadjutors. The mission bears no little fruit, as we learn from the last letters, and its fruit would be still greater were the labourers more in number. Few are living of those sent in former years. Two died this year, Father William Pelham and Thomas Sherborne, a lay brother. There were fifty converts, many of high note, and fifty-four were baptized."

The Franciscans were asked to help in the work; and at the Intermediate Chapter held at Somerset House in 1672, under the presidency of Father Nicholas Cross, Provincial, it was agreed to send some fathers of the English Province thither. The first to set out for that distant mission were Fathers Polycarp Wicksted and

Basil Hobart. The result of their labours may be seen from a paragraph in the " Annual Letters of the Society," where under the year 1673 we read : " Two Franciscan fathers were sent last year from England as coadjutors in the labours of the mission, between whom and ourselves fraternal charity and offices of mutual friendship are exercised, to the common good of the Catholic cause." *

In 1675 Father Masseus Massey was appointed Preses, and with him were Fathers Henry Carew, Basil Hobart and Edward Golding. In 1677 Father Henry Carew became Preses. He was succeeded in 1680 by Father Masseus Massey, who was re-appointed in 1683. In 1686 Lord Baltimore must have asked for more Franciscans, for at the Definitory held on July 15 of that year in London, it was proposed : " What shall we answer to the request of Lord Baltimore for missionaries in Maryland ? " The reply was : " We shall provide two missionaries if we find fathers apt and willing to go."

But in the year 1689 the government was taken out of the hands of Lord Baltimore by the Convention of England. Mr. Copley was appointed Governor by commission from William and Mary in 1692, when the Protestant religion was established by law. How it fared in those days with Catholics may be gathered from the following paragraph in the " Annual Letters : "

" Our missions in the West Indies, of Maryland, and indeed of New York, underwent the same fate with

* *Records of the English Province S. J.*

those of England. In the latter (New York) there were only two priests, and these were forced in this storm to change their residence, as was also the Catholic Governor himself. One of them travelled on foot to Maryland, the other, after many perils on the sea, having been captured and plundered by Dutch pirates, at length arrived safe in France. In Maryland great difficulties are suffered. Our fathers yet remain to render what consolation they can to the distressed Catholics."

However, in 1699, two fathers were again sent thither as missionaries, Bruno Taylor and James Haddock. The latter died there in 1720; and this is the last we hear of the English Franciscans in Maryland.

In the midst of their labours for the glory of God and the good of souls, the English Franciscans had suffered an irreparable loss. Father John Gennings, having witnessed for many years the growth of the Province and the progress of the work which he had so happily commenced, having reached the truly patriarchal age of over ninety years, went at last to his reward. He had continued to work on the English mission until the year preceding his demise, when he signed the acts of the Chapter for the last time; and feeling death approaching, he hastened back to Douai, wishing to breathe his last among his children at St. Bonaventure's College, which had been the scene of the greatest work of his life. There he calmly expired on November 12, new style, in 1660. The following is a translation of his Latin mortuary bill:

JESUS, MARY, FRANCIS.

In the year of our Lord 1660, on November 12, there died at the friary of the English Franciscans at Douai the aged and venerable Father John Gennings, a man of exemplary and blameless life, steadfast in his purpose, and beloved by all. After having laboured in the midst of dangers with great fruit on the English mission, feeling drawn to a stricter life, he embraced the Rule of St. Francis, and restored the English Province of Friars Minor, which had been destroyed by the blind fury of heretics, and founded St. Bonaventure's College at Douai. He was three times Provincial, often Custos and Definitor. And whilst he worthily filled the office of Commissary Provincial in England, feeling that the laying away of his tabernacle was at hand, and wishing to die among his sorrowing brethren and children, he returned to the house of his foundation, where he peacefully slept in the Lord, full of days and merits, about the ninety-fifth year of his age, the sixty-fourth of priesthood and mission, and the fifty-second of religious life. We recommend his soul to your prayers and sacrifices, that he may without delay enter into the joy after which he always sighed.

R.I.P.

VENERABLE HENRY HEATH, O.S.F.

(From the "Certamen Seraphicum.")

To face p. 85.

CHAPTER XI.

BENEFACTIONS AND OBLIGATIONS OF MASSES.

FROM various quarters the English Franciscans received material assistance to help them in carrying on the great work they had undertaken.

They always showed themselves extremely zealous in the observance of their vow of poverty, and made use of what was left or given them in the true Franciscan spirit. From among many proofs we take the following declaration, made at the Chapter of 1683:

For the direction of the consciences of all the Religious of the Province in the perfect observance of the Rule of our Holy Father St. Francis, especially as regards the most high poverty, the Fathers of the Province declare that all alms received either annually or otherwise, have been accepted and are administered according to our Rule and the Apostolic declarations. In witness of which we have made a protestation, which the present Chapter also renews, to the following effect:

Whereas by a precept of our Holy Rule all property is forbidden us in common as well as in private, and with regard to money also the simple use: we, the Provincial and Fathers of the English Province of the Friars Minor of the Stricter Observance, wishing purely to observe our Rule, in imitation of the example left us by the ancient fathers of our Province, for the security of our conscience, and for the edification of those who will come after us, herewith declare :

That we repudiate all property in common as well as in private, admitting only the use of what is necessary, given us either as a free gift, or alms, or as retribution for our labour : not as if we had a strict right to those things, but being content with their simple use. And although, in our quality of Apostolic labourers on the mission, we are often forced to have recourse to money in order to procure the necessaries of life, according to the law of nature and the concessions and declarations of many Popes, yet, even when actually engaged on the mission we cannot do so indiscriminately, or as proprietors, but only with moderation and as procurators of the donors, for past, present or imminent needs. And thus, charging the consciences of our subjects in this matter, we exonerate our own ; and we beseech them by the Poverty and Wounds of Christ, that mindful of their holy profession they strive by the moderate use of temporal things to gain everlasting treasures.

As regards all alms, especially of money, given the Province in general, either for the support of the missions or for the erection and maintenance of friaries or Colleges, we declare that the full and entire ownership thereof remains with the donors, or devolves to the Apostolic See, no matter in what terms the donations are made, lest in the present state of things the pious intention of our benefactors be frustrated, or the Province deprived of the necessary help. Hence we believe and declare that, although according to the laws of the Church the Provincial

Minister has a discretionary power as to the use of things necessary or allowed to the Order, nevertheless the donors alone, or the Apostolic Syndics who are procurators for the Holy See, have a strict right to dispose of them as owners.   Nor can we, nor will we have recourse to such pecuniary alms through the Syndics as our spiritual friends, except inasmuch as we are bound by our Rule to provide for the wants of the sick and the clothing of the brethren, or other similar needs, according to places, and times, and cold climates.

In witness whereof we have signed and sealed this document, February 21, 1676.

F. JOHN A S. CRUCE, *Prov. Min.*
F. FRANCIS A S. CLARA.
F. NICHOLAS A S. CRUCE.
F. DANIEL A S. FRANCISCO.

The General Minister, Joseph Ximenes Samaniego, in a letter dated Madrid, March 24, 1678, expressed himself fully satisfied with this declaration.

It has been thought well to insert the foregoing document, in order that the reader may understand that the English Franciscans were within the limits of their Rule and Constitutions in accepting gifts or bequests as they did.

(Benefactions mentioned in connection with the residences are not given here, to avoid repetition.)

Conspicuous among the early bequests is that of the Fleet Street houses.   Mr. William Lyndsey left us five houses in Fleet Street at the corner of Swan Alley. They were held in trust by some Catholic gentlemen

" upon condition that they should give the profits issuing from the said houses by way of alms to the Friars Minor of the Province of England, until such time as England may be converted, that the said Friars may have a place to shelter themselves, until they can provide a larger building."

Two of these houses fronted Fleet Street, and were let at fifty pounds each yearly. The three others stood back, and one of them was let at seventeen pounds, the two others at nine pounds each per annum.

The first trustees were Mr. Hawkins, Mr. Englefield and Mr. Bolton. Subsequently we find among them the Duke of Norfolk, the Honourable Ralph Widdrington and Edward Burdet, Esq.

The title-deeds of these houses, together with all our other papers, were lost in Oates' plot. But afterwards the Earl of Sunderland gave a warrant for recovering our writings.

These houses were burnt in the great fire of London ; and as by act of Parliament the buildings were to be re-constructed or the ground sold, it was resolved to re-build the houses. It appears that Mrs. Lindsey gave three hundred pounds towards the rebuilding : she was to receive during her lifetime thirty-five pounds annually out of the rents. Mrs. Catherine Sturdy, who was then our Syndic, bore half the charge of rebuilding the three back houses : she was in consequence to enjoy half the profits of the said tenements for the term of forty-one years, she paying out of her moiety half the rent of the ground, which was valued at four pounds and ten shillings per annum.

Her allowance was afterwards reduced to twenty-four pounds yearly; and the last payment due to her was made in 1710.

In 1653 Mrs. Margaret Anderton left two hundred pounds to the English Franciscans for the maintenance of one missionary of ours in England, for which purpose she desired to nominate Father William Anderton for life; and the Definitory consented to this.

The following is a copy of Sir William Powell's declaration, transmitted to us by his grandnephew John Powell:

Whereas I Sir William Powell of Rolleston Parke in ye County of Stafford, Knight, have by my last will and testament bearing date ye 11th day of this instant May, 1654, given and granted an annuity of five pounds per annum to be paid for ever out of ye Lands, which by my said will I have given to my grand-nephew John Powell. Now I doe hereby declare and appoint that the said five pounds shall be annually paid to a good man to pray for my soule, and for my succeeding heirs, and to help poore Catholiques, such a one as Mr. Roper shall appoint, and after his decease, any one whome ye Provinciall of ye Order of Franciscans shall nominate and appoint. In Witnesse whereof I the said Sir William Powell have hereunto sett my hand this 12th of May, 1654.

In the presence of Francis Howard, Jo. Tanfield.

WILLIAM POWELL.

This is a true Coppy, JOHN POWELL.

At the request of Father Francis a S. Clara, a benefactor assigned one thousand pounds, which, in his own name and for purposes to be determined by him, he desired the Mother Abbess of Nieuport (afterwards Bruges) to invest with a merchant or corporation. Half the interest was yearly to be paid her, the other half to be handed over by way of alms to the Guardian of our College at Douai. So long as this alms was received, a Mass was to be said every Tuesday for the said benefactor. At his death the principal was to be paid to the English Franciscan Province, and the Fathers had to celebrate for the repose of his soul Masses and Offices, as they did for one of their own brethren.

This bequest was accepted by the Definitory on June 12, 1656. The following note is appended to the above: "What became of this principal appears not. All I find is a paper, dated April 24, 1665, and signed by Madam Brinckhurst (Abbess) and her council, wherein they desire the Lord Arundel of Wardour to pay our then Provincial four hundred and eighty pounds out of their monies, in the said Lord's hands, for satisfying for the like sum, their then necessities forced them to make use of, and which they took out of our Province's monies, put out at Ghent, in the name of their Convent."

Mr. William Cleve left by his last will and testament an alms of twelve hundred pounds to the Province of the English Franciscans. He had also given another thousand some years before his death. He was to have ten pounds per annum out of the interest during his lifetime, and the use of three hundred pounds during the life of his ghostly Father, to be an annuity for him. One hundred pounds of this money was to be devoted to the building of an infirmary at Douai, which was done by the year 1667.

Mrs. Marthana Wilson signed a declaration to the effect that the profits of these moneys must go towards the maintenance of the friary at Douai, until such time as we can build a new place in England (if God please to be so merciful to this nation as to grant that liberty) ; or else wherever the Religious of the said Province shall judge expedient. This, under her signature, June 18, 1667, she declares to be the donor's wish as he had made known to her, and also to Mr. Hunt (Father Davenport) and Mr. Grey (Father Philip a S. Clara).

There is a note added to the above, saying : " How the aforesaid alms was disposed of does not appear by our Register. And all I can say is that perhaps eight hundred pounds put out on Tettesworth Farm in Staffordshire may be part of it. Likewise five hundred due from Mr. Whitehall upon bond ; and also two hundred more mortgage on Welde House. Upon further enquiry, I find nine hundred put into Lord Widdrington's hands, all paid in to the Provincial's orders at the building of Lincoln's Inn Fields Chapel."

It will not be out of place to mention here that the Widdringtons always were devoted friends to the Order of St. Francis. At Lulworth, in Dorsetshire, is a picture of Sir Edward Widdrington, laid out in the Franciscan habit, with this inscription :

Vera effigies Illustrissimi Domini Edwardi Widdrington, Equitis et Baronetti, ætatis suæ 57. Obiit anno 1671, 13 Junii.*

In 1668 two names were inserted among our special benefactors. The first was that of William Wilson, who was to be considered a Founder of St. Bonaventure's at Douai. Special prayers and Masses were ordered to be said for him, for his wife Marthana Wilson, and for his daughter.

The second was that of Rev. William Vandermote, beneficiary of the Collegiate Church of St. Peter at Lille and member of the Third Order of St. Francis, who was a singular benefactor to our establishment at Douai, and was also affiliated to our Order.

On May 12, 1674, Mrs. Mary Freeman gave one hundred pounds to the Province, in consideration of which the Fathers engaged to say one Mass every month for her husband's soul and one for her own ; a solemn anniversary Mass on the day of her husband's death, and one on her own. Besides, immediately after her death, thirty Masses were to be said for her husband's soul and hers. She died June 20, 1689.

Mr. Slaughter, a great admirer of Mr. Hunt (Father a S. Clara), and much devoted to the Order, with his wife, Lady Gage, put a sum of money in a bank at Paris, with obligation that, after both their deaths, the

* Dr. Oliver's Collections.

profit of it should be paid us or the House of Douai as an alms, upon condition of our praying for the repose of their souls; and he made Sir Daniel Arthur and his heirs trustees to see his will executed.

The following note is added : " This money was paid in by the bank of Paris in the Mississippi year, to the Guardian of Douai, in bank bills (then current money), which were delivered up to Mr. Doué, the Syndic, who has since yearly paid to the House one hundred and sixty florins as part of the principal, and will continue so to do till all the said bills are quite paid off. In this, Mr. Doué did us great service, by getting gradually the full principal of the said bills, which if sold at first would not have yielded thirty in the hundred."

Mrs. Taylor left a sum of money, to be prayed for by our fathers, of which councillor Poole has the disposal, and in my time (Fr. Bonaventure Parry's) has given us two or three sums, still requiring Masses for them, which are all most faithfully discharged here (in England) and at the Mother-house (Douai).   Mr. Fortescue can give an account of this donation and all the conditions of it.

Richard Staley, goldsmith, of London, left all his lands and houses situated in the village of Cheshunt in Hertfordshire to Mr. Edward Burdet, counsellor, of Gray's Inn, after the death of Beatrix, the said Richard's wife, and of her sisters.   And the said Beatrix made a declaration to the Provincial (in 1686), that the intention of R. Staley was that the legacy is for the use of our Province.

In the county of Staffordshire is a farm called Tettesworth, mortgaged by Mr. Hollingshead to Mrs. Garven for eight hundred pounds, in trust for us, afterwards made over to Mr. Foot and his son, in trust as before, and from them conveyed to Mr. Burdet, who, since the Revolution has been at great trouble and charges about it, by reason of a posterior mortgage of a certain person, who sued for his right " in forma pauperis," and pretended the prior mortgage was for superstitious uses ; and in the end obtained a decree in Chancery for proportionable allowance out of the profits of the said farm, as also an abatement of seventy pounds of the above mentioned eight hundred principal. So that this farm, which for some years paid the full interest of eight hundred pounds at six per cent, and somewhat more, amounting to fifty-five pounds per annum, till Lady Day 1696, pays now (1704) and from that year, only forty-six and four shillings, the pounds rest being adjudged by a decree of Chancery to the posterior mortgagee, as above.

Mr. N. Edmundson of Skerton near Lancaster, Father to our Br. Edmundson, has given us a house and garden in Skerton. The writings are in Mr. John Howlden our trustee's hands, and a copy among our writings. What the house and garden yield yearly, I [Fr. Bonaventure Parry] can't tell.

The following benefactions are mentioned about the year 1700.

Sir Nicholas Sheirborn of Stonyhurst made a donation of one hundred pounds.

Mrs. Mary Powell and daughter gave a bond of one hundred and fifty pounds, for which Mr. Burdet was trustee.

The relations of Father Martin (*alias* Charles) Grimston settled an annuity on him, in regard of which the trustees, Sir Walter Vavasor and Lady Winifred Strickland, invested the sum of two hundred pounds in the bank of the Town-house of Paris, the profits of which were to be devoted to the uses of the English Franciscan Province.

Mrs. Ogle gave a donation of one hundred pounds, in consideration of which she was to receive ten pounds per annum during her life. She died in the year 1706.

On June 5, 1716, the Definitory agreed to saying three Masses yearly on the anniversary of the death of Miss Mary Pinnar (January 24), who had left us one hundred pounds.

Also five Masses on the anniversary of Edward Smith, Knight, who had left us a sum of money in his will.

Two donations are recorded in 1719.

Lady Anne Curson of Waterperry gave two hundred pounds for the support of a missionary in England to be nominated by our Provincial. He had to say two Masses every week for her intention.

Mrs. Frances Grey gave one hundred pounds to build an infirmary at Douai. The Fathers engaged to sing two anniversary Masses yearly, one for her, the other for her husband.

In 1740 Sir William Holman, Knight, left four hundred pounds for the support of a missionary of the Order in England, it whatever place it might be thought most expedient.

In the same year three hundred pounds were left by Mr. Joseph Gerard and Margaret, his wife, to be paid by Mrs. Fleetwood. It was agreed to say two hundred Masses for their souls, and to inscribe their names among the special benefactors.

In 1764 Anthony Wright bequeathed to our Fathers the sum of two hundred and fifty pounds. A weekly Mass was to be celebrated at Douai for himself and family.

In 1766 Mrs. Frances Doughty left us thirty pounds : a solemn anniversary Mass was annually to be celebrated for her.

Also in that year Mrs. Mary Blount of Mapledurham gave a donation of thirty pounds, in view of which the Fathers engaged to celebrate a solemn anniversary Mass and some low Masses.

In 1768 Mr. John Webbe left to the fathers twenty pounds : they had to say six Masses annually for the repose of his soul.

In 1770 the Fathers undertook to say one hundred

low Masses for the repose of the soul of Michael Creagh, who had left them fifty pounds.

In 1771 Mr. Thomas Reeves left twenty pounds for Masses.

In the same year Mrs. Elizabeth Gibson bequeathed the sum of four hundred and twenty-seven pounds to the Franciscans ; they agreed to celebrate one solemn anniversary Mass and all the low Masses on that day and the following day for her relatives. These obligations were to last for twelve years.

In 1773 Mrs. Mary Markham bequeathed to the fathers the sum of thirteen hundred pounds. Besides a certain number of Masses to be said by the incumbent of Rowington and other fathers on the mission, there was to be at Douai every year a solemn anniversary Mass with all the low Masses of the day for her repose, on February 12.

In 1776 " Dominus Blundell de inch " gave ten pounds, the fathers engaging to celebrate one solemn Requiem and all the low Masses of the day at his death.

Mrs. Plowden, Mr. Mostyn and Mrs. Monington gave twenty pounds each in the same year, with obligation of one solemn Requiem and all the low Masses of the day, and moreover one solemn anniversary with the office of the dead.

Also in the same year Mr. Alexander Craw left us one hundred pounds, with the following obligations : one solemn Requiem and all the low Masses of the day ; one solemn anniversary with the office of the dead ; a certain number of Masses to be said by our fathers on the English mission.

In 1782, Agnes Kempster left twenty pounds, the fathers undertaking to say twelve Masses annually at Douai.

In 1794, Mrs. Elizabeth Walgrave left us one hundred pounds, simply stipulating that the fathers should pray for the repose of her soul.

Subsequent benefactions will be found in another chapter.

OBLIGATIONS OF MASSES.

In the old church at Douai a solemn Mass had to be sung every year in the chapel of St. Mary Magdalen on the octave day of her feast, for the founders of the chapel (the foundation dated from the year 1669).

The following is a list of the obligations of Masses at Douai in the year 1719.

Missæ quotidianæ.

1.   Pro Dno Gulielmo, etc., quæ est illa Comitis ad utriusque intentionem.

2.   Pro quadam Anna benefactrice.

3.   Pro Dno Henrico Fletcher, etc. (the founder of the new church).

Per septimanam.

1.   Pro Dno Lyndsey et uxore, una.

2.   Pro Dno Thoma Weakes, alia.

Anniversariæ solemnes.

1.   Pro Dno Gulielmo, 7 Martii.

2. Pro marito Dnæ Franciscæ Grey, 24 Martii.

3. Pro filia Dni Gulielmi, 7 Maji.

4. Pro Dna Francisca Grey, 31 Maji.

5. Pro Dna Mabilla Webb, 11 Sept. quamdiu solvitur retributio.

6. Pro Dno Gulielmo, ejus uxore et filia simul, 5 Octobris.

7. Pro Dno Thoma Weakes, 11 Decembris.

8. Pro Dno Thoma Stoaks, 14 Decembris.

Pro determinato tempore.

1. Pro Dna Lucia Creagh, 8 Feb. ad 20 annos.

2. Pro Dna Barbara Creagh, 26 Apr. pro totidem annis. Finietur hæc obligatio anno 1739.

CHAPTER XII.

ALTERNATE JOYS AND SORROWS.

THE Franciscans continued steadily multiplying and spreading in England.

In the metropolis the English Friars Minor were not the only representatives of the Order. From the year 1671 they held their Chapters at Somerset House "in Conventu Regali Reverendorum Patrum Ordinis Sancti Patris nostri Francisci Arabidorum," the home of the Spanish Franciscans, where they were not only allowed to meet on those occasions, but also entertained in royal fashion.

Another addition came in 1677, this time a Flemish Recollect. At that time there was a fair number of Flemish merchants in London, who were desirous of having a priest to hear their confessions and preach to them in their own language. It was almost natural for them to address themselves to the Franciscans, who were very popular in Flanders; and they, on being asked, showed themselves quite willing to accede to the request. The merchants then sought the consent of the English Franciscans, promising that no inconvenience would arise, and that they guaranteed all that was necessary for the father's maintenance. The English Definitory gladly welcomed their Brother from across the Channel, putting only one condition to the arrangement, which was that the Flemish father should be under the jurisdiction of the English Provincial.

But a storm against the Catholic Religion was brewing in England : it burst out in 1678. It is not within the scope of this work to describe the doings of Titus Oates and Bedloe ; suffice it to say that, in the fierce persecution which followed, eighteen Catholics were convicted and executed ; ten of these were priests, whilst the opportunity was taken of putting to death seven others, together with Oliver Plunket, the Venerable Archbishop of Armagh, solely for the sake of their religion. The Venerable Franciscan fathers, John Wall, Charles Mahoney and Francis Levison, shed a lustre on the Order on that occasion by laying down their lives for the faith, whilst several of their brethren suffered imprisonment.

On October 14 of that ominous year, 1678, the English Franciscans were holding their Intermediate Chapter in London. It seems that they had to hurry, or to break up before completing the usual documents, for the acts of that Congregation are incomplete, and were collected so far as was possible from the fragments : "Dispositiones, quantum poterant ex fragmentis ejusdem Congregationis, quæ in initio magnæ in Catholicos persecutionis celebrata fuit, collectæ."

In those days also the Franciscans lost all their papers and deeds, and it was not until the year 1686 that they got them back by means of

The Earl of Sunderland's Warrant for retrieving our Writings taken away in the Popish Plot time.

Robert Earl of Sunderland, Baron Spencer of Wormleighton, President of his Majesty's most honourable Council, and principal Secretary of State.

These are in his Majesty's name, to authorise and require you forthwith to deliver unto Mr. Charles Pora the following writings, or such of them as shall be in your custody, viz., one bond of Charles Clark, to pay unto Ralph Dixon for the use of the English College at Douai twenty pounds. A deed of mortgage made by Sir George Browne, and Dame Elizabeth his wife, and William Thorold of several parcels of land in the county of Lincoln, to pay yearly to the use of the English College at Douai twenty pounds. Two indentures made by William Brew and George Alexander unto Susan Lyndsey, of two tenements in Fleet Street, and divers other tenements there and in Swan Alley, all going for the remainder of ten thousand years. A will whereby it appears that William Lyndsey gave the aforesaid tenements and premises and the rents to the English College, or Recollects, in Douai, with all the ancient deeds from April 25, in the 4th of Edward VI. A deed by which it appears that William Lyndsey and Susan his wife for 1440 pounds paid, held of the manor of Tottenham and other lands in Tottenham, Stoe Barshenley, Sonshall, Waden and Wedbarn, at a rent charge of 80 pounds per annum till paid: this estate belongs to the English College at Douai. A deed made relating to a rent charge, by Sir Francis Englefield, of 26 pounds, 18 shillings and 4 pence per annum, out of the rectory and parsonage of Wooten Basset to Edward Roberts, Gentleman, dated May 1st, 12th of King Charles II., resigned again to St. Francis; with several other writings in two little trunks taken from Mr. Jolly's house in Drury Lane; as also a box of books, a silver hilted sword, and several mathematical instruments, taken likewise from the said Mr. Jolly's house; for which this shall be your warrant.

Given at the Court, at Windsor, July 16, 1686.

SUNDERLAND, P.

To Sir Richard Walcupp, Knight, and

To Richard Graham, Esq., or to either of them.

The storm of persecution having passed away, Catholics began to breathe more freely, and in 1686 we find the Franciscans again holding their Chapter in Somerset House. In the suffrages at the end of the decisions of this Congregation prayers are prescribed as usual, with the addition of "pro Catharina Regina Dotrice, cujus munificentia Regia fuimus refecti."

In 1678 the English Franciscans showed by their energy and expansion that the Province had reached the summit of its glory. They established nine new official residences in various parts of the country, and began to build a friary in true Franciscan style in Lincoln's Inn Fields, with a staff of ten, among whom were seven priests.

The following year, 1688, ten Belgian fathers were

called over to England, to help the English Franciscans in the mission work. Their names, beside the five at Lincoln's Inn Fields, were, John Capistran Frans, Mathias Roelhoof, Francis Six, Urban Tanghe and Elias Van Eecke. In October they all took up their places in the various residences to which they had been appointed.

Little did they dream of the wave of destruction which was fast approaching, and would sweep everything before it.

In November the Orange Revolution broke out. The Belgian Fathers had to hurry back home, and many of the English Franciscans also hastened to the continent. So great was the rush to Douai, that there was not room enough for all the fathers who continued to arrive, and the clerics had to be sent out to different Houses of the Order in Belgium.

It was not in England but at Douai that the Chapter of 1689 was held; and it was once more on St. Bonaventure's College that the affections and the efforts of the brethren were centred.

FATHER BERNARD EYSTON, O.S.F.

(From the Portrait at Hendred House.)

To face p. 105.

CHAPTER XIII.

AUTHORS.

BEFORE proceeding with the history of the Province, we will give an idea of the literary productions of the English Franciscans.

A glance at the authors and their writings cannot fail to show that if the English Province produced many men of true piety, solid learning was not neglected among them; thus illustrating the text with which the arms of the Franciscan Order are often adorned, "In Sanctitate et Doctrina."

FATHER JOHN GENNINGS wrote the life and martyrdom of his brother, under the title of "The life and death of Mr. Edmund Genings, Priest, crowned with martyrdom at London, the 10th day of November, in the year MDXCI." It was printed at St. Omers, in 1614. He is also the author of "Institutio Missionariorum," Douai, 1651.

FATHER BONAVENTURE JACKSON wrote a book entitled "Manuduction to the Palace of Truth," printed at Mechlin in 1616, in which he points out the way back to the truth to those who have erred. *   The work was published under the pseudonym of Richard Britton, (Dodd, vol. ii. p. 421.)

VENERABLE ARTHUR BEL published at Brussels, in

* Wadding ad an. 1616.

1624, " A brief instruction how we ought to hear Mass," a translation from the Spanish of Andrew a Soto, dedicated to Anne, Countess of Argyle. Also " The Rule of the Third Order of St. Francis," and in the year 1625, " The history, life and miracles of Joane of the Cross," 8vo, St. Omers. (Dr. Oliver.)

FATHER EGIDIUS or GILES WILLOUGHBY translated into English the golden treatise of St. Peter of Alcantara, " On Mental Prayer." It was published in 1632, and dedicated to Lady Powis. (Dodd.)

FATHER WALTER COLMAN published a poem called " The Duel of Death," which he dedicated to Queen Henrietta Maria, consort of Charles I. He also composed in verse a book on the controversies of the times, and a translation of the Life of St. Angela, of the Third Order of St. Francis. Father Mason says he has not seen the works, and that they were perhaps lost in England, at the time of the author's arrest and imprisonment.

FATHER AUGUSTINE EAST published at Douai, in 1642, the devotional treatise, " The Goad of Divine Love," which is a translation of St. Bonaventure's work, " Stimulus amoris." He dedicated it to Father George Perrot, then Provincial.

VENERABLE HENRY HEATH wrote " Soliloquia, seu Documenta Christianæ Perfectionis," printed at Antwerp in 1652. A translation, " Soliloquies and Documents of Christian Perfection," was published at Douai in 1674; it was reprinted in London in 1844. Another edition of this Latin work was issued at Quaracchi in 1885. The following list of his other compositions is found in the reprint of the " Certamen Seraphicum," Quaracchi, 1885.

Tractatus de peccatis.

Tractatus de Incarnatione.

Tractatus in priora Regulæ capita.

Compendium lib. I. Decretalium, usque ad c. 27. q. 6. d. 95. inclusive.

Collectiones ex novo et vetere Testamento.

Summa 4 librorum Sententiarum ad mentem Doct. Subtilis.

Epitome Universalium Porphyrii et philosophiæ Aristotelis.

Compilatio S. Scripturæ de Pœnitentia et Peccatis.

Tractatus de gratia, cum discussione opinionis Pelagii.

Theologia moralis.

Tractatus de Passione Domini (Latine et Anglice).

Controversiæ præcipuæ inter Catholicos et Protestantes modernos Angliæ.

Controversiæ de Angelis, cultu Sanctorum et imaginum.

Logica ad mentem Doctoris Subtilis.

Philosophia naturalis.

Tractatus de casibus conscientiæ.

Compendium corporis Juris.

Flores S. Augustini de gratia, simul et beati Prosperi.

Summa Concilii Tridentini.

Res gestæ ab Ecclesia a tempore Herodis usque ad mortem Lycinii imperatoris.

Tractatus de discretione tentationum, cum medicinis probatis.

Meditationes piæ.

Tractatus cui titulus : Abnega temetipsum et sequere Christum.

Regulæ humilitatis et patientiæ.

Exercitium quotidianum pro interiori conversatione.

Tractatus de intentione.

Liber similitudinum (anglice).

Tractatus pius pro Religiosis.

Liber sermonum variorum.

Tractatus de illicita in Anglia frequentatione ecclesiarum Protestantium, et Anglicani juramenti fidelitatis susceptione.

FATHER RICHARD MASON, from whose able pen we have the following works :

Sacrarium privilegiorum quorundam Seraphico P. S. Francisco indultorum.   Douai, 1636.

Questionum theologicarum resolutio pariter ac collatio cum sententiis S. Augustini.   Douai, 1637.

Regula et Testamentum S. Francisci, with a treatise De Confraternitate Chordæ, and Manuale Tertii Ordinis S. Francisci. These were printed at Douai in Latin, in 1643; but in the same year appeared his translation into English of the said Manual, 12mo, dedicated to the Dowager Lady Elizabeth Rivers.

Manual of the Confraternity of the Cord, 12mo, Douai, 1654, dedicated to Lady Ann Howard.

The Rule of Penance of the Seraphical Father St. Francis, as approved and confirmed by Leo X., in two vols., Douai, 1644. The first is dedicated to Father John Gennings, the second to the Abbess (Margaret Clare West) and Sisters of the Third Order of St. Francis at Nieuport.

Certamen Seraphicum Provinciæ Angliæ. 4to, Douai, 1649. This is his most valuable publication.

According to the catalogue of the library of the British Museum, he was the author of " Apologia pro Scoto-Anglo," 12mo, Douai, 1656 ; and "Microcosmus," 8vo, Wangen, 1671.

But perhaps his noblest production is a " Liturgical Discourse on the Holy Sacrifice of the Mass" in 8vo. It consists of two parts ; yet, strange to say, the second part was printed first, in 1669, with appendix and table of contents ; the first part appeared in 1670. This most learned and edifying work is dedicated to Henry, the third Lord Arundel, Baron of Wardour (Count of the Holy Roman Empire, and Master of the Horse to the late Queen-mother, Henrietta Maria), whose hereditary devotion to the Holy Sacrifice the author commemorates. In 1675 he published an abridgement of this admirable work.

FATHER JOHN BAPTIST CANES, whose first work was " The Reclaimed Papist," a small 8vo, 1655, dedicated to John Compton, Esq., to whom, it seems, he was chaplain. It is written in the form of a dialogue between a Catholic knight and a Protestant lady.

His " Fiat Lux," or " A general Conduct to a right understanding and charity in the great Combustions and broils about Religion in England," inspires sentiments of moderation and peace. The second edition appeared in 1662, and was dedicated to Elizabeth, Countess of Arundel and Surrey, the mother of Cardinal Howard. This work has an appendix on " Infallibility."

He was also the author of " Diaphanta, or an

Exposure of Dr. Stillingfleet's Arguments against the Catholic Religion." Another treatise against Dr. Stillingfleet was published at Bruges, shortly after the author's death, in 1672. (Wood, Dodd.)

FATHER CHRISTOPHER DAVENPORT, whose works were printed in two vols. fol. at Douai, in 1665 and 1667. The following are the contents:

IN VOL. I.

1. Systema fidei, seu tractatus de Concilio Universali.

2. Tractatus de Schismate, speciatim Anglicano.

3. Historia minor Fratrum Minorum almæ Provinciæ Angliæ.

4. Manuale missionariorum, seu Commentatio super nobiliores quæstiones Regulæ S. Francisci ad missionarios spectantes.

IN VOL. II.

1. Apologia Episcoporum.

2. Liber dialogorum, seu Summa Veteris Theologiæ Dialogismis tradita.

3. Problemata scholastica et controversalia speculativa.

4. Opusculum de medio statu animarum.

5. Paralipomena philosophica de Mundo peripatetico.

6. Religio philosophi, seu peripatetica discussio celeberrimi miraculi restauratæ tibiæ.

7. Epistolium adversus judiciariam astrologiam.

Besides these, we have from him:

1. Supplementum Historiæ Provinciæ Angliæ, in quo est Chronosticon. Douai, 1671.

2. Deus, Natura, Gratia, sive Tractatus de prædestinatione, meritis, peccatorum remissione, et Sanctorum invocatione. Accessit Paraphrastica Expositio articulorum confessionis Anglicanæ, 4to, Lugduni, 1634. This work has the " Placet prælo mandetur " of Father John Gennings, 1633. But, interpreted in its most favourable sense, it pleased neither Catholics nor Protestants. The Spanish Inquisition put it on its Index, and it would probably have been condemned in Rome, if Charles and Laud had not persuaded Panzani, the Papal envoy, to use his influence to stop the prosecution : thus it was possible to go too far, even in a good cause.

He also wrote a Dedicatory Preface to " The Chronicle and Institution of the Order of the Seraphicall Father St. Francis," which had been translated at his request from the French by William Cape (a probo et Catholico viro D. Gulielmo Cape). It was printed at St. Omers in 1618, and dedicated to " the Englishe Poore Clares in Gravelinge."

FATHER NICHOLAS CROSS. The catalogue of the Bodleian Library correctly assigns to him the authorship of " Cynosura; or, a Saving Star which leads to Eternity, being a Paraphrase on the 50th Psalm : Miserere mei Deus," dedicated to the Countess of Shrewsbury. It is a thin folio, printed in London, in 1670. (Dr. Oliver.)

FATHER LAWRENCE A S. EDMUNDO composed a spiritual treatise, the printing of which the Definitory agreed to in the year 1672.

FATHER CHARLES PORA wrote a work in French, having

the following title : " L'amour Reglé, par P. Charles Pora, Recolet, dedié à Monseigneur de Barillon, Marquis de Brange, &c." Paris, 1682. It is a small volume of 328 pages.

FATHER BERNARD EYSTON is the author of " The Christian Duty," 4to, printed at Aire in 1684.

FATHER JOHN CROSS, of whom we have the following works :

" Philothea's Pilgrimage to Perfection, described in a Practice of ten days' solitude," 8vo, printed at Bruges, in 1668.

A treatise " De Juramento Fidelitatis."

" An Apology for the Contemplations on the Life and Glory of Holy Mary, the Mother of Jesus," 12mo, London, 1687, dedicated to Queen Mary, Consort of King James II.

A philosophical course of " Dialectica, Logica, Metaphysica, Physica naturalis, Mathematicæ rudimenta universa, ad mentem Doctoris Mariano-Subtilis."

He was also requested by the Chapter, in 1684, to undertake the task of writing the life of Venerable John Wall.

FATHER ANTHONY LE GRAND was the author of " Institutio philosophiæ secundum principia Renati Descartes," London, 1671. Also " Historia Naturæ," a treatise " De carentia Sensus et Cognitionis in Brutis," and " Apologia pro Renato Descartes." (A. Wood, Athenæ Oxon.)

Dodd says that he also published " Historia Sacra," 8vo, and " Missæ Sacrificium neomystis succincte expositum," 12mo, London, 1695.

Father John Rookwood published at Douai the lives of three Capuchins: Angelus de Joyeuse, Benedict Cansfield and Archangel Gordon.

Father John Baptist Weston composed the able and useful work, "An Abstract of the Doctrine of Jesus Christ; or, the Rule of the Friars Minors, literally, morally, and spiritually expounded," printed at Douai in 1718.

Father Anthony Parkinson was requested by the fathers in 1725 to commit to the press his valuable compilation on the History of the Order in England. It was printed in London in 1726 under the title of "Collectanea Anglo-Minoritica; or, a Collection of the Antiquities of the English Franciscans, or Friers Minors." The Appendix contains an account of "The English Nuns of the Order of St. Clare," before the reformation.

The Statutes for the Fathers on the Mission, "Statuta Fratrum Minorum Recollectorum Almæ Provinciæ Angliæ, pro Missione," were printed in 1713, according to a decision of the Chapter held on May 3 of that year. They were reprinted in 1747. The little volume also contains the Rule and Testament of our Holy Father St. Francis, and some prayers.

Father Gregory Powell published a Manual and Catechism in Welsh. (Dodd.)

Father Pacificus Baker. We have from his pen a controversial work, entitled "Scripture Antiquity;" also "Meditations on the Lord's Prayer, from the French;" "The Christian Advent;" "The Sundays kept holy;" "The Devout Christian's Companion for

the Holy Days;" " The Devout Communicant;"
" The Holy Altar and Sacrifice explained;" "The
Lenten Monitor." Without much originality, all
these works are remarkable for unction, solidity and
moderation. One of his books is an abridgement of
Father Mason's "Liturgical Discourse on the Holy
Sacrifice of the Mass," in the form of a dialogue.

FATHER PHILIP LORAINE wrote the work " Pagano-
Papista Chimæra Infidelitatis Protestantis," in 1750.
(Dodd.)

FATHER FELIX ENGLEFIELD is the reputed author of
"The Miraculous Powers of the Church of Christ."
The work was published in 1756, without name of
either place or author. It is an 8vo of 300 pages, and
has for scope the confutation of Dr. Conyers Middleton.

FATHER LEO PILLING wrote : " A Caveat addressed to
the Catholics of Worcester against the insinuating
Letter of Mr. Wharton," 8vo, London, 1785. Also " A
Dialogue between a Protesting Catholic Dissenter and
a Catholic, on the Nature, Tendency and Import of the
Oath lately offered to the Catholics of England ;" and
" An Argumentative Letter to the Rev. Joseph Reeve,
on his view of the Oath said to be tendered by the
Legislature to the Catholics of England." (Dodd.)

We may mention here that leave was granted the
English Franciscans by the General Definitory, in the
year 1661, to resume the custom, which had existed in
the first Province, of instituting Doctors of Divinity.
The first who received the title was Father Davenport,
the second Father Mason. But at the Chapter of 1692
a resolution was passed "that the title of Doctorship
should now cease in our Province."

FATHER PAUL ATKINSON O.S.F.

(From the Portrait at West Gorton, Manchester.)

To face p 115.

CHAPTER XIV.

THE NEW CHURCH AT DOUAI.   OMINOUS SIGNS.
THE STORM.

THE greatest spiritual conquest of Father Martin Grimston was Sir Henry Fletcher, Baronet, of Hutton, in Cumberland ; for God had chosen him as an instrument to bring about the conversion of this gentleman to the true Faith. And not only did he become a zealous Catholic, but also a most devoted friend to the Order of St. Francis ; and he built at his sole expense the fine new Church of St. Bonaventure at Douai, which obtained a reputation for its architectural beauty.

The first stone of this sacred edifice was laid in October, 1706.* Six years later, on November 13, 1712, it was solemnly dedicated by the Archbishop of Cologne, Prince Joseph Clement, as appears from the following attestation :

On the twenty-sixth Sunday after Pentecost, which was the 13th day of November, in the year of our Lord 1712, by special leave of the Right Rev. Lord Guido, Bishop of Arras, the most Serene and most Reverend Prince Joseph Clement by the Grace of God Archbishop of Cologne, Archchancellor of the Holy Roman Empire, Legate of the Holy Apostolic See, has

---

* *Souvenirs de Douai*, 1822.

solemnly and according to the usual rite dedicated at Douai, in the Diocese of Arras, to God Almighty, in memory and under the title of St. Bonaventure Confessor and Doctor, the Church of the English Franciscans ; and has also consecrated the high-altar enclosing therein the relics of Saints Urban, Vincent and Gaudentia. He has morever prescribed that the feast of the anniversary of the dedication shall be observed every year on the Sunday following the feast of St. Martin, Bishop of Tours.

In witness of which he has ordered these letters to be expedited, signed with his own hand, and sealed with his archiepiscopal seal, at Valenciennes, November 18, 1712.

JOSEPH CLEMENT, Archbishop.
KHREMP, Secr.

The pious founder did not live to see his glorious work crowned : he had gone to his reward six months before the dedication of the noble temple he had raised to the glory of God.

The church had a nave and side-aisles, extending to the present dome. Both the nave and the aisles were terminated by a semicircular apse. We read in a description of the edifices of Douai that the only fault that could be found with it was that it appeared too short. It is rather the other way now ; but the western portion has undergone no alteration, and the organ with its case has never been moved.

After his conversion Sir Henry entirely relinquished all the pleasures and vanities of the world, and took up his abode among the English Franciscans at St. Bonaventure's, Douai, where he passed the remainder of his life. Every day he served Holy Mass in the Church, to the great admiration and edification of the people, who saw him humbly kneeling at the foot of the altar, entirely rapt in God, as if in an ecstasy. He was buried in the sanctuary near the high-altar. His epitaph was inscribed on a marble slab, over the sacristy door, on the gospel side.

D. O. M

IN HUJUS SANCTUARII MEDIO JACET PERILLUSTRIS DOMINUS
HENRICUS FLETCHER ANGLUS
BARONETTUS DE HUTTON IN CUMBRIA, QUEM DUM VIXIT
ANTIQUA GENERIS NOBILITAS, DIVITIARUM AFFLUENTIA,
AC UTRIUSQUE PRO CHRISTI SEQUELA CONTEMPTUS
CUM SINCERA IN DEUM PIETATE, IN PAUPERES CHARITATE
IN OMNES COMITATE, CONJUNCTUS,
ILLUSTRE CHRISTIANÆ VITÆ EXEMPLAR REDDIDERE.
POSTQUAM DIVINUM CONVERSIONIS AD FIDEM CATHOLICAM
MUNUS, SACRA HACCE ÆDE SUMPTIBUS SUIS EXTRUCTA,
ORNATAQUE GRATUS AGNOVISSET, AC POSTERITATI TESTATUM
RELIQUISSET,
PIE AC PLACIDE DIEM OBIIT SUPREMUM
HUJUS CONVENTUS INCOLA, ET NULLIUS VOTI
SÆCULARIS ASCETA,
ANNO DOMINI 1712, MAJI 19, ÆTATIS SUÆ 54.

Some years later, his spiritual guide and friend, Father Martin Grimston, was laid to rest by his side.

A few incidents in connection with Douai must be mentioned here ; not that they are of any consequence, but because we wish to be complete.

In 1730 the Confraternity of St. Dorothy, which had been established long before in the Church of Saint Jacques, was transferred to our church.

In 1761 the Stations of the Cross were erected in our church; but it was decided that the devotions should take place on a day different from that of the Walloon Recollects. The exercise seems afterwards to have been discontinued, for in 1773 it was resolved that the Way of the Cross must be resumed in our church; it must be made some Friday in the month, but with closed doors.

With regard to the House, it was decided in 1732 to rebuild the north side. There was great opposition to this by the neighbouring institute, the "Moulart Seminary," so called after a priest, M. Moulart, the authorities fearing lest the new buildings might interfere with their comfort or pretended rights. It was not until about the year 1747 that this matter was settled to the satisfaction of all the parties concerned.

We have good information as regards the number of English Franciscans in the course of the eighteenth century. In the year 1708 there were forty-two in community at Douai, *viz.*, seventeen priests, one deacon, three subdeacons, five clerics, thirteen lay brothers and three tertiaries.

In 1758 there were forty fathers on the mission in England. The account given to the General Chapter of the "Status Provinciæ" is generally the same: we select that of 1756, which is as follows:

"At Douai in Flanders, we have a friary and college, dedicated to St. Bonaventure, where there is a

Guardian, Vicar, Instructor of clerics and novice master, also two professors of theology, one of Holy Scripture and two of philosophy.

"Under the direction of our Province are two convents of English nuns : one of poor Clares at Aire in Artois, where two fathers reside, the Confessor and his assistant, and two lay brothers for the quest. The other convent is at Bruges in Flanders, for Sisters of the Third Order of our holy Father St. Francis, where there are also two fathers, for the service of the Sisters and the boarders.

" In England we have eleven Guardians, elected at the Provincial Chapter, who are truly the local superiors of all our missionaries living in their respective districts.

" Among our fathers six are jubilarians in the Order, and two professors ' emeriti ' of theology.

"Since our last relation to the General Chapter, Father Baker, an eminent preacher and zealous missionary in England, has published two pious books.

" The number of brethren in the Province is about one hundred, and of nuns in both convents about eighty."

Then follows a list of deceased brethren, and signatures, dated London, January 16, 1756.

Not long after the middle of the century unmistakable signs of coming events became discernible : the nations of Europe commenced to prepare for the great upheaval, which was to sweep across the continent before its close.

Vexatious laws were initiated by the authorities

of the State on the one hand. On the other, the English Franciscans began to experience some difficulty in carrying on the various works in which they were engaged. Perhaps, if we may say so, the spirit of zeal and devotion was declining in England : vocations grew scarce, and the means of support became inadequate. To speak plainly, there was a falling off in men and means ; and this would ultimately in all probability without additional cause have sufficed to bring about the fall of the English Franciscan Province.

In 1773 the fathers were confronted with the law of "the most Christian King," forbidding youths to make their religious profession until the age of twenty-one years completed.

In 1779 there were no Franciscan students at Douai to commence their course of theology. For some years back, instead of four professors only three had been appointed.

Already in 1774 the Definitors had agreed that "the Provincial could not go to the General Chapter to be held in Rome, nor the Custos either. He need not for that reason resign his office, as we have no one else to send, owing to the great number of deaths we have had of late years."

The decrease in the number of men necessitated ere long a diminution in the number of residences.

With regard to means, so early as 1761 it had been found necessary to sell some articles of church-plate left by Sir Henry Fletcher ; and in 1767 the fathers reluctantly decided on disposing in the same manner of a silver crucifix, a gift of the same benefactor.

In 1779 the want became very great, for the Definitors deliberated whether it would not be well, in the actual need of the Province, especially of Douai College, to have handbills printed explaining the urgency of the case; the fathers on the mission could distribute them, and thus charitable people might be induced to come to their assistance. But although at first the Definitors felt inclined to try the experiment, they ultimately shrank from such a step, and decided that no bills should be printed:—" Nulla formula est conficienda."

The want of men began to make itself more keenly felt in 1785, when at the Chapter meeting the Definitors came to the conclusion that there was sufficient reason for applying the exception to the general rule mentioned in the Statutes, and that Guardians might be re-elected immediately after the expiry of their triennial term of office.

Harassing measures of the State increased the troubles of the Franciscans. The Government of France had framed a code of Constitutions expressly for the Recollects. These the "most Christian King" had been forced to sign, and the Pope, fearing greater evils, had yielded his consent. * The State officials wanted to force these measures upon the English Franciscans, and in 1774 they had to consider the

* The " New Constitutions of the Recollects " were drawn up in September, 1770, at a National Assembly of the Recollects of France, in pursuance of an edict of Louis XV., dated 1768. Pope Clement XIV. approved them on April 3, 1773, and King Louis on May 14 in the same year.—*R. P. Hélyot.*

proposition, " Are we bound to accept the General Constitutions of the Recollects of France, approved by the Sovereign Pontiff and the most Christian King ?" They hoped to get over the difficulty by answering, " No, for we belong to the Germano-Belgic Nation of the Franciscan Order. As regards our House of Douai, let the Provincial do the best he can."

But the Government continued drifting on to its doom. In 1790 the French Assembly passed a law prohibiting religious from making vows at all. The Franciscans were now confronted with a measure which threatened them with extinction. With heavy hearts they resolved that the final step would have to be taken, and they would leave their beloved College of St. Bonaventure ; but it was arranged that a few of the religious should remain, until expelled by main force.

They were offered a domicile in Flanders, provided they would open a college for Flemish as well as for English students, and abstain from questing, so as not to be burdensome to the people. To these conditions they readily assented, adding that if the choice of a place was left them, they would prefer Bruges.

In that year, 1790, there were only two clerics at Douai.

The civil power showed the temper in which it was, by ordering two lists of English Franciscans to be drawn up.* They are probably complete.

The first contains the names of the religious on the continent.

* L. Dechristé, *Douai pendant la Révolution.*

AT DOUAI.

Father Peter Bernardine Collingridge, Guardian, 32 years.
   ,,   Lawrence Hawley, Vicar, Guardian in partibus, 38 years.
   ,.   John Hart, professor of theology, 30 years.
   ,,   Albert Jones, 43 years.
   ,,   Constantius Henrion (French), 55 years.
   ,,   Stephen Grafton, professor of philosophy, 28 years.
   ,,   Augustine Roberts, professor id., 27 years.
   ,,   Alexius Whalley, 51 years.
Brother Andrew Weetman, deacon, 24 years.
   ,,   McDonnell, not professed, 16 years.
   ,,   Peter Lovelady, not professed, 25 years.

LAY BROTHERS.

John Spencer (Daniel), 76 years.
Felix Jerningham, 60 years.
Charles Webb, 66 years.
Philip Nowell, 54 years.
Joachim Cooper, 48 years.
Joseph Street, 38 years.
James Deplanques (French), 32 years.

BESIDES:

Father Anselm Millward, with the English ladies at Bruges.
   ,,   Pacific Kington, with the same ladies.
   ,,   Joseph Tate, with the English Clares at Aire.
   ,,   Lewis Kellery, ibid.
Brother Hubert Delecourt (French), ibid.
   ,,   Francis Harcourt, ibid.

The other list contains the names of English Franciscans on the mission.

Father Romanus Chapman, Provincial.
   ,,   Bonaventure Pilling.
   ,,   Leo Pilling.
   ,,   Andrew Weetman.
   ,,   Charles Juliaens.
   ,,   Charles Stuart.
   ,,   Pacific Nutt.
   ,,   James Howse.

Father Joachim Ingram.
,,   Angelus Ingram.
,,   Angelus Ravenhill.
,,   Peter Wilcock.
,,   Henry Waring.
,,   Bernardine Fleet.
,,   Henry Bishop.
,,   Athanasius Baynham.
,,   Paschal Harrison.
,,   Peter Coghlan.
,,   John Anderton.
,,   Gregory Watkins.
,,   Ignatius Casemore.
,,   Anthony Caley.
,,   Nicholas Knight.
,,   Thomas Cottrell.

The Revolution soon broke out. On December 19, 1791, the English Recollects were placed under arrest in their own house. They were:

Lawrence Hawley, Superior.	Alexius Whalley.
John Hart.	Albert Jones.
Pacific Kington.	Lewis Kellery.
Stephen Grafton.	Constantius Henrion.
Augustine Roberts.	Joseph Purcell.

On February 18, 1793, the Administration of the District affixed the seals to the friary; and on August 8 following the fathers received an order to quit the town of Douai before 5 p.m. the next day.

There was no alternative, they had to go: and not only to go, but to hasten, to hurry, in the midst of the greatest dangers on all sides, from which some escaped only after suffering great distress and even imprisonment. But with God's help they all safely reached Belgian soil, and were directed by the Commissary

General, Aloysius Minne, to the town of Tongres or Tongeren in the diocese of Liége, where they arrived in September. The English Carmelites, of whom Father Columban Ferrers was then Superior, had a residence in this place, which they generously gave up to the Franciscan refugees, who were sixteen in number, viz., seven priests, four clerics and six lay brothers. All was soon arranged with the Bishop of Liége and the Commissary General, and the English Franciscans were allowed to remain there in secular dress, until the storm of the Revolution having abated, " they should be able to return to their friary at Douai."

In November of the same year the Intermediate Chapter was held in London. The House of Tongres was now considered a regular establishment, and a Guardian and professors were appointed for it.

It was thought expedient to convoke the triennial Chapter for the following year, 1794. It was duly celebrated in London on July 31, when a Guardian and professor were again appointed for Tongres. A couple of days later, whilst the Fathers of the Chapter were still engaged in their deliberations, lo ! there arrived the brethren from Tongres at the very house. They explained that the French hordes had overrun Belgium, profaning the churches, expelling and ill-treating priests and religious; that they had fled, and, through countless dangers, made their way, as best they could, to London.

CHAPTER XV.

DWINDLING.

IF we consider the troubled state of Europe at the end of the eighteenth century, and the difficulties under which the English Franciscans laboured, we shall not be surprised to hear that after 1794 there was no Chapter until the year 1800. They had, it is true, twice met, but without effecting much. In 1796 they assembled to petition for various dispensations, rendered necessary by the circumstances of the times. Among these they asked leave to hold their Chapters only every four years : this was afterwards refused, but it was probably on the strength of the request that they waited till 1800. In 1799 a meeting was forced upon them by the death of the Provincial, Father Pacificus Nutt : they elected Father Nicholas Knight Vicar Provincial, but no other business was transacted.

The Fathers were awaiting the course of events. They were not without hope of soon being able to return to St. Bonaventure's at Douai. Meanwhile they seemed to be at a loss what to do. They were, however, men of zeal and goodwill; and had it been possible they would, no doubt, have retrieved the Province, for which object they left no stone unturned, as we shall see.

They began by securing the confirmation of all their privileges, in the circumstances in which they then found themselves in England. Permission was obtained for clerics to be ordained " titulo missionis," and leave was granted to wear the secular dress "more aliorum religiosorum in Anglia, sine habitu regulari incedere." But they had to hold their Chapters at the usual time, and at least five " vocales " were to be present for the elections. The need of a suitable place for a noviciate had not failed to impress itself upon the fathers. They had resolved to apply to Sir Edward Smythe, Bart., Co. Durham, for a domicile at Esh, or Ash,* but nothing came of this. Then they addressed themselves to Mr. Webb Weston of Sarnesfield, but with no better result. Finally they decided to admit novices at Osmotherley.

Nor were friends wanting to give them material assistance. In 1800 they counted among their benefactors Mr. Wright, Mrs. Allam and Mrs. Britten. Mrs. Elizabeth Walgrave had given a donation some time previously ; and Mrs. Wakeman left a legacy for Solihull and Baddesley. In 1803 donations were recorded from Thomas Ryder and Mrs. Scarisbrick. In 1806 Mr. Suffield became a benefactor ; also Cesar Johnson, who left some buildings at Birmingham. To these were added later on the names of Nicholas Selby and others.

But death began to make havoc among the fathers. In 1799 the Provincial, Father Pacificus Nutt, had passed away. In 1800 six more deaths were recorded ;

* A short distance to the east of Esh is Ushaw College.

and by 1803 again six fathers had died, among whom were two Definitors.

In 1806 there were still twenty-eight fathers; in 1813 only twenty-one. Father Bernardine Collingridge, Provincial, had been raised to the Episcopal dignity, and was thus lost to the Province.

But the Franciscans struggled on. At the Chapter of 1803 the fathers applauded the resolution that, notwithstanding all the obstacles in the way, the tottering Province should with God's help be preserved. "Conclamatum est a Patribus omnibus capitulariter congregatis, ut posthabitis omnibus obstaculis, Deo adjuvante, Provincia nostra modo collabens præservetur."

This Chapter was held in London; and it was then suggested by the Commissary to send the novices, if any should present themselves, to Wetzlar, a town in Germany near Frankfort. The fathers resolved, however, that they would first try once more to educate them in England, and not send them out of the Province, unless all other means failed. Afterwards they tried at Perthyr.

It could no longer be doubtful that Douai was lost to the English Franciscans. In 1795 the church had served for the meetings of the " Popular Society." In 1797 saltpetre works were put up in it. In 1803 it took the place of the parish-church of St. Jacques, which had been demolished in 1800, and was reconciled on May 28. Finally, long after, in 1852, it was enlarged, the extension covering a great portion of the conventual grounds, and was reconsecrated in 1854, under the new title of " St. Jacques."

The troubles of the times in Europe in the early part of the nineteenth century were such that communication with the General Superiors of the Order had become next to impossible. In these circumstances it was thought expedient to grant faculties to the various provinces to elect Vice-Commissaries, who should have the power of a Commissary General. This arrangement existed in the English Province from 1806 until 1827, and the office was filled at various times by Fathers Stephen Grafton, James Howse, Augustine Roberts, Lawrence Hawley and Francis McDonnell.

In the year 1812 the usual appointment of a Preses to each residence ceased. In the same year leave was obtained to re-elect Definitors immediately after the expiry of their term of office. It was also granted that Definitors who were unable to attend the Chapter, could give their vote in writing or by proxy; but this the fathers declined to accept. In 1814 the recitation of the Divine Office was given up, because of the small number of Religious.

Yet another effort was made in 1818 to open a noviciate in England, this time at Aston. The fathers, finding that means were forthcoming, addressed themselves to the ecclesiastical authorities for their sanction of the scheme.

Bishop Milner sent the following beautiful reply to Father Hawley, ex-provincial:

Wolverhampton, Feb. 13, 1818.

DEAR SIR,

I cannot but approve of your accepting of Mr. Weld's pious offer and establishing your noviciate at

K

Aston; and I pray God to bestow his blessing on it, that it may become a fruitful seminary of worthy labourers in the harvest of the great Master, which, I trust in Him, will be the case, if the genuine spirit of your thrice holy Founder is infused into and preserved in it, such as it was at Douai, when the latter sent the blessed martyr Paul of St. Magdalene on the mission, or even such as it was when I visited the venerable Father James Rogerson in it. This, however, never can be the case, if there be too close a connection between the Religious and our modern gentry, qui omnes quæ sua sunt quærunt et non quæ Jesu Christi. . . .

The new noviciate, commenced under good auspices, did not fulfil the expectations of the Province. Two novices were there in 1823, whom the fathers intended to send to a friary on the continent to make their profession.

In 1826 it was finally decided not to admit any more novices in England, but to send them abroad to be educated; the place ultimately selected was Palestrina, near Rome.

In 1828 the Provincial, Father Ignatius Richards, died prematurely in Rome, whither he had gone on business of the Province; and the novices whom he had sent to Palestrina went away.

In 1829 it was resolved to close the Franciscan school at Baddesley, which had been erected in the previous century.

In 1830 a doubt arose regarding the validity of the

vows made by Fathers Hendren and O'Farrell. There was really no ground for this, considering the indult they had obtained. However, Pope Gregory XVI. sent them, in 1832, a " sanatio in omnibus, quantum opus est, quoad præteritum."

The Chapter of 1832 was held at Birmingham in the month of October. The fathers had then no large residence with sufficient accommodation, and they had to find lodgings in the town. Considering that the Chapter was composed of seven members, and that the meetings extended over about a week, it is not surprising that the expenses at the " Stork " Hotel amounted to thirty pounds, ten shillings and sixpence.

At the next Chapter, in 1835, they elected only a Provincial and Custos, and no Definitors, " ob paucitatem fratrum." During the previous year the Provincial had sent some boys to the Benedictine College at Douai, that they might study there, and make their noviceship afterwards in a Franciscan friary in Belgium. He now submitted his scheme to the fathers at the Chapter, and it was unanimously approved. But two years later the following resolution was passed : " It is inexpedient to hold out any hope to the eight young men now at Douai, to be received into our Order and Province." *

In this same year, 1837, also, it was decided to give up jurisdiction over the Franciscan nuns at Taunton. Three years previously the Poor Clares of Aire, who

* Their names were : John Bond, James Bond, John Geary, John Gilbert, George Gillet, John Bradley, John Coupe, N. Hollahan.

were also under the jurisdiction of the English Franciscans, had become extinct.

Only nine fathers remained in 1838, and all were at the Chapter held that year at Clifton. They elected a Provincial, Father Leo Edgeworth, and two Definitors, Fathers Hendren and McDonnell, adding that the next meeting should be on or before May 1, 1841. But there was to be no further meeting. The General hesitated to confirm Father Edgeworth's election, and in October, 1839, he appointed Father Hendren Commissary. But in December of the same year he suspended the execution of his letters. Meanwhile the Sacred Congregation of Propaganda had taken the matter in hand, and came to a decision in 1840. The result was that in January, 1841, the Vicar Apostolic of the Welsh district, Thomas Joseph Brown, O.S.B., Bishop of Apollonia, intimated to the fathers that, by a Brief from His Holiness, he had been appointed Visitor Apostolic of the Province of English Recollects; and not long after Father Hendren was raised to the Episcopal dignity.

The few scattered Franciscans were left to ponder in retirement over events of past years and over youthful hopes, alas! not realized. But four out of their number were yet spared to see a joyful day; for winter was well nigh passed, and a new spring was at hand: another day was dawning. They lived to welcome their brethren, who hailed from the very shores where their countrymen in the Order had found a home three hundred years before, and to them they handed over the seal of the English Province, as they had received it whilom from the survivors of the first Seraphic Foundation in England.

Old age and other circumstances did not allow of their joining their brethren and seeing the realization of the dream of their youth. But what was then practically impossible will yet be brought about; and, as they showed themselves worthy members of the Seraphic Order in life, our holy Father St. Francis will acknowledge them with us as his children on the great day.

RESIDENCES.

The places served by the Franciscan Fathers of the second Province may be classified in the following manner :

1. Some may be termed "official residences," to which a Superior, called Preses, was appointed at the Chapter meetings, as is customary in the Order. By the title of Preses given to the fathers, these places will be readily distinguished.

2. Towns or villages, where there was a congregation of Catholics, or a mission, constantly served by a Franciscan father. The appointments to these places were made privately by the Provincial, and no mention was made of them at the Chapters.

3. Houses of noblemen or gentlemen in the country, where a priest resided chiefly for the convenience of the family. Changes naturally occurred in such places from various causes, the fathers being but for a short time in some of them, in others longer.

The same may be said of a certain number of missions, especially in later times.

As residences changed sometimes from one class to another, it has seemed best to let them follow in alphabetical order.

It should not appear surprising if some residences of the third sort were not found here, no mention of them occurring in our records.

VENERABLE THOMAS BULLAKER, O.S.F.

(From the Portrait at Lanherne.)

To face p. 125.

ABERGAVENNY, MONMOUTHSHIRE.
(*Title* :—The Immaculate Conception.)

The beginning of this residence dates from the year 1687. "The house of Abergavenny," says the chronicler, "was given us by Mr. Peter Morgan, made first in trust to Mrs. Mary Roberts, with whom afterwards Mr. Williams (Father Pacificus Williams) having some difficulties, and Mrs. Jane Stubbs, sister to the said Mr. Peter Morgan, being his heir, application was made to her to secure to us the said house; upon which she, the said Jane Stubbs, passed the said house in trust to Mr. Walter Williams of Langfoyst for us; and he afterwards passed it in trust to Mr. Edward Burdet (our Syndic) and Mr. Robert Garter, for the same use Mr. Peter Morgan first intended it."

This house was situated in Frogmore Street.

The chief benefactors to the residence were: Mrs. Gunter, for whom a "De profundis" was to be recited every Sunday evening by the priest and congregation, Mr. Brown, and Mrs. Frances Watkins, for whom some Masses had to be said.

Father Pacificus Williams, junior, was appointed the first Preses in 1687, and continued in that office until the year 1701. He was succeeded by Charles Watkins, 1701-1713; Mathew Pritchard, 1713-1715, when he became Bishop; again Charles Watkins, 1716-1725; Lewis Lewis, 1725; Charles Watkins, 1726-1738; Leo Barker, 1738-1739; Gregory Powell, 1740-1755; Anselm Copley, 1755; Gregory Powell, 1764-1767; Alexius Whalley, 1767-1770; Andrew Weetman, 1770-1773; Augustine Hickins, 1773; Angelus Ingram,

1774-1776; Gregory Watkins, 1776-1779; George Lancaster, 1779-1781 ; Andrew Weetman, 1781 ; Gregory Watkins, 1782-1785 ; Henry Waring, 1785-1787 ; Bernardine Fleet, 1787 ; Gregory Watkins, 1788-1791 ; Paschal Harrison, 1791-1794.

In 1793 a sum of money left by Mr. Weld was, according to his intention, spent on the building, as also sixty pounds left by Mr. Jones, and one hundred pounds left by Miss Prodger.

Father Gregory Watkins was appointed Preses in 1794 ; Thomas Cottrell, 1800-1803 ; Gregory Watkins, 1803-1805 ; Peter Jones, 1805 ; Stephen Grafton, 1806-1808 ; Gregory Watkins in 1808-1809.

This was the last appointment of a Preses, and the place ceased to be an official residence.   But the fathers continued to live there for a long time after, and there also the Chapter meeting was held in 1835.

Father Stephen Grafton died there on December 23, 1847.

ASTON
(near Stone, Staffordshire).

When the Franciscans, as well as other priests and religious, had been expelled from Douai by the French revolutionists, they saw the necessity of making arrangements for their novices, and various means were tried to this end. Finally in 1818 it was decided to sell the ground at Garway, and establish the noviciate-house at Aston. They readily obtained Bishop Milner's consent, who encouraged them in their efforts to continue the Franciscan Province.

In 1821 it was called "Aston friary" (Conventus Astoniensis). The noviciate was then established there, and Father Stephen Grafton was novice master. In 1823 there were two novices. But no further appointment was made; and "Aston Hall" soon ceased to have an official existence.

BADDESLEY, WARWICKSHIRE.

Father Henry Bishop, who came on the English mission from Douai in 1756, was the founder of this residence, and was living here in 1758. It was also here that he closed his laborious career in 1811. We find in the archives "an inventory of the goods belonging to the Chapel of Our Blessed Lady at Badesley Green, July 11, 1776."

The great benefactor and patron of the place was Mr. Ferrers. He also allowed the father his board, and running of a horse. In return he received the spiritual blessings of numerous Masses for himself and relatives.

The Franciscan school of Edgbaston was transferred to Baddesley at the end of 1789. The following year, 1790, it was in full working order. In 1800 some regulations were drawn up by the fathers assembled in Chapter for the good government of the school.

Five times the Franciscan Chapter was held here: in 1808, 1811, 1814, 1817, and 1820.

In 1824 the fathers received a legacy of two thousand pounds for the maintenance of three boys at the school from Mrs. Mary Frith. In return they had to say two Masses for the repose of the soul of George

William Frith on his anniversary, July 5 ; one to be said here, the other at Aston.

But notwithstanding all the efforts of the fathers the school was not destined to last, and in the year 1829 they came to the conclusion that it should be closed.

———

BECKFORD, GLOUCESTERSHIRE.

This place is mentioned in the year 1758 by Father Felix Englefield, then Provincial. Mr. Wakeman was the patron. In the above named year Father Lawrence Robinson resided here.

———

BEOLEY, WORCESTERSHIRE,

Beoley lies on the borders of Warwickshire, two miles from Redditch. We find but one Franciscan whose name is mentioned in connection with this place : it is Father John Wheeler, who resided here in the year 1771.

———

BIRMINGHAM AND EDGBASTON.

At the Chapter meeting of 1687, held at the residence of the Provincial, Father John Cross, in London, the erection of nine new residences, projected in the course of that year, was approved. The seventh on the list of these new residences was Birmingham. Father Leo Randolph, a man of experience, for he had already been thirty years on the mission, was selected as the first Preses. He commenced that same year the building of St. Mary Magdalen's Chapel, the plans of which were approved in November : it was called after his own name in religion "a S. Magdalena." The following year, 1688, he obtained an assistant priest. Father Urban Tanghe, one of the ten Belgian Recollects who had recently come over to share the labours of their brethren on the English mission, was sent to help him.

In the same year 1688 it was also decided to transfer the Franciscan noviciate hither from Lincoln's Inn Fields as soon as possible; and accommodation was to be provided in the building accordingly. One hundred pounds previously given as alms by Sir Hercules Underhill were devoted to this object; and the incumbent was to say a yearly Mass for the repose of his soul.

But not long afterwards the chapel and residence were entirely destroyed by the mob. The spot being in a very exposed position, it was thought desirable to sell the ground. This, however, seems to have been a matter of some difficulty; and it was only done after Father Leo Randolph's death by Father Grimston, who obtained thirty pounds for it.

After the untoward event Father Randolph lost no time in looking for another site; and it seems that he was not long in finding one at Edgbaston. For shortly after his death Father Bonaventure Parry, then Provincial, wrote: "The present incumbent, Mr. Anthony Parkinson, can give an account of all Mr. Randolph's books, papers and church-stuff, at Edgbaston."

After Father Leo Randolph, the office of Preses was filled by Philip Sadler, 1698-1701; Anthony Parkinson, 1701-1710; Philip Sadler, 1710; Anthony Lambert,

1711-1716; William Lockier, 1716-1719; Thomas Holmes, 1719-1725 ; George Lancaster, 1725-1728.

The first direct mention of the Edgbaston school occurs about this time: it is in connection with the accounts of the year 1727. It is also mentioned that in 1730 Father Bernard Parker was teaching there.

But from a note written more than thirty years later, it is certain that the school had then already been some years in existence. For it says that "about the beginning of the school, Lady Curson greatly helped towards the establishing of it " by her generosity. Now this Lady Anne Curson of Waterperry made two bequests, in consideration of which the fathers had to say four weekly Masses. The first bequest was made in 1719, the other in 1722. This makes it appear certain that the beginning of the school dates from Father Holmes' term of office ; and a commencement was probably made about the year 1720. Another note which speaks of an agreement between Father Holmes and the Provincial, confirms this conclusion.

In 1731, at the Chapter meeting, the fathers decided that "as our school in Warwickshire has to contend with many difficulties, we leave everything regarding it to the prudent disposition of the Provincial " (Father John Capistran Eyston).

The school and mission always remained two distinct concerns. Among the regulations drawn up in 1735, the first provides that the incumbent shall pay to the master of the school sixteen pounds per annum for his board, etc.

In 1740 Father Alexius Martin, who was then

teaching, was recalled from the school. He had been incumbent before. If other changes were judged expedient in that year, they were left in the hands of the Provincial.

In 1747 it was decided that the incumbent alone must have the care of income and expenditure ; and twice a year, viz., about the feast of the Annunciation of our Blessed Lady, and that of St. Michael, he shall give an account to the master of the school and the Guardian of the district. The account to be duly signed, and forwarded to the Provincial.

A new house was to be rented in 1750 for the school, and forty pounds were allowed for alterations and additions. The following letter of Father Baker, then Procurator of the Province, contains some interesting details. It is addressed to Father George Lancaster.

Sir,

The affair of changing the house at Edgbaston, and going to Mr. Ran's, has been considered, and consented to, on the following conditions :

1. That Mr. Holmes allows forty pounds and no more, towards the expenses of the building and alterations to be made. The rest of the expense to be paid by the Congregation and those who desire the change ; for no after changes will be answered for here.

2. That the plan sent by Mr. White be followed, and no alterations made in it that may make the expenses greater than what has been given in, viz., sixty-five pounds. At least that no more be demanded here, than the forty pounds given and allowed towards it.

3.   That a lease be taken for twenty-one years, with power on our side to quit the house, and give up the lease at the expiration of 5, 10, 15, or 21 years, but we not to be turned out, if we choose to stay, till the expiration of the lease.

4.   The lease to be made in the name of some honest, substantial Catholic in Birmingham, the person left to you, who are best acquainted with them ; and to your judgment it is left to manage the affair.   The forty pounds will be remitted to you ; and Mr. Holmes desires you will be so good as to take the trouble of managing it, and inspecting the buildings that are to be made.

In your last to me, you say the project will be very commodious ; but in your thoughts a great many blocks are in the way.   Had you mentioned them, they would have been considered on here.   But not naming them, it must be left to your prudence and judgment to remove them as well as you can.   As for any security for the money we lay out, I don't see any we can have, unless Mr. Ran will oblige himself to refund all or part of what we lay out on his house, in case by mob, or other forcible means we be driven away before the expiration of five years of the lease. If he will not do this, we must run the hazard, and trust to Providence, our only security ; and if turned out, sit down by the loss.

Another difficulty we apprehend here is, whether there will not be danger of making a talk in the country, and of making our persons' landlord an enemy to us by quitting his house, and for which, I suppose, he must have a quarter's warning. You may see by this that Mr. Holmes and his Council readily come into the proposed change, as far as they can contribute towards it; but leave the management of the difficulties to you, to get over them. And if you can make all things easy, you may treat and conclude with Mr. Ran as soon as ever you please. But this must be done by you, for Mr. Holmes does not think it proper to let Mr. White, or Mr. Brown either, have the management, as being young and inexperienced in these affairs. If you have any objections to what I have sent you in Mr. Holmes' name, you'll let him know by letter, and he will further consider of them.

As to repairs, it is left to you to make the agreement with Mr. Ran, as you shall judge most proper, though we decide the landlord ought to be at the expense of those which are absolutely necessary. By repairs here we mean that the stable and out-buildings, as well as the dwelling house, be in good and tenable repair when we enter upon the premises, as we shall be obliged to leave them in a tenable condition whenever we quit them. As for repairs while we inhabit the house as before said, what is necessary to keep it *sarta tecta*, sound against wind and weather, that the landlord be obliged to do, or allow it in his rent.

As Mr. White tells me in his letter, the landlord is to pay all taxes and poor rates and other levies by the Parish, we expect that nothing of this kind be incumbent upon us, but altogether be paid by the landlord.

I am, etc.,

P. BAKER.

January 27, 1749-1750.

A regulation was made in 1766, to the effect that the incumbent's authority should extend also to the professors and the direction of the school.

In 1782 Mrs. Mary Weld left three hundred and fifty pounds to the school, for the education of a boy not under twelve years old, afterwards to be sent to our college at Douai. Mrs. Ann Monington left two hundred and fifty pounds for a like object.

In 1784 Sir James Brockholes, Knight, of Lancashire, bequeathed four hundred pounds to the fathers, which were applied to the school. Some Masses and Offices of the dead were to be celebrated for the repose of his soul.

In 1788 the school appears still to have been in its usual working order, and is mentioned in the accustomed manner. But it was transferred to Baddesley, probably the following year.

Having traced the vicissitudes of the Edgbaston school, we must now resume the relation of matters connected with the mission.

Among the chief benefactors, who contributed towards the maintenance of the incumbent, were Mr. Ferrers, Sir Hercules Underhill, Mr. Mense, Mr. Ralph Bucknall, Mr. Jackson, Mr. Sparrows of Barton Park, Mr. Savage of Stafford, and Mr. Powell.

Father George Lancaster was succeeded in 1728 by Bernard Parker. He was followed in 1731 by Lawrence Loraine. Then again George Lancaster, 1732-1734 ; Alexius Martin, 1734-1737 ; George Lancaster, 1737-1741 ; Robert Painter, 1741-1746 ; Bernard Yates, 1746-1749 ; Bernardine Carruthers,

1749-1752; Anselm White, 1752-1755 ; Bernardine Carruthers, 1755-1758; Anselm White, 1758-1761 ; Thomas Dixon, 1761-1764; Bernard Barker, 1764-1767 ; Charles Juliaens, 1767-1770; Athanasius Baynham, 1770 ; Pacificus Nutt, 1771-1773 ; Henry Bishop, 1773-1776 ; James Howse, 1776-1779 ; Charles Juliaens, 1779-1781; James Howse, 1781 ; Bonaventure Pilling, 1782-1785. During his term of office, on May 6, 1783, St. Peter's Chapel was opened. Then followed James Howse, 1785-1787 ; Pacificus Nutt, 1787; he was then Provincial.

Whilst he held the post of Preses, in 1791, Mrs. Johnson bequeathed two hundred pounds for the support of the incumbent at our chapel in Birmingham. Her name, and that of her husband John, were put down among the special benefactors.

The next Preses, Augustine Kemble, was appointed in 1800 ; Constantius Henrion in 1803 ; Henry Bishop in 1805 ; Ignatius Casemore in 1806; Henry Bishop in 1808 ; Augustine Roberts in 1809 ; continued in 1811. He was the last Preses.

In 1821 the mission of Birmingham received one half, *i.e.*, one hundred pounds, of the legacy of William and Elizabeth Lewin, for which one Mass was to be said every three weeks. The other half was for the mission of Solihull.

It only remains to add that although Birmingham had ceased to be an official residence, the Franciscans had the care of the mission for a long time after. And six times the Chapter meeting was held here : in 1821, 1823, 1824, 1827, 1830 and 1832.

BRAMBRIDGE, HAMPSHIRE.

The patron of this residence was Mr. Wells. Father Gregory Martin was here in 1758, as we find in the writings of Father Felix Englefield.

BRANSFORD.

At the Provincial Chapter held in the year 1665, it was decided to send Father Lewis of Nazareth to serve this residence.

· BRISTOL.

Although from the year 1647 there was a titular Guardian of Bristol, it never was an official residence. But some of our fathers served there on the mission in the nineteenth century.

Father Edgeworth began his labours at Bristol in the spring of 1825; and Father O'Farrell followed him thither on December 24, 1830. To meet the rapid increase of Catholicity, Father Edgeworth purchased, in the spring of 1831, a large plot of ground at Clifton for the erection of a spacious church. The ground was first broken on August 11, 1834, and on October 4, the feast of St. Francis, the foundation stone was laid. Within the area purchased he erected a small chapel in honour of St. Augustine, where Mass was first said in 1842. The church was opened six years later, in 1848; Father Edgeworth had then retired to Antwerp.

Father O'Farrell was first attached to St. Joseph's Chapel in Trenchard Street, where he laboured with the zeal of an Apostle. Afterwards he contrived to purchase the well built and graceful church of the

Irvingites, now St. Mary's on the Quay. It was
solemnly dedicated by Bishop Baines on July 5, 1843,
and Father O'Farrell was installed the first incumbent.
He continued to minister there many years.

It must be added that the Chapter meeting of 1838,
which was the last of the second Province, was held at
Clifton.

***

BURTON.

This place was at one time served by the Franciscan
fathers, for we find in 1773 the following entry :

" Mr. Ingram (Father Angelus Ingram), as incumbent
of Burton, receives from Healy's annuity ten pounds
per annum. And from the Carpue's family at half
yearly payments one pound eleven shillings and sixpence."

There are many places called Burton, and sufficient
evidence is not forthcoming to show which is intended.
It would seem, however, that it was in Yorkshire.

***

CANTERBURY.

At a Definitorial meeting held under the presidency
of the Provincial, Father John Cross, July 15, 1686,
the following question was put : " What use shall we
make of the nine hundred pounds, now in the hands of
Lord Widdrington ? "   This gentleman * acted at that
time as Syndic or agent to the Franciscans.   The
reply was that the sum in question should be devoted
to the recovery of the site of the old Franciscan

---

* In the writings of the old Franciscans he is styled "Lord,"
presumably erroneously. See also p. 91.

°friary at Canterbury.   From this it would appear very probable that we had a residence in that city.   At all events it was undoubtedly contemplated.

CHEESEBURN GRANGE, NEWCASTLE.

At the end of the eighteenth century this place was in the hands of R. Riddle, Esq.

After the breaking up of the community at Tongres, Father Joseph Tate, who had been Guardian there, resided here for some time, between 1794 and 1800.

Father Bernardine Fleet also lived here at the beginning of the nineteenth century.

CHIPPING, LANCASHIRE.

The project of securing a priest for the service of this locality originated with Paschal Howlden, a lay brother, who died at Douai in 1729.   The details are found in the following entry, made in 1704 :

Howlden's Fund for a Missioner.

Brother Paschal Howlden, before his holy profession put out a sum of money, as I take, about one hundred and fifty pounds, to raise a little fund of about seven or eight pounds a year, for a missioner of ours, to serve the poor in the parishes of Laithgrim [Leagram] and Chipping, in the county of Lancaster.   His brother John Howlden being trustee, who promises to pay it honestly.   And for this the incumbent is desired and required to say ten Masses yearly, viz., three for their father, three for their mother, two for their brother, and two for their sister.

The fathers residing at White Hill had to serve Chipping, as appears from the will of Cuthbert Hesketh, in 1710.

COCKPIT HOLE, BUCKINGHAMSHIRE.

The Franciscans must have had a residence in this locality, for in 1767 it was proposed to build a new house here.

EAST HENDRED, BERKSHIRE.

Father Pacificus Price was chaplain to the Eyston family in 1687. A century later, about the year 1788, Father John Evangelist Anderton resided here. His address was, " At B. Eyston's Esq., Hendred, near Abingdon."

An entry made about the year 1703 seems to find its proper place here. " Mr. William and Mr. John Eyston's concerns are in Mr. Charles Eyston their good worthy brother's hands."

The following interesting account is taken from the manuscript of the late Charles John Eyston, of Hendred, Berks. It relates to St. Amand's Chapel.

My Father, George Eyston, Esq., began the Repaire of this Chappell on Wednesday in Easter Weeke, in yᵉ yeare 1687 whᶜʰ happened to be that yeare on the 30ᵗʰ of March, and it was completely finished on the 17ᵗʰ of September yᵗ yeare, one Andrew Bartlet painted and guilded it, and had 42 pounds for doing it as appears yet by his Bill and Acquittance wᶜʰ are to be found amongst the Papers wch belong to the Chappell.

Saturday, September 24, 1687, Father Pacificus alias Philip Price (who then lived in the Family), a Franciscan Fryer, and one who afterwards was twice Provincial of his Order blessed the Altar Stone,* being assisted by Father Francis alias Wm Hardwick, Father John Baptist alias Wm Weston, two of the same order, after that was done Vespers were said with as much solemnity as the place would allow. The day following being Sunday the 25th of September, there were seaven Priests who said Mass in it. The Priests were Mr. Price, who said the first, Mr. Prosser and Mr. Evans, two clergy priests, Mr. Francis Hildesley, Soc. Jesu, Mr. Anthony alias Francis Young, Mr. Weston above mentioned and Mr. Hardwick, the three last were Franciscan Fryers. The company who were at the opening of the Chappell were Sir Henry More of Fawley and his Family, Sir John Courson and his first Lady, Mr. John Massey, actually then Deane of Christ Church in Oxon, Mr. Robert Charnack, and one Mr. John Augustine Bernard, the former Fellow of Maudeline College, and the latter Fellow of Brazen Nose College in Oxford. Mrs. Perkines of Ufton, Mr. Perkins of Beenham, Mr. Hildesley of Little Stoke and his brother Martin, Mr. Francis Hide, jun. of Pangborn, father to the present

---

* Among the "Facultates pro Missionariis nostris ad Bene-placitum R. A. P. Ministri concedendæ," the 6th is, " Consecrandi calices, patenas, altaria portatilia, et alia vestimenta ad SS. Eucharistiam celebrandam necessaria." (Copy of 1704.)

Mr. Hide, and some other Catholic gentlemen came hither for the service in the morning. But only Sir John Curson and his Lady and my Uncle Ber. Winchcomb and his first wife were at the consecration of the Altar Stone the day before. And the year following there were meanes found to have both the altar and the Chappell privileged as may be seen by the Bulls which are amongst the writinges which relate to the chappell. From the time of its being opened till the Prince of Orange came in and invaded the nation the Chappell was open to all comers and goers. The Blessed Sacrament constantly kept with a lamp burning; mass dayly celebrated in it. But when he and his army passed over the Golden Myle some loose Fellows (whether by orders or not I cannot tell) came hyther went into the Chappell pretended to mock the Priest by supping out of his Chalice, which they would have taken away had it been silver, as they themselves afterwards gave out ; however, having torn down the JESUS MARIA from the altar, which holy names were printed upon Pannells in the same frames where the JESUS MARIA are now wrought in Bugles, they retired takinge an old suite of Church stuffe with them to Oxford, where they drest up a manikin with it, and set it up there on the Topp of a Bon-Fyer. This happened on Monday, December 11th, 1688, and this is all the mischief they then did, besides breakeing the lamp and carrying away the Sanctus Bell. Mass from y[t] day ceast there until Monday, June 24th, 1689, when Mr. Weston above mentioned by accident fortund to bee here and then he sayd

Mass in it againe and from that time till now *i.e.* Aug. 1718 wee have generally used it.

FALMOUTH.

This mission was founded by the charitable Rowland Conyers, Esq., who departed this life on April 28, 1803.

Bishop Sharrock, Vicar Apostolic of the Western District, secured the services of Father Ignatius Casemore as first incumbent. He arrived in January, 1805, and continued to serve this mission for over thirteen years.

FAWLEY AND WHATCOMBE, BERKSHIRE.

Mr. Edmund Young settled eight pounds a year for a Franciscan missionary to serve the poor in these parts of Berkshire after the death of his brother, Father Anthony Young, a S. Francisco, who acquainted Father Price, then Provincial, with it, in a letter dated November 20, 1695.

Two legacies are chronicled in 1791 for the support of the Franciscan missionary in the Fawley district: Mr. T. Moore bequeathed seven hundred pounds, and Mrs. Young four hundred pounds.

Father Nicholas Knight served Whatcombe and Fawley in 1775; he resided at Miss Young's, Whatcombe House.

In 1810 it is again stated that the incumbent has for some time resided at Whatcombe.

GARWAY, MONMOUTHSHIRE.

We read in the records, about the year 1704, that
" Mr. Thomas Williams of Garway, gave us the estate
of Garway, as appears by his declaration, towards
building a house in those parts, or meanwhile maintain
a missioner thereabouts ; and passed it by will in trust
to Robert Grimond, who being dead, his heirs and
executors are content to dispose of it as we think fit,
either by sale or otherwise, provided security be given
for our faithful performing the said Thomas Williams'
will.   Mr. Hancock [Father Alexius Hancock] has
undertaken for the present to manage the concerns
relating to this house."

In 1735 the fathers considered that it would be well
to sell the residence of Garway Hill, and devote the
price to the maintenance of one or more missionaries
in those parts, until with the help of God another
residence could be procured, and the pious intentions
of our benefactors further fulfilled.

The Father who served " the Garway Hills " was not
bound to any particular residence.   Father Felix
Englefield, writing in 1758, says that the priest used to
live at Hilson ; but at that time Mr. Lorymer allowed
him his board, and he resided at Perthyre.

The incumbent here also served Broad Oak, Ross, for
which he received three pounds yearly.

Mr. Martin Turner's fund for an English Franciscan
serving in Monmouthshire was applied to this
place.

In 1818 it was finally decided to dispose of the
Garway estate and to hand over the proceeds to the

Preses at Aston, where the noviciate was then being established.

———

GREENWICH.

It appears that in the year 1634 we had a residence in the house of the only Catholic gentleman in the town. The Provincial Chapter met in that house in the above mentioned year: and this was the second Chapter of the second Province held in England, the first having been held in London in 1632.

———

GRIMOLDBY GRANGE, LINCOLNSHIRE.

This place is mentioned in 1782 as being at that time served by a Franciscan Recollect.

———

GROVE PARK, WARWICKSHIRE.

Father George Lancaster resided here in 1730.

It was decided in 1742 that the incumbent of Grove Park must say one Mass weekly for the repose of the soul of Lady Anne Curson, so long as he receives the alms.

In 1758 Father Arnold resided here.

The patron of the living was H. J. Dormer.

———

HEREFORD.
(*Title* :—St. Thomas.)

The residence of Hereford dates from the year 1684, when Father Pacificus Williams, then Definitor, was appointed Preses. He was succeeded by Alexius Hancock, who was there from 1686 until 1719, performing his duties all those years with great zeal.

Father Michael Hawarden was sent in 1688 as assistant.

In 1696 it was decided to sell or otherwise dispose of the house at Hereford; and to place the proceeds in the hands of a Syndic or other trustworthy friend, until another house could be obtained, more suitable for the use of the Province.

Two years later, in 1698, it was resolved to sell the house to Mrs. Agnes Brett. It was not long ere the sale was concluded, for Father Bonaventure Parry, Provincial, says in a note :

" The residence house and grounds at Hereford are sold and alienated : belonging now to Mrs. Agnes Brett, who nevertheless is to make good to us the sum of one hundred pounds, which Mr. Alexius Hancock lately laid down for repairing the said house, with Superiors' leave. The articles of agreement between Mr. Hancock and the said Agnes Brett, are in Mr. Hancock's hands. Thus stood things when I made my visit here in August, 1702."

Father Hancock was succeeded as Preses by :

John Baptist Gibson, 1719-1728 ; Michael Hawarden, 1728-1731 ; John Baptist Gibson, 1731 ; Michael Hawarden, 1732-1734 ; John Baptist Beaumont, 1734 ; Athanasius Chapman, 1735-1741 ; Alexius Martin, 1741-1752 ; Augustine Hickins, 1752-1755 ; Alexius Martin, 1755 ; Augustine Hickins, 1756-1758 ; Thomas Eccles, 1758-1764 ; Nicholas Knight, 1764-1767 ; Bernard Barker, 1767-1773 ; George Lancaster, 1773-1776 ; Andrew Weetman, 1776-1778 ; Henry Waring,

1778; John Anderton, 1779-1781; Henry Waring, 1781; Alexius Whalley, 1782-1784; Lawrence Hawley, 1784; Leo Pilling, 1785-1787; Leo Haddon, 1787; Andrew Weetman, 1788-1790; Paschal Harrison, 1790; Leo Haddon, 1791-1794; Thomas Cottrell, 1794-1800; Andrew Weetman, 1800-1803; Leo Sumner, 1803-1805; Ignatius Casemore, 1805; Gregory Watkins, 1806-1808; Andrew Weetman, 1808; Lawrence Hawley was appointed in 1809, and continued in 1811.

This was the last appointment.

HEXHAM.

(*Title*.—St. Anthony of Padua.)

This was the second on the list of the nine residences begun in 1687. We have the following details from Father Bonaventure Parry's writings:

" At Hexham in Northumberland we have a residence, the ground of which was given, as I take it, by Mr. Ben. Carr, of the said town: of which, and what belongs to it, Mr. Constantine Jackson can give best account."

Father George Golding, the first Preses, was here 1687-1695; George Goodyer, 1695-1698; Bernardine Metcalfe, 1698-1701; Constantine Jackson, 1701-1717; Bernardine Metcalfe, 1717-1719; Gregory Jones, 1719-1725; Bonaventure Hutchinson, 1725-1729; Peter of Alcantara Gordon, 1729-1731; Bernardine Metcalfe, 1731-1734; Pacificus Baker, 1734-1737; Lawrence Robinson, 1737-1743; Bernard Yates, 1743-1746; Peter of Alcantara Gordon, 1746-1749;

Bonaventure Hutchinson, 1749-1752 ; Leo Francis, 1752-1758 ; Paul Dixon, 1758-1761 ; Robert Painter, 1761-1764 ; Bernard Yates, 1764-1767 ; Henry Bishop, 1767-1770; Joachim Arnold, 1770 ; Alexius Whalley, 1771-1773 ; Charles Juliaens, 1773-1776 ; Thomas Cottrell, 1776-1779 ; Henry Bishop, 1779-1781 ; Bruno Babe, 1781; Lawrence Hall, 1782-1791 ; Angelus Ravenhill, 1791-1793 ; Bernardine Fleet, 1793 ; Andrew Weetman, junior, 1794-1800 ; Paschal Harrison, 1800-1805 ; Alexius Whalley, 1805 ; Thomas Cottrell, 1806-1808 ; Alexius Whalley, 1808 ; Bernardine Fleet, 1809-1812.

After him the appointments cease.

HIGHDEN, SUSSEX.

Highden, now called Highdown, is in the neighbourhood of West Grinstead. In 1758 Father Placid Payne was at Highden, and another Franciscan, Father Houghton, was at West Grinstead. But "Houghton" is an alias, and it is uncertain what his real name was.

The patron of both Highden and West Grinstead was Mr. Caryll.

HOAR CROSS, IN YOXHALL PARISH, STAFFORDSHIRE.

This residence is mentioned by Father Felix Englefield in 1758, when Father Anselm Copley was living there.

The patron of the place was Mr. Talbot.

HOLT, LEICESTERSHIRE.

We find what follows chronicled concerning this place in 1704, by Father Bonaventure Parry: "In Leicestershire, at Mr. Byerley's near Leicester, there are Mr. Gervais Cartwright's books, which I recommended to Mr. Augustine Hickins, either to be sold, or brought to Mr. Neville's of Holt, where the said Mr. Hickins at present resides."

HOLYWELL, FLINTSHIRE.
(*Title* :—St. Winifred.)

This was one of the residences which the Franciscans resolved to found in the year 1687 ; it was the fourth on the list.

Father Michael Russell was appointed Preses.

About the year 1704 Father Bonaventure Parry wrote : "We had a residence in King James's days at Holywell in Flintshire ; but nothing of it now remains."

HORTON, GLOUCESTERSHIRE.

Father Felix Englefield resided here in 1757, when he was Provincial. One of his letters is dated : "Datum in nostra residentia de Horton, hac die 20 Martii, an. 1757."

He was still there the following year.

Mr. Paston was the patron of the place.

IDSWORTH, HAMPSHIRE.

This residence is mentioned in 1758, when Father Thomas Holmes was here.

The patron was H. C. Dormer.

LEE HOUSE, LANCASHIRE.

The residence of Lee House in Thornley was founded in 1738, when the Chapter accepted the conditions proposed by Thomas Eccles of Thornley for a resident missionary in his house.

Father Germanus Holmes, Confessor of the Faith, is said to have served the mission here some time from White Hill, when he resided in that place.

Father Leo Francis was here in 1758.

The obligations of the incumbent at Lee House were:

To say one Mass every Sunday in perpetuity.

Three Masses yearly, *viz.*, one for Francis Eccles, one for his father and one for his mother.

LEOMINSTER, HEREFORDSHIRE.
(*Title*:—The Holy Trinity.)

At Leominster, or Lemster, a residence was founded with the approval of the Chapter in 1687; and Father Felix Price was appointed Preses. He filled the office for five or six years.

The following entry of Father Bonaventure Parry will tell us what became of it.

Lemster Residence.

In Mr. John Cross's time there was a little sort of residence established at Leominster, by the industry and endeavours of Mr. Felix Price: which soon after, in the Revolution, was entirely demolished.

LLANARTH, MONMOUTHSHIRE.

Father Samuel Fisher, called in religion Bonaventure,

served this mission for many years, from 1835 until 1865. He continued to reside here two or three years longer, and then retired to Pontypool.

LONDON.

There have been Franciscans in London from the beginning of the second Province. Either the Provincial or his Commissary for England resided here, and also the titular Guardian of London; and to one of these the fathers had to report themselves upon their arrival in England. As early as 1632 a Chapter meeting was held here; and from the year 1637 the Chapter assembled here almost regularly. The meeting place in 1671 was " The Royal Friary of our Holy Father St. Francis, of the Reverend Fathers of Arabida." At this place the fathers often met afterwards. In 1672 it is designated as " Somerset House ;" in 1674 again as " the Royal Friary of the Reverend Franciscan Fathers of Arabida ; " in 1677 as " Somerset Palace, the residence of her most serene Highness, the Queen of England." In 1678 the Chapter assembled " in London, at the beginning of the great persecution ; " in 1686 again " at the Royal Friary of the Franciscan Fathers of Arabida, in Somerset House."

In 1655 two fathers, Adam Batten and Ambrose Bevans, were appointed exclusively for the purpose of catechising children in London, either at their homes, or at the father's residence.

In 1656 Father Anthony Le Grand was appointed Vicar or assistant to the titular Guardian of London.

He was also made professor of philosophy here ; and Father Adam Batten was appointed assistant professor in 1657.

In 1686 it was resolved to open a school of classics at Putney, under the presidency of Doctor Slaughter, and the fathers were advised to send to that school youths whom they considered fit pupils.

Towards the end of the same year the fathers deliberated whether the school should be continued, and it was decided that they should use their utmost endeavours to keep it on. But before long a far more important step was to be taken.

In November, 1687, it was resolved to acquire the spot near the arches in Lincoln's Inn Fields, lately in the possession of the Countess of Bath, on the conditions formulated by Edward Burdet, our Syndic. The fathers were directed to ask contributions of their friends towards the erection of the conventual buildings and chapel, under the title of our Holy Father St. Francis.

The foundation was begun without delay : the Superior and members of the community were selected, and the religious exercises arranged, even as regards lesser details. Father Peter a S. Maria was appointed Preses. The others were : Father Alban Ayrey, Vicar ; Father Angelus Bix, preacher ; Father Francis Hardwick, visitor of the sick ; Father Paul Atkinson, prefect of the choir and catechist ; Father Angelus Fortescue, preacher ; Father William Lockier, preacher ; Michael Hawarden, cleric ; Henry Moore, lay brother, and Peter Lalor, lay brother. It was decided that the Religious

should wear the Franciscan habit, and sandals, according
to custom as regards shape and colour; that is, they
should wear brown, not grey habits. Sermons were to be
preached on Sundays, and catechism was to be given
twice in the week. A course of philosophy was also in-
augurated. The Little Hours were to be recited at seven
o'clock in the morning, after which the antiphon " Hæc
est præclarum vas " was to be sung, except on Sundays
and feasts, when this was to be done after High
Mass.

On the occasion of the opening a gentleman, Mr.
Sadler, presented a fair large silver chalice, a pair of
silver cruets and a silver basin to the chapel at
Lincoln's Inn Fields, on condition, however, that
they should be returned to him in case the chapel were
given up.*

In the following year, 1688, the noviciate was
opened here, with Father Paul Atkinson as novice
master, and three novices. The staff had increased
to nineteen and was composed as follows :

Father Peter a S. Maria, Preses ; Father Felhoen,
professor of theology ; Father Angelus Bix, titular
Guardian of Canterbury ; Father Francis Hardwick,
Vicar ; Father Francis Six ; four Belgian fathers (PP.
Brabantini) ; Father Paul Atkinson ; Father Angelus
Fortescue ; Father William Lockier ; Father John
Capistran Frans ; three novices ; two lay brothers ;

* The chalice and cruets mentioned above were reclaimed
and handed over to him after the destruction of the place.
But he bequeathed them to his son Philip, one of the English
Franciscans ; and after his death they were given back to the
fathers, and sent to Douai.

Brother Cuthbert, tertiary, to be incorporated. This took place in the month of October.

But man proposes and God disposes. On November 4 of the same year the Prince of Orange landed with a powerful army on the Devonshire coast. That same day, which was the 22nd Sunday after Pentecost, crowds of people attacked our residence with great violence, and tried on that, and also the following day, until midnight, to destroy both the old and the new chapel, together with the house, and to expel the Religious. But the fathers were protected by soldiers and horse sent by King James.

These were days of great danger and anxiety. November 14 was approaching: that was the birthday of Queen Elizabeth. It had been arranged that on that day the Prince of Wales should be taken to Portsmouth, and thence, if necessary, to France, whilst the King should go to Salisbury, and place himself at the head of the army. Knowing that in these circumstances he could not keep us safe from the mob, which appeared determined to destroy the place, His Majesty commanded Bishop Leyburn to intimate his will to us. This he did by sending a note, which we give textually.

FOR MR. CROSSE.

Verie Rd. Father,

I am comanded by the King to lett you know, that since the rabble hath already been very insolent and troublesome to you, atte your residence in Lincolns-inne-fields, and is like to be more hereafter; it is his Majesty's desire and pleasure, that for the prevention of future dangers and inconveniences, you with the rest of your fathers retire from that place.

> I am, Verie Rd Father,
> Your most affectionate servant,
> LEYBURN.

In pursuance of this order, the Franciscans withdrew from the place on November 16, having first removed their goods and obtained a guard of soldiers from the King for the security of the house and chapel.

What happened afterwards may be gathered from a note made a few years later.

"The London residence house was by the arches in Lincoln's Inn Fields, where there was a very decent chapel and convenient lodging rooms. But before we had enjoyed it long, the Revolution coming on, it was plundered and gutted by the mob. But three or four years after, being repaired by the Syndic at our cost, was then inhabited by the Portuguese Envoy, till our lease expired ; after which we had no more to do with it. By this place 'tis incredible what we lost. Perhaps if I should say upwards of three thousand pounds, I should not be much in the wrong."

Notwithstanding the loss of their residence, a comparatively great number of Franciscans continued to live and to work in London. About the middle of the eighteenth century there were eleven ; towards the end six, as we shall mention in the proper place.

The fathers were now reduced to the necessity of having to rent a room, where they might keep their books and other effects. At the beginning of the eighteenth century, one of them writes: " The room where our books are, costing three pounds a year, has already consumed almost the value of them. Wherefore I heartily wish some course were taken before winter, to dispose of them at a cheaper rate. There be many duplicates, and very many useless among them, which being taken out, much less room will serve them."

But although the fathers afterwards sold part of the books, they found it necessary to keep on the room.

After the disastrous days of November, 1688, one more Preses was appointed, Father Charles Pora. He was subsequently made titular Guardian of London, and died about the year 1695.

Here are some addresses of the Franciscans in the eighteenth century. Father Pulton's and Father Baker's letters are addressed, " At Mr. Wright's the Goldsmith "—sometimes, " the Banker "—" at the sign of the Golden Cup, Henrietta Street, Covent Garden." From 1729-1734, " at Mr. Cabry's, Fan maker, at ye Golden Fan, over against Gray's Inn Gate in Holborn." Letters written by Fathers Cantrill, Parkinson and Smyth have also this address: " Mr. Baker, at Mr. Anderton's in Little Wild Street, near Lincoln's Inn Fields."

In 1758 there were eleven Franciscans in London : Fathers Cantrill, Loraine, Baker, André, Greswold, Ingram, Dixon, Wheeler, Chapman, Rogerson, and Stevens. For nine of them there were livings, the patrons of which were, the Portugese Embassy of three ; Lady George Howard of three ; the Bavarian Embassy of one ; Mrs. Eyre of one ; Mr. Bird of one.

About the year 1790 there were six fathers in London: Chapman, Needham, Cox, Stevens, Leo Pilling and Juliaens. The last named was still at Sardinian House, Lincoln's Inn Fields, in the early years of the nineteenth century. He died in 1807. A faithful brother, Francis Harcourt, was his assistant: he had accompanied the fathers when they were expelled from Douai.

LOWER HALL, LANCASHIRE.

In 1796 Mr. Brewer left ten pounds for this residence. Afterwards Lady Stourton became the chief benefactress of this place.

Father Michael Hawarden resided here in 1703. He was still here in 1717, but went away that year, having been appointed Vicar at Douai. He left a note in Father Eyston's hands, wherein he mentioned that five boxes of books were laid up in the new private place at Lower Hall.

Father Painter resided here in 1758.

Among the benefactors of this place were Mrs. Langdale and Mrs. Hesketh, for whom Masses had to be said.

MAPLEDURHAM, OXFORDSHIRE.

Father Felix Englefield mentions this place in his writings. The patron was Mr. Blount.

In 1758 Father Edward Madew resided here; he was then titular Guardian of Newcastle.

MICHELGROVE, HAMPSHIRE.

This place was the seat of the Shelley family.

Father Angelus Fortescue was chaplain to Sir John Shelley in the year 1700.

MONMOUTH.

(*Title*:—Our Holy Father St. Francis.)

In the year 1687 this residence was founded at the same time as eight others. Father Pacificus Williams was appointed Preses, and filled that office until the year 1705. This worthy and zealous man, having been sometime on the spot, thought it desirable to purchase the old priory; and in this he at length succeeded. The following entry, made when he was still alive furnishes us with the details :

" The priory of Monmouth was purchased by Mr. Williams, senior, alias Father Pacificus a S. Francisco, by the means of a Syndic, and with the consent or approbation of Superiors ; and therefore belongs to the Province. But the present tenants, Mr. John Williams and his wife, have their lives in it, paying the Syndic fourteen pounds yearly. The writings are in Mr. Burdet's (the Syndic's) custody."

Afterwards the fathers had some trouble in asserting their ownership of the priory, which was called into doubt.

The next Preses was Father Jerome Parry, 1705-1714. Then Bernard Baskerville, 1714-1716 ; Lewis Lewis, 1716-1719 ; Alexius Jolley, 1719-1722 ; Lewis Lewis, 1722-1725 ; Bernard Baskerville,

1725 ; Lewis Lewis, 1726-1732 ; John Beaumont, 1732-1734 ; Athanasius Chapman, 1734.

The following year it was thought well, if possible, to sell the residence, and apply the proceeds to the maintenance of one or more missionaries in the district, until with God's help another residence could be procured and the pious intentions of the benefactors further fulfilled.

It appears that the property was eventually sold for two hundred pounds. Father Chapman was succeeded by: Anthony Parkinson, 1735-1737 ; John Baptist Gibson, 1737-1743 ; Bonaventure Bedingfield, 1743-1747 ; Bruno Babe, 1747-1749 ; Placid Aston, 1749 ; Thomas Eccles, 1750-1758 ; Augustine Hickins, 1758 ; Thomas Dixon, 1759-1761 ; Angelus Ravenhill, 1761-1764 ; Thomas Eccles, 1764-1766 ; Bruno Babe, 1766-1770 ; Nicholas Knight, 1770-1773 ; Lawrence Lorain, 1773 ; Alexius Whalley, 1774-1776 ; Peter Wilcock, 1776-1779 ; Edward Madew, 1779-1782 ; Ignatius Casemore, 1782-1785 ; Augustine Kemble, 1785-1787 ; Lawrence Eccles, 1787 ; Augustine Kemble, 1788-1790 ; Angelus Ingram, 1790 ; Augustine Kemble, 1791-1793 ; Anselm Millward, 1793 ; Andrew Weetman, senior, 1794-1800 ; Joseph Pursell, 1800-1803 ; Ignatius Casemore, 1803-1805 ; Bernardine Fleet, 1805 ; Joseph Tate, 1806-1808 ; Stephen Grafton, 1808 ; Constantius Henrion, 1809-1812.

This was the last appointment.

———

MOUNT ST. MICHAEL.

The foundation of this residence was decided upon in 1686, for in that year the Chapter considered the proposal of acquiring a plot of ground on which to build a house, for the dwelling of a missionary, and for the accommodation of pilgrims, at the foot of Mount St. Michael, " in the diocese of Llandaff," as the record says, by means of alms received, or to be received by Father Pacificus a S. Francisco.

The reply to the proposal was in the affirmative. The scheme, however, seems not to have been very successful, for there is no further mention of this residence.

OSMOTHERLEY, YORKSHIRE.

(*Title* :—Our Lady of Mount Grace.)

The residence of Mount Grace dates from the year 1665, when it was accepted by the Chapter. The following year Father William Shepheard was sent thither with the injunction to conform himself in all things to the instructions he would receive from Father Francis a S. Magdalena.

The beginning of this place is thus recorded by Father Bonaventure Parry, who had been Preses here.

" Osmotherley House in Yorkshire was given us by Lady Walmsley, with all the outhouses, a little garden and field, for which she also bought an estate in the Dales of twenty pounds annually and gave it us for ever, on condition of keeping and maintaining one in the said house, for performing duties there for the benefit, devotion and comfort of pilgrims. Which has been successfully continued above thirty years ; and may so for many more, provided good, zealous persons be placed there."

In 1674 Father Francis Osbaldeston, or a S. Magdalena, was still " Rector " of Mount Grace. He was succeeded the following year by Marianus Napier. Then came Francis Hardwick in 1680 ; and the following year, still as " Rector," Father Bernardine Langworth. He governed the residence many years, and during his tenure of office the title of Rector was altered to that of Preses. He was told to repair the old chapel in 1686.

In his time also Lady Elizabeth Pierrepont presented a fine set of vestments to the chapel. And in connection with this subject we have the following interesting document from Father John Cross.

BROTHER JOHN OF THE HOLY CROSS,

of the Seraphic Order of St. Francis, Jubilate Reader and Dr. of Divinity, and Minister Provincial of the Province of England, to the REV. FATHER BERNARDINE LANG-WORTH, *of the same Order and Province, Preses of the House and Chapel of the Holy Virgin Mary of Mount Grace, in the Parish of Osmotherley, of the Province, County and Diocese of York, health and everlasting salvation.*

Whereas the Right Honourable Lady Elizabeth Pierrepont, of the illustrious family of the Earls of Kingston, and daughter of the high born Robert E. of Kingston, for the love of God, the exercise of Divine worship, and through her special devotion to the ever immaculate Mother of Jesus, has given to the said Chapel of the Holy Virgin Mary of Mount Grace, aforesaid, a suit of Church stuff, for the service of God, and the use of the said Chapel, there to remain, and to be preserved, without ever to be removed from the said Chapel, *viz.*, a vestment, stole, maniple, veil, pall, antependiums for the altar and two sideboards, or credences, of white flowered satin, with flowers of gold, laid with gold lace, and gold-coloured fringe; an alb, amice, altar cloth, and corporal, of fine linen, and laced, all marked C.P., and whereas, according to the sacred Constitutions of our Holy Order, it is not lawful to alter the intention of benefactors, in gifts given to the use thereof: to the end that the said Right Honourable Lady's charitable donation aforesaid be not made void, it is our will, and we do expressly command in virtue of Holy Obedience, that the gift forementioned be carefully and faithfully preserved, in, and for, the use of the said Chapel only: and never to be misapplied, contrary to the intention of the illustrious Donor abovesaid. And that this ordination, together with the exhibition of the gift above mentioned, be by you, and by your successors, for ever read and represented, to yours, and their immediate successors respectively, after every provincial Chapter; and that once yearly, within the Octave of the Immaculate Conception of the Mother of Jesus, one Mass be applied by you, or your companion, residing at the said Chapel, for the space of one hundred years (if times permit), and whilst the said place or Chapel shall remain under our government, for the present and eternal welfare of the said Right Honourable Lady, our benefactress. And that a copy of this order be inserted in the Register of the Province.

Given at our residence in London, this 18th day of November, in the year of our Lord 1686, with the consent of the Diffinitory then assembled, under our handwriting, and the great seal of our Office.

BR. JOHN OF THE HOLY CROSS,
Minister Provincial.

In 1688 Father Masseus Woolmer was sent to this residence as assistant priest.

Father Bernardine Langworth remained Preses here until the year 1701, with a short interruption in 1692-1693. In the former year Father Bonaventure Parry was Preses, in the latter Father Angelus Bix.

It was probably through the exertions of Father Langworth that a school for young gentlemen had been established here. After his time it began to languish; but in 1702 the fathers decided that an effort should be made to restore it to its former flourishing condition; and in this they were successful. Mrs. Jennison, who had charge of the temporalities of the place, obtained thirty pounds from the Provincial towards the needs of the school. But the improvement was mainly due to the exertions of Father Ambrose Ogle. For Father Bonaventure Parry, who had formerly known the place, wrote:

" Ambrose Ogle is the present incumbent at the Chapel, of whom I have an extraordinary character from all hands.   He manages the school to admiration, which has increased very much, the house being almost quite full of scholars.   The housekeeper, Mrs. Jennison, performs her part too, to the full content and satisfaction of all."

This difficulty once got over, another trouble was not long in coming.   The ownership of the property was called in question at the Bishop's Court at North-allerton, and the neighbouring justices threatened they would get to the root of the matter.   In these circumstances, the deeds could not be found.   Mrs. Juliana Walmsley had been the purchaser, and had given the place to the fathers.   Subsequently all the deeds and writings belonging to the house were in Mr. Calvert of Borrowbrig's hands.   This was all the fathers knew.   But they hoped that if trouble came, Mrs. Walmsley's heirs would be able to do something in their favour.

The matter came before the Chapter in 1723, and it was asked : " What is to be done, now that the justices of the realm call our ownership of the residence of Mount Grace in question ? "

The reply was : " Our residence is at present in danger ; but we must endeavour to retain possession by all lawful means possible."

This storm also passed, and the fathers enjoyed many years of peace and tranquillity afterwards in this place.

Mr. Thomas Coates, of Stay House, was a great benefactor to the fathers here.   Besides investing one hundred pounds for the incumbent, he gave fifty pounds to supply the altar with wax, altar breads, and wine. One of the conditions of the donation was, " that the family of Stay House be served by the incumbent of Osmotherley as formerly, with all necessary services and rites of the Holy Catholic Church, once in six weeks, or as need shall require."

To this place were also applied five hundred pounds, part of the legacy of Mr. Talbot, which he had intended as a fund for a Franciscan missionary in Northumberland. But not being able to find a place then, the Superiors assigned it for the time being to Mount Grace.

Among the benefactors are also mentioned Anthony Anderton, Christopher Peart, Barbara Ormandy, all before the middle of the eighteenth century ; after that, Rudolph Robinson in 1766 ; Thomas Peart in 1776 ; and in 1787 John Catton, of St. Columb's in Cornwall.

There were as usual obligations of Masses for the benefactors. We now return to Father Langworth's successors in the office of Preses. These were Bernard Price, 1701-1704 ; Bruno Taylor, 1704-1707 ; Ambrose Ogle, 1707-1728 ; Bernardine Metcalfe, 1728 ; Peter of Alcantara Adams, 1729-1732. During his term the roof was extensively repaired. Peter of Alcantara Gordon, 1732-1738 ; Bernard Yates, 1738-1740 ; Matthew Collingridge, 1740-1749 ; Bernard Yates, 1749-1752 ; Matthew Collingridge, 1752-1758 ; Robert Painter, 1758-1761 ; Matthew Collingridge, 1761-1764 ; Lawrence Eccles, 1764-1770 ; Ambrose Payne, 1770 ; Bruno Babe, 1771-1773 ; Bernardine Fleet, 1773-1776 ; Bruno Babe, 1776-1778 ; Lawrence Eccles, 1778 ; Lawrence Hall, 1779-1782 ; Lawrence

Eccles, 1782-1785 ; Thomas Cottrell, 1785-1787 ; Peter Wilcock, 1787 ; Thomas Cottrell, 1788-1790 ; Henry Waring, 1790 ; Peter Coghlan, 1791-1793 ; Ignatius Casemore, 1793-1800 ; Bernardine Fleet, 1800.

Already in 1796, after the expulsion from Douai, it had been resolved to open a noviciate at Osmotherley, and to appoint a novice master for the place. A further step was taken in the year 1800 towards making the place a regular friary, and Father Henry Waring was appointed Guardian.

But the plan was not destined to succeed, and the appointment of a Preses was resumed, the office being filled by Alexius Whalley, 1803-1805 ; Joseph Pursell, 1805 ; Augustine Roberts, 1806-1808 ; Ignatius Casemore, 1808 ; James Howse, 1809-1812. He was the last.

Pembridge Castle, Monmouthshire.

Pembridge Castle was served one Sunday in the month from Perthyre (or Perthyr), for which Mr. Townly gave a salary of six guineas per annum. Thus Father Felix Englefield in his notes, 1758.

Perthyr, in Rockfield Parish, Monmouthshire.

The patron and chief benefactor of this residence was Mr. Lorymer. Some Masses were to be said for him annually ; and the "Si quæris" in honour of St. Anthony of Padua was to be recited every Tuesday for his intention.

In 1758 two Franciscans resided here—Fathers Augustine Hickins and Thomas Eccles.

An effort was made in 1815 to make this the noviciate house, and the residence was called " Conventus Perthyranus." But after three years trial the undertaking was abandoned, and the noviciate transferred to Aston.

READING.

All we know of this place is what is found in Father Bonaventure Parry's writings. " Mr. Grimston," he says, " did once hire a chamber in the town of Reading for the convenience of poor Catholics to serve God; but I know not whether he has it now."

This is Father Martin Grimston, who came on the mission in 1695.

ROLLESTON PARK, STAFFORDSHIRE.

The residence of Rolleston dates from the year 1654, as appears from the will of Sir William Powell, Knight. He was grand-uncle to Father John Powell.

ROUGHEY, OR ROFFEY, SUSSEX.

We learn from a memorandum in Father Collingridge's time that, towards the beginning and in the early part of the nineteenth century, this place was attended on the first Sunday of every month by the incumbent of West Grinstead.

For this service Mr. Webbe Weston, Esq., of Sutton Place, near Ripley, in Surrey, paid twelve pounds a year to the Procurator of the Franciscans.

ROWINGTON, WARWICKSHIRE.

A bequest was made about the year 1686 by Thomas Atwood, Frances his wife, and Jane Milburne, from the parish of Rowington, for an English Franciscan to serve the place. They also stipulated that the sum they had left, one hundred pounds, or the interest, might afterwards be applied to a house of the Order in England, according to the wishes of Superiors. There was an obligation of Masses attached to this legacy.

The fathers came to a favourable decision, having considered the proposal, on April 27, 1686, and accepted the incumbency of the place.

We find Rowington mentioned in 1758 in connection with Baddesley. We hear of it once more in 1773, when it is decided that "the incumbent, who has for some time past received twenty pounds per annum from Mrs. Mary Markham's fund, must say one Mass every fortnight for the repose of her soul."

SARNESFIELD COURT, NEAR WEOBLY, HEREFORDSHIRE.

This was once the residence of the Monington family, and was for some time served by the Jesuit fathers.

A Franciscan, Father Leo Haddon, was resident priest at this place about the year 1787, as appears from the Procurator's notes. About ten years later an attempt was made to open a noviciate here; but the plan did not succeed.

SHIREFIELD, HAMPSHIRE.

We have a complete description of this residence

in the year 1758. The incumbent of Shirefield was chiefly maintained by Mr. Holman's legacy for the missionary serving the poor in Hampshire. In connection with this fund fifty-two Masses had to be discharged annually. He had also an allowance of Mr. Sheldon for serving Shirefield ; of Mr. Betts for serving Bishop's Waltham ; and of Mr. Young for serving Stockbridge.

The father who was in residence here had also to attend to the spiritual needs of Catholics at Barton Stacey, Uphusborn, Basingstoke and Whitchurch (Hants), in case there was no other priest available for duty in those parts.

———

SIZARGH, NEAR KENDAL, WESTMORELAND.

This place was at one time served by the fathers of the Society of Jesus. Father Lawrence Eccles, O.S.F., was here in 1807.

———

SOLIHULL, WARWICKSHIRE.

This residence must have existed before 1758, for in that year it was in full working order ; and among the chief benefactors were Mr. Ferrers, Mrs. Elizabeth Levison, Mrs. Dorothy Levison, and Mrs. Ashley ; for all of whom there were obligations of Masses.

The mission very probably dates from about the year 1750 ; for Mrs. Elizabeth Levison, who may be considered one of the founders, is mentioned in connection with the place as being still alive in 1758.

In 1761 Elizabeth Palmer left twenty pounds, the interest of which was partly to be given to the incumbent, who had to say five Masses for the repose of her soul; the rest to be distributed among the poor of Shirley Street.

In 1815 William Collins left the rents of some lands to the Franciscan missionary at Solihull, with the obligation of saying six Masses annually for the repose of his soul and those of his relatives.

In the same year, Mrs. Anne Barron bequeathed two hundred pounds to our mission at Solihull, in consideration of which ten Masses annually had to be said for ten years; after that two per annum.

In 1821 this mission received the half, or one hundred pounds, of the legacy of William and Elizabeth Lewin. One Mass had to be said every three weeks for their eternal repose.

In 1824 a sum of fifty pounds was left by Mrs. Elizabeth Green for our Missionary here.

STOKESLEY, YORKSHIRE.

This place was permanently served by one of the Franciscan fathers of Osmotherley, as appears from Father Englefield's writings.

Previous to the year 1758 Mr. Bradshaw Pearson had left one hundred pounds for the priest's remuneration.

STONECROFT, NEAR HEXHAM.

This residence owes its origin to Ursula Mountney of Stonecroft, who left by will, in the second half of the seventeenth century, twenty pounds towards the support of a Dominican or Franciscan priest here.

Not long after the Franciscans began to serve the place. In 1686 the resident father, owing as it appears to some legal difficulty, was in danger of being evicted. The Definitors deliberated on the matter, and resolved to write to the patron of the place, Sir Rudolph Clavering, asking him to do all in his power to maintain the incumbent in possession.

Father Peter Atkinson died here in 1687.

In 1690 it was decided that the property in Stonecroft and Hubush should be let to farm to some discreet Catholic, qualified to entertain a priest for the service of Catholics in Hexham and Warden, and the neighbourhood.

TICHBORNE, HAMPSHIRE.

This residence is mentioned by Father Felix Englefield in 1758. In that year two Franciscans were living here together, Fathers Beaumont and Ravenhill.

The patron was Sir H. Tichborne.

TOR ABBEY, DEVONSHIRE.

Father Beaumont served this mission for six years, about the middle of the eighteenth century.

Many years later another Franciscan ministered here, Father Pursell, who arrived on September 23, 1820. But he was then in weak health, and died the following year.

TUSMORE, NEAR BRACKLEY, NORTHAMPTONSHIRE.

This residence is mentioned about the year 1790,

when Father Augustine Kemble lived here, as appears from the Procurator's notes.

———

UFTON COURT, BERKSHIRE.

Father Felix Englefield mentions this place in his list of residences drawn up in 1758. The patron was Mr. Perkins.

Father Felix Price served the residence in the above year; and Father Athanasius Baynham was here towards the close of the eighteenth century.

———

UGBROOKE, DEVONSHIRE.

The seat of the Cliffords. The place is mentioned as having been served nearly always by the Jesuit fathers.

A Franciscan, Father Peter Frost, resided here in 1758, as we know from Father Englefield's list. This kind and zealous priest laboured here for about ten years; for though his register only commences with October, 1757, it seems that he had arrived in the previous year. He continued until June, 1766, when, to the sincere regret of the Clifford family, he was destined by his Superiors to take charge of the school at Edgbaston. (Dr. Oliver.)

———

UGTHORPE, YORKSHIRE.

A proposal was submitted to the Franciscan Chapter in 1684, " whether the Province would accept the incumbency of Ugthorpe in Yorkshire, now held by the Rev. Father George Smith, of the Order of Hermits of St. Augustine, who receives twelve pounds per annum for his services; with this condition, that our missionary shall receive two pounds annually during Father Smith's lifetime, and after his death ten. On the understanding, however, that those ten pounds shall revert to the Augustinian fathers, if they obtain from the Holy See faculties for the English mission." The proposal was accepted, and the deed of agreement with Father Smith was put in the archives.

We find the following entry in the "Catalogue of writings" in 1704 : "Georg Smyth's Covenant concerning Ugthorp, July 24, 1684."

UPHALL, LINCOLNSHIRE.

We find this residence mentioned in the year 1782. Mr. Thomas Hall, alias Father Lawrence Lorain, was then here.

WARDOUR, WILTSHIRE.

Father Angelus a S. Francisco, or Richard Mason, served this mission in the second half of the seventeenth century, in succession to Father William Smith, S.J., who died on September 13, 1658. Father Angelus was again succeeded by a Jesuit.

WARKWORTH, NORTHAMPTONSHIRE.

This place was served by the Franciscans in the second half of the eighteenth century. In Mr. Holman's time he had Father Bedingfield for chaplain.

Father Hall was here in 1758, when Mr. F. Eyre was the patron. Father Kemble also resided here before 1790.

WARWICK.
(*Title :*—St. Mary of the Angels.)

Warwick is the eighth on the list of nine residences decreed in 1687. Father Nicholas Dalyson, or Dallison, laboured here constantly, with one interruption about the year 1700, from the beginning till the year 1707.

He saw his foundation pass through various vicissitudes, for in 1704 the Chronicler writes :

" About the same time as Mr. Randolph set up at Birmingham, Mr. Dalyson also begun a chapel at Warwick, where he purchased the ground it stood upon. But this, as well as all the others throughout the whole kingdom, was destroyed too : but the ground is not alienated. The things belonging to this place, Mr. Dalyson can give good account of."

Father Dalyson was succeeded as Preses by Francis Dodd, who was here from 1707 until 1740, with an interruption in 1731, when the office was filled by George Lancaster ; then Lawrence Lorain, 1740-1744 ; John Baptist Gibson, 1744-1747 ; George Lancaster, 1747-1755 ; Anthony Lancaster, 1755-1758 ; Henry Bishop, 1758-1764 ; Placidus Payne, 1764-1767 ; Peter Frost, 1767-1770 ; George Lancaster, 1770-1773 ; Thomas Dixon, 1773-1788 ; Henry Bishop, 1788-1793 ; Angelus Ingram, 1793 ; Henry Bishop, 1794-1800 ; Lewis Kellery, 1800-1805 ; Lawrence

Eccles, 1805; Paschal Harrison, 1806-1808; Joseph Howse, 1808; Henry Waring, 1809-1812.

No further appointments.

This is the place to mention that in 1749 the fathers decided that one hundred pounds were to be distributed among the poor Catholics of the parish of Burbuck* and vicinity, to fulfil our obligations, according to the directions given by Father Dodd, Preses of Warwick, before his death, in 1747.

WATER HALL, BUCKINGHAMSHIRE.

Father Bonaventure Bedingfield resided here in the year 1758. The place is mentioned in Father Felix Englefield's list.

The patron was Mrs. Markham.

WEST GRINSTEAD, SUSSEX.

This mission was served by the Jesuit Fathers from 1701 to 1755. In the preceding year Mr. Caryll had addressed himself to the Franciscans at Douai, who sent Father Placid Payne, then newly ordained, to serve the place, until a final arrangement could be made.

As Father Felix Englefield was Provincial at this time, we shall relate the circumstances in his own words.

"July, 1758. Mr. Edward Caryll made a foundation at this time, for one of ours to serve the poor Catholics

----

* It is written Burbuck in the original, but probably Budbrook is meant.

at West Grinstead, which place formerly belonged to that noble family ; and for which he gave the sum of thirteen hundred pounds ; which gift and donation was accepted by our Chapter in July, 1758. And in which, in gratitude for so great a charity, it was ordered that at his death there should be a solemn High Mass and Dirge, with all the Masses of the day, performed at Douai. And five hundred Masses discharged by our missioners, as the Rev. Father Provincial for the time being should appoint. That his anniversary should be kept, and a weekly Mass performed by the incumbent, as well as nine anniversaries for his relations.

" *Note.*—That Mr. Caryll is to receive the income of the said sum from us during his life; and that one hundred pounds of it is to go for the purchase of the place, in case it is to be sold."

At the time mentioned above, July, 1758, Father Payne had completed the furnishing of the residence, towards which the Province contributed the sum of eighteen pounds.

Father Felix Englefield says that Father Houghton resided here in 1758.

The following are the names of the Franciscans who served this mission : Fathers Payne, Dixon, Copley, Chapman, Pilling, Cottrell and McDonnell, who became Provincial in 1815. He was the last.

—

WEYMOUTH, DORSETSHIRE.

Father Leo (Francis) Edgeworth served this mission from the month of August, 1824, until the spring of 1825, when he went to St. Joseph's Chapel, Bristol.

WHITE HILL, LANCASHIRE.
(*Title* :—The Holy Cross.)

The foundation of the residence of White Hill, " in the chapelry of Goosnargh, and the parish of Kirkham," dates from the year 1687.

Some years later, after the " great Revolution," we find the following description of it :

" The residence of White Hill was procured by Father Michael Jackson, and consists of a Chapel, and a little dwelling-place at one end ; the ground of which was given us by Mr. Cuthbert Hesketh, upon conditions expressed in his deed, that is in Mr. Michael Jackson's hands, and a copy in ours. The same Mr. Cuthbert Hesketh put out two hundred pounds, Mr. Gabriel Hesketh and Mr. Evan Gerard being trustees, the interest of which being ten pounds per annum, for maintaining a missioner of ours, who is obliged to say two Masses per week for the said Mr. Cuthbert and his wife ; to serve the poor Catholics of the parishes of Goosnargh and Chipping ; and if permitted make his abode and live at the Chapel of White Hill.

" The Chapel being uncovered by the mob, the walls are ordered to be taken down, and all the materials either sold or laid up safe."

The sacred edifice, however, soon rose out of its ruins, and the residence flourished for more than one hundred years in the hands of the Franciscans.

A certain number of Masses had to be said annually for the following benefactors, besides Mr. Hesketh, the founder : Jane Adamson, Richard Holden, James Ayrer, the Cardwell family, Gilbert Slater, Jane

Armstrong, Thomas Slaughter and Alice his wife.

In 1688 Father Joseph Trappes was sent as assistant to Father Michael Jackson, who was the first Preses, and held that office until 1710. He was succeeded by Henry Appleton, 1710-1738; Charles Tootell, 1738-1752; John Evangelist Tootell, 1752; Robert Painter, 1753-1755; Charles Tootell, 1755-1758; Leo Francis, 1758-1761; Charles Tootell, 1761-1764; Robert Painter, 1764-1767; Leo Francis, 1767-1770; Bernardine Fleet, 1770-1773; Lawrence Eccles, 1773-1776; Bernard Yates, 1776-1778; Alexius Whalley, 1778; Peter Wilcock, 1779-1782; Anthony Caley, 1782-1784; Peter Wilcock, 1784; Ignatius Casemore, 1785-1787; James Howse, 1787; Nicholas Knight, 1788-1790; Ignatius Casemore, 1790; Peter Wilcock, 1791-1794; Henry Waring, 1794-1800; Pacificus Kington, 1800-1803; Joseph Tate, 1803-1805; Bonaventure Martin, 1805-1808; Joseph Tate, 1808; Anselm Millward, 1809. This was the last appointment.

WHITE KNIGHTS, NEAR READING.

The Franciscans served this residence for a very considerable time. We have the following entry in Father Pulton's handwriting:

A memorandum at Mr. Clifton's going from White Knights in 1734, the original being left with Mr. Greswold, his successor there.

My bridle, saddle, whip, boots, spurs and spatterdashes I leave to my successor, if a Brother of our

Province, who may have the use of them ; of my two tomes in folio of Père Henno's Divinity, and of all the other books in my closet, all of which belong to the body of the English Franciscans, or to some particular members thereof, whose names are in them, or else R..A. [Recollectorum Anglorum].

Another Franciscan, Father Healy, is mentioned as being here 1773-1775.

WITHAM, ESSEX.

Father McDonnell served this mission from 1826 to 1839. In 1832 he was appointed Visitor of the Province, previously to the Chapter at which he was elected Provincial. His expenses on this occasion are thus set down in the accounts: "Journey to London, Taunton, Birmingham and Witham, £11 18s. 10½d."

WOOTTEN HALL, WARWICKSHIRE.

Father Felix Englefield mentions this place in 1758, when Father George Lancaster resided here. Father Peter Frost died here in 1785.

Among the Franciscans who were here afterwards was Father Caley at the end of the eighteenth century, and Father Bishop at the beginning of the nineteenth.

WORLABY, NEAR BRIGG, LINCOLNSHIRE.

This was the residence of the Webb family.

Towards the close of the eighteenth century the place was served by some Franciscans. Father Anthony

Caley was here in 1783. Afterwards Father Ignatius Casemore.

The altar picture belonging to the Chapel was afterwards taken to Gainsborough.

———

YORK.

(*Title*:—The Blessed Sacrament.)

"In the year 1687," says the chronicler, "Mr. John Cross, then Provincial, established a residence and school for youth at York; where were two preachers, and two masters of humanity, first begun in Jubber Gate, and afterwards continued in Castle Gate."

The first Preses of the residence was Father Bonaventure Parry. Father Bernardine Barras was his assistant and taught the school.

In 1688 Fathers Elias van Eecke and Mathias Roelhoof, two of the ten Belgian fathers who had come to help on the English mission, came as assistants.

But on November 22 of this year all were forced to fly. For some years afterwards, however, a Preses continued to be appointed.

Father Gregory. Jones, alias Andrews, was Preses from 1689 to 1695. After him Father Bernardine Barras in 1695. Then Daniel Selby in 1696. He was the last.

In 1704 the chronicler added: "The house was hired : so no more a residence now."

———

MEMBERS OF THE SECOND ENGLISH FRANCISCAN PROVINCE.

IT is morally certain that the names of all the fathers will be found here. For although in 1634 we must account for five Religious, of which number only three can be traced, it is not improbable that the other two are lay brothers, whose names are not given.* Further, there is, it is true, a break in the record between 1640 and 1647 ; but fortunately we have in the latter year a list of deceased since 1640. The death of some of the Religious is not mentioned ; but, on the other hand, we have on four occasions a general statement as regards the number of deaths. In the year 1634 it is said that " five Religious have died," among whom was William a Sancto Augustino. In 1653 " at the College of Douai three of the brethren have died." In 1655 " at the College of Douai two of our brethren have died ; on the Mission one." In 1656 " the number of deceased since the last Provincial Chapter is five." Reference may be made to these statements in case of doubt. With regard to aliases, great care has been taken to discriminate the individuals accurately. It should be borne in mind that the fathers were often known by their baptismal names on the mission, not by their religious names. All are priests, unless otherwise stated.

* Lay brother, properly speaking, means a member of the First Order ; but it is also used for Tertiaries in the writings of the old Franciscans.

FATHER WALTER COLMAN, O.S.F.

(From the " Certamen Seraphicum.")

To face p. 191.

ADAMS, PACIFICUS, was approved for preaching and hearing confessions in 1693, and sent on the English Mission in 1696. He died in 1700 or 1701.

ADAMS, PETER OF ALCANTARA, was approved for preaching and hearing confessions in 1725. Appointed Preses of the residence of Mount Grace, 1729-1732. He is again mentioned in 1734 and 1737.

ADSHED, PAUL, lay brother, died at Douai in the year 1731.

ANDERTON, JOHN EVANGELIST, was approved for preaching and hearing confessions in 1752 ; appointed professor of philosophy at Douai, 1752-1755 ; Vicar at Douai, 1755 ; novice master, 1753-1756 ; sent on the mission and appointed titular Guardian of Coventry, 1758—he then resided at Edgbaston ; confessor of the Poor Clares at Aire, 1761-1764 ; confessor of the nuns of the Third Order at Bruges, 1764-1770 ; confessor at Aire, 1770-1773 ; confessor at Bruges, 1773 and 1774 ; titular Guardian of Newcastle, 1776-1779 ; Preses of the residence of Hereford in 1779 and 1780 ; titular Guardian of Oxford in 1781 ; elected Custos, 1782-1785 ; titular Guardian of Greenwich 1785-1788—about this time he was staying at Basil Eyston's, Esq., Hendred ; again Custos, 1788-1791 ; appointed titular Guardian of London in 1793, and again in 1796. He died before the year 1800.

ANDERTON, WILLIAM A S. ANTONIO, was approved for preaching and hearing confessions in 1634 ; appointed confessor of the Poor Clares at Aire, 1634-1640. He was, as well as Father Bel, as Challoner assures us, of the number of priests deputed by the Archbishop of Cambrai in virtue of a Brief of Pope Urban VIII. to enquire "into the cause and manner of death of several priests" lately executed under the penal statutes, and to transmit the account thereof to Rome. He was titular Guardian of York, 1647-1653; of Newcastle, 1659-1662, and again, 1665-1668; Definitor, 1668-1671. He died on the English mission either in that or the following year.

ANDRÉ, PHILIP, was before his ordination, in 1728, appointed professor of philosophy for three years. Having been ordained, he was approved for preaching and hearing confessions in 1729. He was professor of theology from 1731-1740; confessor at Bruges in 1740; Guardian of Douai, 1741; titular Guardian of Newcastle and confessor at Aire, 1743-1746; titular Guardian of Worcester, 1746-1749; Definitor, 1749-1752; titular Guardian of London, 1752-1755; Custos 1755-1758; titular Guardian of Greenwich, 1758-1761; Custos again 1761-1764; elected Provincial in 1764; declared a jubilarian in 1771. He died in England in 1772.

ANDREWS, BERNARDINE, was approved for preaching and hearing confessions in 1663, and for the mission at the same time. He was titular Guardian of Bristol, 1671-1674. He died in England in 1679 or 1680.

APPLETON, HENRY, was approved for preaching and hearing confessions in 1704; sent on the mission in 1705; Preses of the residence of White Hill from 1710 until his death. He was titular Guardian of Newcastle from 1723 to 1726 ; titular Guardian of Canterbury in 1731, and again of Newcastle in 1732. He died in England in 1737 or 1738.

APPLETON, *alias* HANNAN, HENRY, was approved for preaching and hearing confessions in 1746. He was professor of philosophy at Douai, 1746-1749 ; professor of theology, 1749-1761, in which year he was sent on the mission. He was titular Guardian of Greenwich, 1761-1764 ; Definitor in 1764, in which office he died in England, in the year 1767.

ARMSTRONG, PETER, A S. MARIA, was appointed professor of philosophy at Douai when still a cleric in 1663. Afterwards ordained, approved for preaching and hearing confessions, and continued professor of philosophy in 1665. He was professor of theology from 1668-1674. He then came on the mission, and was made titular Guardian of Norwich at the time of the erection of that Guardianate in 1675. Appointed titular Guardian of York in 1677. He had to hide himself in 1680, on account of the persecution, and his whereabouts could not be ascertained at the time of the Chapter, which was not held in England, but at Bruges, owing to the same circumstances, and which he should have attended. He was again appointed titular Guardian of York in 1683 ; and of London in 1684 ; Definitor in 1686. Appointed Preses of the residence of Lincoln's Inn Fields, when the new friary was commenced there in 1687. He was again titular Guardian of London in 1689 and 1690 ; of Worcester, 1692-1695 ; Custos in 1695, in which office he died in the year 1697 or 1698.   He had been decorated with the title of Doctor of Divinity.

ARNOLD, JOACHIM, was approved for preaching and hearing confessions in 1749, and for the mission in 1753.   In 1758 he was at Grove Park, Warwickshire. Appointed Preses of the residence of Hexham in 1770 ; titular Guardian of Greenwich, 1771-1774 ; and of Coventry, 1774-1776 ; Definitor in 1776, in which office he died in England in 1778 or 1779.

ASTON, PLACID, was approved for preaching and hearing confessions in 1737 ; Vicar of Douai and novice master, 1743-1746; confessor at Aire, 1746-1749 ; Preses of the residence of Monmouth, 1749-1752 ; titular Guardian of Cambridge from 1752 till his death, which occurred in London in 1754 or 1755.

ATKINSON, PAUL, CONFESSOR OF THE FAITH, was approved for preaching and hearing confessions in 1683.   He was professor of philosophy at Douai in 1684 and 1685, and was appointed professor of theology in 1686.   He became a member of the community of the new friary at Lincoln's Inn Fields in 1687, in quality of " Catechist" and " Prefect of the choir."   He resided for a time at Tichborne, and was elected Definitor in the year 1698.   In 1700 he was condemned to perpetual imprisonment for the Faith, and closed his long martyrdom at Hurst Castle (formerly a prison, now a signal-station) in October, 1729.   He was buried in the old Catholic cemetery on the hillside above Winchester.

His gravestone is thus inscribed :

H. S. E. R. P. *

PAULUS ATKINSON FRANCISCANUS,

QUI OCT. 15, 1729, ÆTAT. 74,

IN CARCERE DE HURST VITAM FINIVIT,

POSTQUAM IBIDEM 30 PEREGERAT ANNOS.

R. I. P.

ATKINSON, PETER, was approved for preaching and hearing confessions in 1680. Appointed novice master at Douai in 1683. He came on the English mission in 1684, and died at the village of Stone Croft near Hexham in 1686 or 1687.

AYLMER, AUGUSTINE, was approved for preaching and hearing confessions in 1695. From that year until 1701 he was professor of philosophy at Douai. Appointed professor of theology in 1701, he continued in that capacity until 1707, when he became Guardian of Douai, which office he held for three years. In 1710 he was elected Custos of the Province.

AYREY, ALBAN, A S. AGATHA (baptismal name JAMES), was approved for preaching and hearing confessions in 1674, and sent on the mission. He was appointed chronologist in 1675, and the fathers were directed to forward to him all their historical documents. He was titular Guardian of Norwich, 1683-1686. In 1687 he became Vicar of the newly erected friary at Lincoln's Inn Fields. He was chaplain to the Spanish ambassador, Pedro Ronquillo, in 1688,

---

* This means : Hic sepultus est Reverendus Pater.

but was requested to continue preaching at Lincoln's Inn Fields chapel, and also at Somerset House. Two of his sermons are extant : one delivered at Weld House, London, on the third Sunday of Advent, December 12, 1686 ; and the other preached at Somerset House before the Queen Dowager on the second Sunday after Easter, April 10, 1687. He became confessor to the nuns of the Third Order at Bruges in 1692 ; titular Guardian of Norwich from 1698 until 1701. He was elected Definitor in 1705, and died in that office the following year.

BABE, *alias* PRICE, BRUNO, was approved for preaching and hearing confessions in 1743 ; sent on the mission and appointed Preses of the residence of Monmouth in 1747 ; titular Guardian of Oxford, 1755-1758 ; about this time he resided at Ufton Court, Berkshire. Titular Guardian of Worcester, 1761-1764 ; Preses of the residence of Monmouth, 1766-1770, and of the residence of Mount Grace, 1771-1772 ; titular Guardian of York, 1773-1776 ; again in 1778 ; and of Newcastle, 1779-1781 ; Preses of the residence of Hexham in 1781 ; titular Guardian of Norwich in 1782. He died in England in 1783 or 1784.

BAKER, PACIFICUS (baptismal name ARTHUR), was approved for preaching and hearing confessions in 1725 ; professor of philosophy, 1725-1728. From 1728 to 1732 he was novice-master at Douai, and 1729-1730 also Vicar. In 1732 he was sent on the mission. He was appointed Preses of Hexham, 1734-1737 ; titular Guardian of York, 1735-1738, and again

1740-1743 ; Definitor, 1743-1746 ; titular Guardian of York, and also Procurator of the Province, 1746-1752 ; titular Guardian of Greenwich, whilst remaining Procurator, 1752-1755 ; Custos, 1755-1758 ; titular Guardian of London, 1758-1761 ; Provincial, 1761-1764 ; again Provincial, 1770-1773. He died in England on March 16, 1774, aged 80 years. He was considered an eminent preacher, and wrote several books of piety. He was a Jubilarian in the Order.

BARKER, BERNARD, was approved for preaching and hearing confessions in 1755. He came on the mission in 1762. He was Preses of the residence of Birmingham, 1764-1767, and of the residence of Hereford, 1767-1773 ; titular Guardian of Canterbury in 1773, in which office he died on the mission in 1775 or 1776.

BARKER, LEO, was approved for preaching and hearing confessions in 1734 ; professor of philosophy at Douai, 1734-1737 ; appointed to explain the Franciscan Rule to the community in 1737 ; Preses of the residence of Abergavenny, 1738-1740. He died at Douai in 1753.

BARRAS, BERNARDINE, was appointed assistant teacher in the school attached to our residence at York in 1687. Approved for preaching and hearing confessions in 1689. He was incarcerated for the faith in the dungeon of the Kidcote prison, at the end of York bridge, for several months in 1689. Appointed Preses of York in 1695. He died there the following year.

BARRETT, EDWARD, was approved for preaching and hearing confessions in 1716, and for the mission in 1717. He was titular Guardian of Cambridge, 1732-1735 ; and of Norwich, 1737-1740 ; Definitor, 1740-1743 ; titular Guardian of Worcester, 1743-1746, in which year he died in England.

BASKERVILLE, BERNARD, A S. CRUCE, was approved for preaching and hearing confessions in 1680 ; professor of philosophy at Douai, 1680-1684 ; professor of theology, 1686-1692 ; titular Guardian of Cambridge, 1689-1692 ; Definitor, 1695-1698 ; titular Guardian of Cambridge, 1698-1701 ; again Definitor, 1701-1704 ; titular Guardian of Bristol, 1704-1707 ; Definitor, 1710-1713 ; titular Guardian of Bristol, 1713-1716 ; Preses of the residence of Monmouth, 1714-1716 ; Definitor, 1716-1719 ; Provincial, 1719-1722 ; again Preses of Monmouth in 1725, and titular Guardian of Bristol, 1725-1728. In the latter year he died, a jubilarian, in England.

BASKERVILLE, BONAVENTURE, was approved for preaching and hearing confessions in 1691. Sent ou the mission in 1692. He was appointed titular Guardian of Canterbury in 1704, and died the following year.

BASKERVILLE, THOMAS, professed cleric, died at Douai in 1689.

BATTEN, or BATTING, ADAM. He was the first that delivered a Latin discourse on the occasion of the Chapter in 1656. He was appointed Secretary of the Province in 1656, and agent iu temporal affairs to the

Poor Clares at Aire.   In 1657 he was appointed head professor of philosophy in London, where Father Anthony Le Grand was already teaching.

BAYNHAM, ATHANASIUS, was approved for preaching and hearing confessions in 1761 ; Vicar of Douai, 1762-1764 ; professor of philosophy, 1764-1767 ; confessor of the Poor Clares at Aire in 1767 ; Vicar of Douai, 1768-1770 ; Preses of the residence of Birmingham, 1770-1773 ; titular Guardian of Coventry and confessor at Aire in 1773 and 1774 ; Guardian of Douai in 1776 and 1777 ; confessor at Bruges in 1778 ; titular Guardian of Greenwich, 1779-1782 ; Definitor, 1782-1785 ; titular Guardian of Cambridge, 1785-1788, and of Oxford, 1790 ; Custos, 1791-1794. About this time he resided at Ufton Court near Reading. He was appointed titular Guardian of York in 1794, and of London in 1800.   He died in 1802 or 1803.

BEAUMONT, JOHN BAPTIST, eldest son of Joseph and Hannah (olim Harding) Beaumont, of Stone Easton in Somersetshire, received the Franciscan habit at Douai. He was approved for preaching and hearing confessions in 1725, and sent on the mission the following year. He was appointed Preses of Monmouth in 1732, and of Hereford in 1734 ; titular Guardian of Bristol, 1734-1737. For six years, before the arrival of Reverend Charles Needham in 1745, he was Chaplain at Tor Abbey.   About the year 1758 he resided at Tichborne in Hampshire.   It was then decided to recall him from the mission.   He had a brother, William, a Jesuit, of whom mention occurs in 1761, in which year Father

John Beaumont was sent to Douai. He was becoming old and rather weak-minded in 1764, and it was thought well to keep him at home. He was a jubilarian in the Order, and died at Douai in the year 1774.

BEDINGFIELD, BONAVENTURE (baptismal name CHARLES), was approved for preaching and hearing confessions in 1731. Sent on the English mission in 1732; titular Guardian of Canterbury, 1737-1740; Definitor, 1740-1743; Preses of the residence of Monmouth, 1743-1747; titular Guardian of Bristol, 1743-1746; Definitor, 1746-1749; titular Guardian of Cambridge, 1749-1752; Definitor, 1752-1755; titular Guardian of Greenwich, 1755-1758. At this time he resided at Water Hall, Buckinghamshire. He was also at one time chaplain to Mr. Holman of Warkworth, Northamptonshire; Definitor, 1758-1761; titular Guardian of York, 1761-1764; Definitor, 1764-1767; titular Guardian of Worcester, 1767-1770; Definitor, 1770-1773; titular Guardian of Greenwich, 1773-1776. He was declared a jubilarian in the latter year, and died at Douai in 1782.

BEE, MICHAEL, lay brother, died at Douai in 1735.

BEL, VENERABLE FRANCIS (baptismal name ARTHUR), MARTYR, was born at Hanbury, near Worcester, in 1590. At the age of twenty-four he went to the English College at St. Omers, and thence to Valladolid, where he was in due time ordained priest. He took the habit of St. Francis at Segobia in 1618.

Shortly after his profession he was called away from Spain and incorporated in the English Province by order of the Commissary General. Here is a translation of his letter:

FATHER ANDREW A SOTO,

*Commissary General of the Order of Friars Minor
of the Regular Observance and Confessor to her
Most Serene Highness, the Infanta of Spain, to the
Reverend Father Francis Bel, eternal salvation in
the Lord.*

Whereas our Most Reverend Father General, Benignus of Genoa, has committed to me the care of sending to England and Scotland such fathers as seem suitable to labour in the Lord's vineyard, for the comfort of Catholics, who groan under the heavy yoke of persecution, and for the restoration and preservation of our Order in those parts; and as he has given me power to call English and Scotch Religious from any Province whatever: I enjoin you, in whose zeal and piety I trust, in virtue of Holy Obedience, to come to these parts at your earliest convenience, in order to be sent into the Lord's harvest there, or to prepare yourself for the mission here among your countrymen, until you shall be judged fit to go. I herewith recommend you to our Prelates as well as to the Faithful of the places where you happen to stop on the way.

Given at Brussels, on the last day of December, 1619.

FATHER ANDREW A SOTO,
Commissary General.

In 1622 he was appointed confessor to the Poor Clares at Gravelines, and afterwards to the nuns of the Third Order of St. Francis at Brussels. In the decree of the erection of the English Province, promulgated in 1630, he was mentioned as one of the Definitors. He was also at that time appointed Guardian of Douai and professor of Hebrew. In 1632 he was named Provincial of Scotland. He was appointed titular Guardian of London in 1637 and Definitor in 1640. He was apprehended for the Faith on November 6, 1643, and suffered martyrdom in December of the same year.

BENSON, THOMAS, A S. ANNA, was approved for preaching and hearing confessions in 1657, and at the same time appointed novice master; confessor of Poor Clares at Aire, 1659-1662; Procurator of the Province, 1665-1671; Definitor, 1671-1674; again Procurator, and titular Guardian of Canterbury, 1674-1677; Definitor, 1677-1680; confessor at Bruges, 1678-1681; titular Guardian of Oxford, 1680-1683; Guardian of Douai, 1683-1686; Definitor, 1686-1689; titular Guardian of Greenwich, 1689-1692; Definitor, 1692-1695; titular Guardian of Cambridge, 1695-1698; Definitor, 1698-1701; titular Guardian of Oxford, 1701-1704. He died in 1705.

BEVANS, AMBROSE, was approved for preaching and hearing confessions in 1655, and at the same time sent on the mission, and appointed Catechist for the city of London. He is mentioned again as being on the mission in 1665. In 1668 he was recalled to Douai;

but afterwards he was sent back to England, where he died in 1685 or 1686.

BEVERIDGE, JEROME, was approved for preaching and hearing confessions in 1713 ; sent on the English mission in 1722; titular Guardian of Coventry in 1732 and 1733, and of Norwich in 1734 and 1735; titular Guardian of Worcester, 1740-1743 ; and of Oxford, 1750-1753.　He died, a jubilarian, at Douai in 1765.

BISHOP, HENRY, was approved for preaching and hearing confessions in 1755.　The following year he was sent on the mission.　In the year 1758 he resided at Baddesley.　He was Preses of the residence of Warwick, 1758-1764 ; titular Guardian of Coventry, 1764-1767 ; Preses of Hexham, 1767-1770 ; Preses of Birmingham, 1773-1776 ; titular Guardian of Worcester, 1776-1779 ; Preses of Hexham, 1779-1781 ; titular Guardian of Worcester in 1781 ; Definitor, 1782-1785 ; —about this time he resided at Rowington ;—titular Guardian of Coventry, 1785-1786, and of Canterbury in 1787 ; Preses of Warwick, 1788-1789 ; titular Guardian of Worcester in 1790 ; Preses of Warwick, 1791-1792 ; titular Guardian of Cambridge in 1793 ; Preses of Warwick, 1794-1795 ; titular Guardian of Coventry, 1800-1803, when he was declared a jubilarian ; Preses of Birmingham in 1805 ; titular Guardian of London, 1806-1807 ; Preses of Birmingham in 1808 ; titular Guardian of Norwich, 1809-1810. The following year he died at Baddesley.　He lies buried near the sacristy door ; and on a slab inserted in the wall we read the following inscription :

Hic jacet
R. P. HENRICUS BISHOP, O.S.F.
Hujus Capellæ Fundator.
Obiit 19 Junii a.d. 1811, Æt. 86.
R. I. P.

His portrait in oil, formerly at Baddesley, is now at St. Francis', West Gorton, Manchester.

BIX, ANGELUS, was approved for preaching and hearing confessions in 1674; Vicar of Douai, 1675-1676; titular Guardian of Oxford, 1677-1680; and of Canterbury, 1680-1683; he was confessor at Aire in 1680; and at Bruges, 1681-1684; titular Guardian of Canterbury, 1686-1689; in 1689 he was appointed to the staff of the newly founded friary at Lincoln's Inn Fields. His sermon preached on Good Friday, April 13, 1688, at Somerset House, was published by command of Queen Mary d'Este, Consort of King James. Afterwards he was confessor at Aire, 1689-1692; titular Guardian of York in 1692. He died in England in the year 1695.

BIX, JOHN EVANGELIST, was approved for preaching and hearing confessions in 1687. He died about the year 1704.

BOLE, NICHOLAS, was approved for preaching and hearing confessions in 1710. He was organist at Douai. Afterwards he was sent on the mission, but returned to Douai in 1719, to superintend the completion of the new organ, which had been commenced

under his supervision. The following year he came
again to England. Appointed titular Guardian of
Greenwich in 1723, when he also became assistant
Procurator to Father John Capistran Eyston, titular
Guardian of London, whose place he had to take in his
absence ; he was also recommended to visit him
frequently and to give him every possible assistance.
He died on the mission in 1727 or 1728.

BOOTH, JOHN, lay brother, died at Douai in 1686.

BROWN, alias CARRUTHERS, BERNARDINE, was approved
for preaching and hearing confessions in 1747, and at
that time also sent on the mission. He was Preses of
Birmingham 1749-1752 ; and again appointed to the
same office, 1755-1756. He was a teacher at the
school of Edgbaston, where he died in 1757. His
death, as Father Felix Englefield writes, was a great
loss to the school.

BROWNE, ADAM, A S. MICHAELE, was sent on the
mission in 1650. He was titular Guardian of Greenwich, 1653-1657 ; in 1655 he was appointed Catechist
for the city of London, and in 1657 professor of philosophy in London ; titular Guardian of London, 1659-
1662 ; Definitor, 1662-1665 ; titular Guardian of
London, 1666-1669 ; Custos, 1671-1674 ; again appointed titular Guardian of London in 1674, he died
the following year in that city.

BUDDEN, JOSEPH, lay brother, died at Douai in 1729.

BULLAKER, VENERABLE JOHN BAPTIST A S. BONA-
VENTURA (baptismal name THOMAS), MARTYR, was born
at Chichester about the year 1604. At the age of

eighteen he went to the college of St. Omers, and from thence, after a short stay, to the English seminary of Valladolid. When about nineteen, he was admitted to the Franciscan Order in the famous friary of the Spanish Recollects at Abrojo near Valladolid. He finished his studies at Segobia, and came from there on the English mission. He was first imprisoned at Plymouth and Exeter, but afterwards, being discharged, he entered upon his missionary labours. He was declared incorporated in the English Province in 1638, and was appointed titular Guardian of Oxford in 1640. He suffered at Tyburn, October 12, 1642.

Bullen, or Bulley, Michael, was approved for preaching and hearing confessions in 1671 ; titular Guardian of Newcastle, 1683-1686. He died on the English mission in 1706 or 1707.

Burgaigne, George, was appointed titular Guardian of Dorchester in 1632. He died probably before the year 1634.

Burton, Augustine, a young father who died in 1707.

Butterfield, alias Drue, Robert, a youth whose profession was declared invalid in 1631, and who in consequence returned to the world.

Caley, Anthony, was approved for preaching and hearing confessions in 1779 ; appointed Preses of the residence of White Hill, 1782-1785 ; titular Guardian of Canterbury, 1785-1786, and of Worcester in 1787. About this time he resided at Wootten Hall Again titular Guardian of Worcester, 1791-1794 ; elected

Definitor in 1794.   He died before the year 1800.

CANES, JOHN BAPTIST, A S. VINCENTIO, or VINCENT, was born on the borders of Nottinghamshire and Leicestershire, and brought up a Protestant. When arrived at the age of eighteen, he was sent to the university of Cambridge, and remained there two years. His docility of heart led him to the discovery of the truth, and he consecrated himself to God and the service of religion in the Franciscan Order. Already before his ordination he commenced teaching philosophy at Douai. He was approved for preaching and hearing confessions in 1640, and continued professor of philosophy. In 1647 he taught theology. The following year he came on the mission. He was titular Guardian of Worcester, 1650-1653; again appointed to teach theology in 1653; elected Definitor in 1656. He became popularly known as "Fiat Lux" (Be light made), the title of one of his works on the religious troubles in England. He was selected by the Catholic body to defend their cause against Dr. Stillingfleet, their most virulent antagonist, and he succeeded to the general satisfaction. He was a man of acute and vigorous mind, and sprightly humour; and united to ardent zeal the most delicate forbearance and charity. His life was wholly employed in the service of religion.

Dodd says that he lived sometimes in Lancashire, but for the most part in London, and was remarkable for the plainness of his dress and conversation. In 1671 he was made titular Guardian of Greenwich. He died at Somerset House in June, 1672, and was buried in the chapel belonging to the Palace.

CANTABRIGIENSIS, or of CAMBRIDGE, LEWIS, came on the English mission as Secretary of the Province in 1632. He died probably before the year 1634.

CANTRILL, BRUNO, was professor of philosophy at Douai, 1701-1703. He asked leave of the General to go to another Province, but it was not granted. He was professor of theology, 1707-1722; titular Guardian of Canterbury, 1716-1719; Custos, 1719-1722; sent on the mission, and appointed titular Guardian of Greenwich, in 1722; and again 1728-1731; Definitor, 1731-1733, when he was elected Vicar Provincial on the death of Father Philip Sadler. About this time his address was: At Mr. Cabry's, Fan Maker, over against Gray's Inn Gate. He was Provincial, 1734-1737; Procurator in 1738; again Provincial, 1743-1746. He died in England in 1759.

CAPE, ANTHONY, died at Bruges about the year 1671.

CAPE, ANTHONY, A S. JOSEPHO, was a lay brother about the year 1639.

CAPE, PETER, A S. JOSEPHO, was approved for preaching and hearing confessions in 1634; appointed professor of philosophy in 1650; titular Guardian of Worcester, 1653-1656; Guardian of Douai, 1656-1659; Custos, 1659-1662; titular Guardian of Greenwich, 1662-1665; Definitor, 1665-1668; appointed Commissary in 1668. He died in England in 1670 or 1671.

CAREW, HENRY, A S. FRANCISCO, was sent to the mission of Maryland in 1675, and appointed Preses there in 1677. He died on his return voyage from Maryland in 1682 or 1683.

CARTWRIGHT, GERVASE, A S. FRANCISCO, a native of Nottingham, was approved for preaching and hearing confessions in 1653, and sent on the mission. He was titular Guardian of Cambridge, 1659-1662; Definitor, 1662-1665; titular Guardian of Canterbury, 1665-1668; Custos, 1668-1671; titular Guardian of York, 1671-1674; master of novices at Douai, with the title of Guardian of Cambridge, 1674-1677; Definitor, 1677-1680; titular Guardian of Coventry, 1680-1683; Provincial, 1683-1686. In 1689, at the time of the Revolution, he was arrested, and thrown into Leicester gaol, where he was kept two years and four months. He had been sentenced to death; but the Prince of Orange commuted this sentence into that of exile. In consequence, he was forced to leave the country, and went to Belgium, where he took up his abode at the residence of the English Franciscans at Bruges, attached to the convent of the nuns of the Third Order, to whom they were confessors. He went to his reward on August 24, 1691, and was buried in the cloister of the convent. On his tombstone was the following inscription:

D. O. M.

R. ADM. P. GERVASII CARTWRIGHT

IN ANGLIA PRO FIDE AD MORTEM DAMNATI

AT EXILII POST DIUTURNOS CARCERES TANDEM MULCTI,

VENERANDÆ EXUVIÆ HIC QUIESCUNT,

QUAS 24 AUGUSTI 1691 SANCTE DEPOSUIT,

ÆTATIS 63, PROF. 44, SACERD. 40.

His head was reverently enshrined in the wall of

the same cloister, with a glass before it, so that it was visible to all.

CASEMORE, IGNATIUS (baptismal name WILLIAM), was born at Reading, September 13, 1751; and after making his first studies among the Jesuits embraced the Franciscan Rule of life. He was approved for preaching and hearing confessions in 1779; appointed Preses of the residence of Monmouth, 1782-1785; and of White Hill, 1785-1788; titular Guardian of Norwich, 1788-1789. About this time he resided at Worlaby near Brigg, in Lincolnshire. Titular Guardian of Cambridge, 1791-1792; appointed Preses of Mount Grace in 1793; of Monmouth in 1803; and of Hereford in 1805. In this year Bishop Sharrock, Vicar Apostolic of the Western District, sent him as first incumbent to Falmouth, where he continued for more than thirteen years. During this time he had also the honorary titles of Preses of Birmingham in 1806; of Mount Grace in 1808; titular Guardian of Cambridge, 1812-1815; of London, 1815-1818; of Coventry in 1818; and again in 1824. In 1818 he resigned the incumbency of Falmouth owing to declining health, and retired to the Convent of Poor Clares at Coxside, Plymouth, where he died November 29, 1824, aged seventy-three years; and was buried in their cemetery.

CHAPMAN, ATHANASIUS (baptismal name FRANCIS), a native of Warwickshire, first studied at the English College, Rome, where he received minor orders in 1722. But he left at the end of the same year, and joined the English Franciscans at Douai in 1727. He was approved for preaching and hearing confessions in 1731, and sent on the mission the following year. Appointed Preses of Monmouth in 1734; and of Hereford, 1735-1741; titular Guardian of Worcester in 1737; of Bristol, 1738-1740; of Cambridge, 1746-1749. In the latter year he died in England.

CHAPMAN, JOACHIM, a professed cleric, died at Douai in 1725.

CHAPMAN, ROMANUS, was approved for preaching and hearing confessions in 1743; professor of philosophy at Douai, 1743-1746; professor of theology, 1746-1747; Vicar at Douai, 1748; confessor at Bruges, 1749-1752; and at Aire, 1752-1755; sent on the mission, 1756; titular Guardian of Canterbury, 1758-1761; and of Norwich, 1764-1767; Definitor, 1767-1770; confessor at Bruges, 1770-1773; titular Guardian of Canterbury in 1770; and of Cambridge, 1774-1775; Custos, 1776-1779; Provincial, 1779-1782. He was declared a jubilarian in 1784; Provincial, 1788-1791. About this time he resided in Chapel Street, Grosvenor Square. He died in London, December 4, 1795.

CHASE, STEPHEN, lay brother, died at Douai in 1750.

CHUNE, ANTHONY, lay brother, died about the year 1702.

CLARK, FRANCIS, was approved for preaching and hearing confessions in 1776; Vicar of Douai, 1779-1782, in which year he died.

CLARK, SAMUEL, A S. HENRICO, was appointed titular

Guardian of York, 1659-1662 ; Definitor, 1662-1665 ; again titular Guardian of York, 1665-1668 ; and of Worcester, 1674-1677 ; Custos, 1677-1680 ; titular Guardian of Newcastle, 1680-1683 ; Custos, 1683-1686 ; titular Guardian of Oxford, 1686-1689 ; Definitor, 1689-1692 ; titular Guardian of Oxford, 1692-1695 ; Definitor, 1695-1698 ; titular Guardian of Oxford, 1698-1701 ; Custos, 1701-1704. In 1705 he became very infirm, and had an apoplectic seizure. It seems that he resided then at the house of Lord Fermore, vulgo Tusmore. He died in 1707.

CLARKE, or CLERCKE, ANTHONY, was one of the first members of the Douai community, when the English Province was in its infancy, in 1618. He was declared a jubilarian in 1668, and styled " Venerable Father." He died in England about the year 1674.

CLARKE, HUBERT, a young priest mentioned in 1695.

CLARKSON, AUGUSTINE, was approved for preaching and hearing confessions in 1752; professor of philosophy at Douai, 1752-1758 ; confessor at Aire, 1758-1761 : and again in 1764 ; titular Guardian of Coventry, 1767-1770 ; and again in 1771. He died at Douai in 1775 or 1776.

CLAY, DANIEL, A S. FRANCISCO, an Irish Franciscan who was, at his request, after satisfactory probation, incorporated in the English Province in 1655. He was confessor to the nuns of the Third Order at Nieuport, 1655-1659 ; Guardian of Douai, 1659-1662 ; Custos in 1662. In 1663 he was deputed to go to the General Chapter instead of the Provincial. In the same year

he resigned his office of Custos, and was appointed
Commissary.   He was titular Guardian of Oxford,
1665-1668; elected Provincial in 1668 and again in
1677.   He died in 1681.

CLEMENSHAW, EGIDIUS, lay brother, died at Douai,
in 1781.

CLIFTON, BERNARDINE (baptismal name JAMES), was
professor of philosophy at Douai, 1707-1713.   In 1710
he was approved for preaching and hearing confessions.
Professor of theology, 1713-1717; confessor at Aire,
1719-1722; Custos, 1722-1725.   Whilst Custos, he
remained professor of theology, but in 1722 he had to
leave Douai for a time, as he defended theological
theses which were by some ill-minded persons interpreted in a wrong sense.   He wished to have them
submitted to Rome, but the Definitors decided not to
proceed in the matter.   He was Guardian of Douai,
1725-1728; Definitor, 1728-1731; titular Guardian of
London, 1731-1734; Custos, 1734-1737; Guardian of
Douai in 1737: titular Guardian of Greenwich and
confessor at Bruges in 1738.   He worked with great
zeal for some time on the English mission; and it is
recorded of him that "he was a man of singular learning and true piety, winning all hearts by his kindness.
He was a lamp, burning inwardly with love for Holy
Religion, and spreading around him a brilliant light in
the darkness of the heresy of Jansenius, by the famous
thesis which he defended in our College of St.
Bonaventure at Douai, on July 16, 1716, a monument
of his genius, a torch of the true Faith, and a

two-edged sword against Jansenism.   He earned the applause of the faithful children of the Church, and incurred the hatred of her enemies.   A great promoter of religious discipline, he directed others more by his example than by his words.   He cheerfully bore a banishment of two years duration."

He died at the residence of the fathers adjoining the convent of the nuns of the Third Order at Bruges in 1738, and was buried in the cloister of the same convent, where the following epitaph was inscribed over his grave :

D.O.M.

HIC JACET R.A.P. FR. BERNARDINUS CLIFTON S.T.L. EMERITUS, HUJUS MONASTERII CONFESSARIUS ACTUALIS, CONVENTUS FRATRUM MINORUM RECOLLECTORUM ANGLORUM DUACI EX-GUARDIANUS, ALMÆ PROVINCIÆ ANGLIÆ OLIM DEFINITOR, AC ITERATO CUSTOS.

OBIIT SUMMO SUI POST SE RELICTO DESIDERIO,
29 DECEMBRIS, ANNO 1738, ÆTATIS 58, PROFESSIONIS 39, SACERDOTII 32.

CODRINGTON, ANTHONY, was approved for preaching and hearing confessions in 1719.   Professor of philosophy at Douai, 1719-1723.   In the latter year he tendered his resignation, owing to timorousness.   But as his aptitude for teaching was generally known, he was instead appointed professor of theology.   In 1726 he again urged his incompetency, but the Chapter refused to listen to his excuses, and he continued teaching till his death, which occurred in the year 1731.

COGHLAN, PETER, was approved for preaching and hearing confessions in 1785 ; professor of philosophy, 1785-1788 ; sent on the mission in 1790 ; appointed Preses of the residence of Mount Grace in 1791. He died before the year 1800.

COLLINGRIDGE, BERNARDINE (baptismal name PETER), was born in Oxfordshire, March 10, 1757. In early life his vocation balanced for a time between the institute of St. Ignatius and the Franciscan Order, and finally he decided for the latter. When still a cleric he was appointed professor of philosophy, in 1779, which post he filled till 1785. In 1784 he had been approved for preaching and hearing confessions. He was professor of theology, 1785-1788 ; Guardian of Douai, 1788-1791 ; Definitor, 1791-1794. At the termination of his Guardianate at Douai, he had gone to Baddesley as President of the Franciscan school. Thence he went to the Portuguese Chapel in London, to replace Father Bonaventure Pilling, who had departed this life in 1801. But soon after he was made assistant to Rev. John Griffiths, of St. George's Fields. During this time he had been made titular Guardian of Oxford in 1794 ; Definitor, 1800-1803 ; Custos, 1803-1806 ; and in the latter year he was elected Provincial. In the course of the following year, 1807, Bishop Sharrock, Vicar Apostolic of the Western District, secured him for his coadjutor. He resigned the office of Provincial on July 7 of that year, and was consecrated at St. Edmund's College on October 11 as Bishop of Thespiæ. For a time this learned and saintly prelate resided at Chepstow, at Taunton, at Clifton, at Trenchard Street

Chapel House, Bristol; but finally at Cannington, where he died suddenly on March 3, 1829, and was buried on the 10th, which would have been his seventy-second birthday.

It is said in praise of him that a more zealous, disinterested and unostentatious prelate could not be imagined. (Dr. Oliver.)

COLLINGRIDGE, MATTHEW, was appointed for preaching and hearing confessions in 1734. He was Preses of Mount Grace, 1740-1749; titular Guardian of York, 1749-1752; again Preses of Mount Grace, 1752-1758; titular Guardian of York, 1758-1761; again appointed Preses of Mount Grace in 1761. He died on the mission in 1764.

COLLINGRIDGE, RICHARD. When he was still a cleric, in 1711, his aptitude for science was noticed, and he was told to prepare for teaching philosophy. He was accordingly appointed professor of philosophy in 1713, and at the same time approved for preaching and hearing confessions. Guardian of Douai, 1719-1722; titular Guardian of Newcastle, 1725-1728; Definitor, 1728-1731; again titular Guardian of Newcastle in 1731. He died in England in 1732.

COLMAN, WALTER, in religion CHRISTOPHER A S. CLARA, CONFESSOR OF THE FAITH, was descended of a good family in Staffordshire. He studied first at the English College of Douai, and then returned home. But after some years, being disgusted with the pleasures and vanities of the world, he renounced all to enter the Franciscan Order. He was approved for preaching and hearing confessions in 1634, and came soon after on the English mission. His taste for literature is shown by his writings. When he had worked some years on the mission, he went to Douai for a time to renew his spiritual fervour by means of regular discipline and recollection. He then returned to England to resume his former labours. He was imprisoned for the Faith, and condemned to death at the Old Bailey Sessions in 1641, but was not executed. He died a lingering death in Newgate prison in the year 1645.

COOK, FRANCIS, lay brother, died at Douai in 1746.

COOPER, JOACHIM, lay brother, was born in 1742. He was at Douai in 1790. Afterwards, the Franciscans having been expelled from France, he resided in Preston, where he died in 1812.

COPLEY, ANSELM (baptismal name CHARLES), was approved for preaching and hearing confessions in 1735, and afterwards sent on the mission. He was titular Guardian of Norwich, 1744-1746; Guardian of Douai, 1752-1755; Definitor, 1755-1758; Preses of Abergavenny in 1755. Shortly afterwards we find him at Hoar Cross in Staffordshire. He was again Guardian at Douai, 1758-1761; Definitor, 1761-1764; titular Guardian of Oxford, 1764-1767; Custos, 1767-1770. He served the mission of West Grinstead, 1768-1776, in which year he was declared a jubilarian. He died at Douai in 1777 or 1778.

COPLEY, RICHARD, was approved for preaching and

hearing confessions in 1691, and for the mission in 1698.   He died in 1703 or 1704.

COTTRELL, THOMAS, was approved for preaching and hearing confessions in 1767; sent on the mission in 1774; Preses of the residence of Hexham, 1776-1779; titular Guardian of Oxford, 1782-1785; Preses of Mount Grace, 1785-1786; titular Guardian of Norwich in 1787, at which time he resided at West Grinstead; again appointed Preses of Mount Grace in 1788; titular Guardian of Canterbury in 1791-1792, and of Coventry in 1793; appointed Preses of Hereford in 1794, and of Abergavenny in 1800; titular Guardian of Greenwich, 1803-1804, and of London in 1805; Preses of Hexham, 1806-1807; titular Guardian of Greenwich, 1808-1814; titular Guardian of Cambridge in 1815; he died a jubilarian in 1816 or 1817.

COX, BONIFACE, was, when still a cleric in 1758, appointed professor of philosophy, which office he filled all his life.   In 1761 he was approved for preaching and hearing confessions.   He died at Douai in 1764.

COX, FELIX, was approved for preaching and hearing confessions in 1749.   He was sent on the mission in 1750.   About the year 1758 he resided at White Knights in Berkshire.   He was confessor at Bruges, 1761-1764; Guardian of Douai, 1764-1765; confessor at Aire in 1766; Procurator of the Province and titular Guardian of Cambridge, 1770-1773; Custos, 1773-1776; again Procurator in 1776, and also appointed Chronologist; titular Guardian of London in 1778;

Custos, 1779-1782; titular Guardian of London, 1782-1785; Custos, 1785-1788, in which year he died.

CRISP, BENEDICT, A S. JOSEPHO, was approved for preaching and hearing confessions in 1653. He is mentioned again in the year 1665.

CROSS, alias MORE, JOHN, A S. CRUCE, a native of Norfolk, was approved for preaching and hearing confessions in 1656, and was professor of philosophy from 1655 until 1660; professor of theology, 1662-1666; in 1663 and 1664 he was also Vicar at Douai; confessor at Bruges in 1666 and 1667. He taught theology again from 1668 till 1671, when he came on the mission. He was declared Doctor of Divinity in 1672. In the same year he went to the National Congregation of the Order at Mechlin, as deputy of the English Province. He was elected Provincial in 1674, and again in 1686. He was one of the royal chaplains attached to the Court of St. James, and at the Orange Revolution in 1688 followed King James II. to St. Germains. It is recorded of him that he was a man of acute mind, who cultivated piety no less than science. Whilst labouring with the greatest zeal on the mission for the good of souls, he found time to compose some philosophical treatises, in which he followed the doctrine of the Doctor Subtilis, of whom he showed himself a worthy disciple. Having returned from the mission to Douai, he fell into a mortal illness, during which he never ceased sighing for his eternal reward. He peacefully slept in the Lord, amid the prayers and tears of his brethren, on December 13, 1689, being in the sixtieth year of his age, the forty-second of his religious profession and the nineteenth of his missionary career. He was buried at Douai, before the high altar of the old Church.

CROSS, NICHOLAS, A S. CRUCE, sometimes called LACROIX, a native of Derbyshire, was appointed for preaching and hearing confessions in 1647, and also appointed secretary and sent on the mission. He was titular Guardian of London, 1650-1653; Definitor, 1653-1656; again titular Guardian of London, 1656-1659; Definitor, 1659-1662; Provincial, 1662-1665: he assisted at the National Congregation of the Order held at Antwerp in 1663. Since 1653 he had filled the office of Procurator. He was made Commissary in 1666. He was confessor and chaplain to Anne, Duchess of York, and when she fled on account of the persecution, he accompanied her to Scotland. He was again elected Provincial in 1671 and in 1680. We have his sermon " on the joys of Heaven," which he preached at Windsor before the Queen April 21, 1686. He is also said to be the author of a paraphrase on the psalm "Miserere," dedicated to the Countess of Shrewsbury. Three several times he suffered imprisonment for the Faith. He was for the fourth time elected Provincial in 1689 ; but this time failing health compelled him to resign before the end of his term, on May 12, 1691. He then retired to Douai, where he died on March 21, or according to others August 8, 1698, in the eighty-third year of his age, the fifty-ninth of his religious profession, the fifty-eighth of priesthood. He was buried in the sanctuary of the old church, and his name is mentioned, together with those of Fathers

Angelus Mason and John Cross, on the slab on which Father Gennings's epitaph is inscribed.

CUDWORTH, ANTHONY, A S. MARIA, was approved for preaching and hearing confessions in 1660; appointed Vicar of Douai in 1662; titular Guardian of Cambridge 1665-1668; Definitor, 1668-1671; titular Guardian of Canterbury in 1671; Procurator and Secretary in 1672 and 1673; Guardian of Douai, 1674-1677. Although he was then in a weak state of health, his services were so much appreciated that he was made Procurator and Definitor, 1677-1680; titular Guardian of Cambridge in 1680. He died in 1681.

DALYSON, or DALLISON, NICHOLAS, was approved for preaching and hearing confessions, and also for the mission in 1681; titular Guardian of Worcester, 1684-1687. He was appointed the first Preses of Warwick in 1687, and continued in that office until 1698; titular Guardian of Coventry in 1689 and 1690; and of Worcester, 1698-1701. He was again Preses of Warwick from 1701 till his death; titular Guardian of Coventry, 1704-1707, in which year he died.

DAVENPORT, CHRISTOPHER, in religion FRANCIS A S. CLARA, alias HUNT, born at Coventry in 1595, was converted to the Catholic Faith whilst a student at Merton College, Oxford. He received the Franciscan habit on October 7, 1617, at Ypres in Flanders. The following year, having made his profession, he joined the community of Douai, of which he became one of the first members. In 1624, when Father Jackson, then Guardian of Douai, came on the English mission,

Father Davenport was appointed to replace him. He went to the General Chapter in Rome in 1625, where he so well pleaded the cause of the English Franciscans that he obtained a decree for the restoration of the Province. The next year he was re-appointed Guardian of Douai, and continued to teach his brethren, a task on which he had entered when the new college at Douai was opened in 1621. By the decree of the erection of the second English Province, under the title of the Immaculate Conception, dated 1629, he was made the first Custos. He was appointed titular Guardian of London in 1632; Definitor, 1634-1637; Provincial, 1637-1640; Guardian of Douai, 1647-1650, again Provincial, 1650-1653. He was declared Doctor of Divinity in 1661; Provincial, 1665-1668; in the latter year his jubilee in the Order was solemnly celebrated. He was a learned man, well versed in every branch of philosophical and ecclesiastical science, and he combined zeal with discretion. His works, in two folio volumes, were printed at Douai in 1665. His eminent qualities enabled him to render great service in the cause of Religion. Among his spiritual conquests he reconciled to the Church Anne Duchess of York in August, 1670. He was one of Queen Catherine's chaplains, and resided at Somerset House. It was there that, worn out in the service of Religion, he closed his mortal career, early on Whit Sunday, May 31, 1680, aged eighty-five years. According to his wish, he was buried in St. John's Church of the Savoy. In the record of his death he is described as "the very reverend and venerable Father in Christ,

Francis a S. Clara, of blessed memory, three times Provincial Minister; who, having completed his triple jubilee, as religious, priest and missionary, showed himself a prudent and most loving father to his brethren and children until the end, helping them in all their needs.   On the English mission he was a vigilant pastor and faithful labourer for fifty-seven years; making himself all to all, he gained both rich and poor; his name is held in veneration both at home and abroad."

DAVENPORT, IGNATIUS, A S. MAGDALENA, was approved for preaching and hearing confessions in 1657. He came on the mission in 1660; titular Guardian of Greenwich, 1665-1668; and of Cambridge, 1671-1674; Definitor, 1674-1677; again titular Guardian of Cambridge in 1677.   He died in England in 1679 or 1680.

DAVISON, BERNARDINE (baptismal name JOHN), born at Catterick in Yorkshire, February 27, 1791, was approved for preaching and hearing confessions in 1817, and appointed titular Guardian of Norwich; from 1817-1820 he was Confessor of the Poor Clares who had come to England from Aire, and were then at Plymouth.   In 1820 he went to Lee House; and afterwards to Osmotherley.   He was titular Guardian of Cambridge in 1820; of Coventry in 1821; of Worcester in 1823; of Newcastle in 1824; of Oxford in 1827; of Worcester in 1829; Definitor and titular Guardian of York, 1832-1835; titular Guardian of Bristol in 1835. He was one of the signatories at the last chapter meeting held at Clifton in 1838.   He went as assistant priest to Newport in 1841. In ministering to the sick he caught the typhus fever, of which he died, February 2, 1842, a martyr of charity.

DAY, NICHOLAS (baptismal name JOHN), born at the mill in the parish of St. Cross, or Halywell, near Oxford. He came out of the Province of the Immaculate Conception in Spain to Douai in 1618. He was professor of theology in the English Custody previous to the erection of the Province; Definitor, 1630-1637; titular Guardian of Dorchester, 1637-1640; elected Definitor again in 1640; and Custos, 1647-1650; confessor of the nuns of the Third Order at Nieuport, 1648-1650 ; subrogated Definitor, 1651-1653 ; titular Guardian of Cambridge, 1653-1656. He was a jubilarian in the Order. From the Franciscan Register it would appear that his death occurred in 1656. But Anthony Wood in his " Athenæ Oxonienses " says that he died in 1658, and was buried near the west end of St. Ebbe's Church at Oxford.

DE LA RUE, ALBERT, lay brother, died in 1717.

DE LA SOUCH, PETER JOHN, was approved for preaching and hearing confessions in 1678. He died about the year 1690.

DELBAR, CYPRIAN, lay brother, died at Douai in 1767.

DE LEAU, LEWIS, was approved for the mission in 1722; titular Guardian of Oxford in 1733 ; of Worcester, 1734-1737 ; of London, 1740-1743 ; Definitor, 1743-1746 ; titular Guardian of London in 1746. He died a jubilarian at Douai in 1757 or 1758.

De Leau, Orontius, lay brother, died at Douai in 1747.

Delecourt, Hubert, lay brother, described in the civil list of 1790 as " French." He was then at Aire.

Deplanques, James, lay brother, of French nationality, born in 1758; he was at Douai in 1790; his death occurred in 1824.

Dickenson, Theodore, was approved for preaching and hearing confessions in 1678; in 1686 it was rumoured that he was living with the " Cordeliers " (a name given to the Observants as well as to the Conventuals); and it was resolved to take information on the subject. The inquiry must have proved satisfactory, for in 1691 he was sent on the mission. He was titular Guardian of Worcester, 1707-1710; and of Cambridge, 1713-1717. He died a jubilarian at Douai in 1720.

Dickinson, Matthew, was approved for preaching and hearing confessions in 1749; professor of philosophy, 1749-1752; Vicar of Douai and novice master, 1752-1755; continued Vicar, and appointed professor of theology, 1755-1758; confessor at Bruges, 1758-1761; Guardian of Douai, 1761-1764; sent on the mission and elected Definitor in 1764. He died in England in 1767.

Dixon, Jerome, was approved for preaching and hearing confessions in 1752. He died at Aire in 1756.

Dixon, Paul, was approved for preaching and hearing confessions in 1734; he came on the mission in

1735; he was titular Guardian of Canterbury, 1743-1746; Preses of the residence of Hexham, 1758-1761; he served West Grinstead, 1761-1768.

DIXON, THOMAS, was approved for preaching and hearing confessions in 1755, and was sent on the mission the following year. He was Preses of the residence of Monmouth, 1759-1761; and of Birmingham, 1761-1764; titular Guardian of Norwich, 1767-1770; Preses of Warwick from 1773 until his death which occurred in 1775 or 1776.

DODD, FRANCIS, was approved for preaching and hearing confessions in 1704, and sent on the mission; Preses of Warwick, 1707-1740; titular Guardian of Coventry, 1710-1713; Definitor, 1713-1716; titular Guardian of Coventry, 1716-1719; Definitor, 1719-1722; titular Guardian of Coventry, 1722-1725; and again in 1728; titular Guardian of Oxford in 1731; again, 1734-1737 and 1740-1743. He died a jubilarian in England in the year 1747.

DOODELL, SEBASTIAN, lay brother, died at Douai in 1749.

DUCKWORTH, EGIDIUS, lay brother, died at Douai in 1726.

DUNTON, ROBERT, was approved for preaching and hearing confessions in 1693. Vicar at Douai, 1698. He died the same or the following year.

DUROLO, JOSEPH, lay brother, died at Douai in 1674.

EAST, AUGUSTINE, A S. CLARA (baptismal name

LEWIS), was approved for preaching and hearing confessions in 1634, and appointed professor of philosophy; Definitor, 1647-1650; Guardian of Douai, 1650-1653. He taught Holy Scripture, 1647-1653; Custos, 1654. He came on the mission in 1655, and was imprisoned for the Faith, but afterwards liberated. He was titular Guardian of Greenwich, 1656-1659; and of Cambridge, 1662-1665; Custos, 1665-1668; titular Guardian of York, 1668-1671; of Greenwich in 1672 and again 1677-1680. He died at Paris in the month of May, 1680. About the middle of the seventeenth century a few of the English nuns of the Third Order at Nieuport went to Paris on account of the troubles of the wars in Flanders. They had a house with enclosure there, and our fathers were from time to time appointed their confessors. This accounts for Father East's death occurring there. He is the translator of St. Bonaventure's "Stimulus amoris."

ECCLES, BONAVENTURE, a professed cleric, who obtained dispensation from his vows in 1823.

ECCLES, LAWRENCE, was approved for preaching and hearing confessions in 1758; Preses of Mount Grace, 1764-1770; titular Guardian of Newcastle, 1770-1773; Preses of White Hill, 1773-1776; titular Guardian of York in 1776 and 1777; Preses of Mount Grace in 1778; titular Guardian of York, 1779-1782; Preses of Mount Grace, 1782-1785; Preses of Monmouth in 1787; titular Guardian of York in 1788 and 1789; Preses of Warwick in 1805; titular Guardian of Greenwich, 1806 and 1807; of Norwich, 1808; of Cambridge, 1809.

He was a jubilarian in the Order. He resided about this time at Sizargh, near Kendal. He died in 1810.

ECCLES, THOMAS, was approved for preaching and hearing confessions in 1746; Preses of the residence of Monmouth, 1750-1758. About this time he lived at Perthyr. Preses of Hereford, 1758-1764; again Preses of Monmouth in 1764. He died at Douai in 1767.

EDGEWORTH, JOSEPH, a professed cleric, secularized in 1824.

EDGEWORTH, LEO (baptismal name FRANCIS), was born in London, April 26, 1799. He was still a cleric in 1820, when he was appointed professor of philosophy. After his ordination he was made incumbent at St. Peter's, Birmingham. In August, 1824, Bishop Collingridge placed him at Weymouth, where he remained until the spring of 1825, when he was sent to St. Joseph's Chapel, Bristol. During the frightful riots at the beginning of November, 1831, he so distinguished himself by his humanity and heroism as to deserve a civic crown. To meet the rapid growth of Catholicity in Bristol, he purchased a large plot at Clifton for the erection of a spacious church. The ground was first broken on August 11, 1834, and on October 4 following he laid the foundation stone. In the Order he had held the honorary titles of Guardian of Oxford, 1823-1826; of Cambridge in 1827 and 1828; of Canterbury in 1829; again of Cambridge, 1832-1835; of York, 1835-1838. At the Chapter held at Clifton in the latter year, he was elected Provincial, but the General hesitated to confirm him in that office. The enterprise of the contemplated church at Clifton was far too gigantic for his limited means. He became involved in such inextricable difficulties, that he had to seek refuge on the continent from the importunities of his creditors; and he went to Antwerp, where he died suddenly on November 16, 1850, aged fifty-one years. (Dr. Oliver.)

EDMUNDSON, PETER, A S. MARIA, a professed cleric, of whom great hopes were entertained. At the time of the persecution kindled by the Prince of Orange, he was sent with three other clerics from Douai to the friary of the Recollects of the Province of St. Joseph at Bruges, in order to make room for our missionaries who fled from England. It was in that House that he closed his mortal career at the early age of twenty, in the first year of his profession, on April 6, 1690. His death is recorded among the memorable events; and it is mentioned that the words of praise bestowed by Alexander of Hales on St. Bonaventure could be applied to him, that "it seemed as if in him Adam had not sinned."

ELLIS, ANGELUS, was approved for preaching and hearing confessions in 1731. He died in 1737.

EMERTON, FRANCIS, lay brother, died at Douai in 1767.

ENGLEFIELD, FELIX, a young priest who died at Douai in the year 1704.

ENGLEFIELD, FELIX, was appointed professor of philosophy when still a cleric, in 1731. Not long after he was ordained, and approved for preaching and hearing confessions in 1732. He was professor of theology, 1734-1746; titular Guardian of York in 1744 and 1745 ; Definitor, 1746-1749 ; titular Guardian of Oxford in 1749 ; and of Greenwich in 1750 and 1751. He went to the General Chapter in Rome in 1750 iu place of the Provincial, Father Thomas Holmes, who was prevented by age and infirmities from going himself. He was Custos, 1752-1755; Provincial, 1755-1758. About this time he resided at Horton in Gloucestershire. He died at Douai iu 1767. Among his writings is a complete list of Franciscans on the English mission in 1758, with their addresses.

EVANS, CHARLES, was approved for preaching and hearing confessions in 1731. He died at Douai in 1752.

EVERINGHAM, PETER, vulgo CATRIS or CATRICE, was on the English mission some years before 1665, when it was resolved to recall him. He is again mentioned as being on the mission in 1686. He died near Cheshunt in Hertfordshire in 1687.

EYSTON, BERNARD, A S. FRANCISCO, (baptismal name JOHN), descended from a distinguished family in Berkshire, was approved for preaching and hearing confessions in 1653, and appointed professor of philosophy. He was professor of theology, 1656-1668, when he was declared Doctor of Divinity. He was a man of rare ability, and even in official documents styled, "Eminent Father Bernard." He was confessor at Aire, 1668-1671.   He was then appointed prefect of studies, and also novice master.   In 1672 his sight began to fail, so that he had to discontinue teaching. Confessor at Bruges, 1674-1677. Having prepared many labourers for the Lord's vineyard, he wished to share their work, and came on the mission in 1677.   He laboured for some time with great zeal and fruit ; but the religious troubles following upon Oates' Plot, together with his infirmity, for he was lame, forced him to return to the Continent. He was Definitor, 1680-1683 ; confessor at Aire, 1683-1686 ; Definitor, 1686-1689 ; confessor at Bruges, 1687-1691 ; and at Aire, 1691-1695 ; he was again made prefect of studies at Douai in 1693 ; confessor at Bruges, 1696-1697 ; and at Aire, 1700-1706. He retired to Douai, an octogenarian, and spent his time in writing pious treatises. One day, having made his preparation for the celebration of Mass, he took suddenly ill, and after receiving Extreme Unction, fell asleep in the Lord, a jubilarian of his profession and priesthood, in the year 1709, which was the eighty-second of his age, the sixty-fifth of his religious life, the fifty-eighth of priesthood ; and he was buried in the cloister on the south side.

His portrait in oil is at Hendred House.

EYSTON, BONAVENTURE (baptismal name WILLIAM), was approved for preaching and hearing confessions in 1704, and for the mission in 1710. In 1728 he made application for a transfer to the Dominican Order, which was granted.

EYSTON, JOHN CAPISTRAN (baptismal name CHARLES), was approved for preaching and hearing confessions, and also for the mission in 1704 ; titular Guardian of Worcester and Procurator of the Province, 1716-1719 ; Definitor, 1719-1722 ; titular Guardian of London, 1722-1725. During this time he remained Procurator. Definitor, 1725-1728. About this time he was at East Hendred. He was titular Guardian of London, 1728-1731; Provincial in 1731, in which office he died on the mission, July 31, 1732.

FISHER, BONAVENTURE (baptismal name SAMUEL), was born at Uppingham in Rutlandshire on October 20, 1792. He was approved for preaching and hearing confessions in 1818, and began his missionary labours at Taunton in the same year. After contributing greatly by his zeal and abilities to the propagation of the Catholic Faith in the town and neighbourhood, he had the consolation of seeing the foundation stone of a public chapel laid in the Crescent in April, 1821, and of witnessing its opening in July, 1822. In the Order he was honoured with the titles of Guardian of Worcester in 1821 ; of London, 1823-1826 ; of Canterbury in 1826 ; of York, 1827-1828 ; of Newcastle in 1829 ; of Bristol in 1832 ; and of London in 1835 ; from 1823-1834 he was confessor of the Poor Clares of Aire, then at Coxside, Plymouth. He was one of the signatories at the last Chapter meeting at Clifton in 1838 ; from the year 1835 until 1865 he was incumbent of Llanarth, in Monmouthshire. He afterwards retired to Pontypool, where he died, January 14, 1875.

FLEET, BERNARDINE, was approved for preaching and hearing confessions in 1767, and at the same time appointed professor of philosophy; Preses of the residence of White Hill, 1770-1773; and of Mount Grace, 1773-1776; novice master, 1779-1782; confessor of Poor Clares at Aire, 1782-1785; Preses of Abergavenny in 1787; titular Guardian of Canterbury, 1788-1789; and of York, 1790-1793; Preses of Hexham in 1793; appointed titular Guardian of Norwich in 1794; Preses of Mount Grace in 1800; titular Guardian of Newcastle in 1803; Preses of Monmouth in 1805; titular Guardian of York in 1806; and of Canterbury in 1808. About this time he resided at Cheeseburn Grange, near Newcastle. He was elected Definitor and appointed Preses of Hexham in 1809; titular Guardian of Newcastle in 1812; and of Oxford in 1814. He died a jubilarian in the Order in 1815.

FLEMING, JEROME, was approved for preaching and hearing confessions in 1728, and also appointed professor of philosophy. The following year he became professor of theology; confessor at Aire, 1734-1737; Vicar of Douai and novice master, 1737-1740, when he was sent on the mission. He was titular Guardian of Oxford in 1744. He died in England in 1750.*

FORTESCUE, ANGELUS, A S. MARIA, renounced a plentiful estate to embrace Franciscan poverty. He was approved for preaching and hearing confessions, and also for the mission, in 1686. In November, 1687,

* Father Thomas Flynn, O.S.F., a native of Ireland, who was at Plymouth about the year 1800, did not belong to the English Province.

he was appointed as preacher to the staff of the newly formed community at Lincoln's Inn Fields. He was titular Guardian of Newcastle in 1691; and of Worcester, 1695-1698; elected Definitor in 1698. A severe trial was now in store for him. Whilst chaplain to Sir John Shelley, Bart., of Michelgrove in Hampshire, he was infamously calumniated by some malevolent tongues. Thereupon he was, not without danger of his life, imprisoned for five months in London, after which his friends succeeded in obtaining his release. A judicial inquiry was then held, but nothing could be proved against him. He was thereupon declared innocent by the civil court, by the Chapter of the Franciscans, and by the Bishop. The two following letters were written to vindicate his character: the first by Sir John Shelley to the Provincial Chapter, the other by the fathers of the Chapter to Sir John.

GENTLEMEN,

Here is a persecution pointed indeed directly against Mr. Fortescue, but the design is too plainly laid against the whole. If you are unanimous in his defence, I resolve to stand by you, and then one thing I expect as necessary to confound H. G. (whose wild passion, with the instigation of cunninger knaves, has made a tool through him, to undo you all, at least in these parts), viz., to give Mr. Fortescue under your hands such a character, as your, and my long experience assures us he deserves. Not that any of us can think a man of his known integrity wants it, but by that means I shall be better enabled to parry the violent thrusts of our malicious enemies. And now to convince the whole world of the good opinion I and my family have of Mr. Fortescue's solid virtue towards God, and sincerity towards us, notwithstanding the calumnies so barbarously spread against him, specially that notorious one of a Lampoon, upon the testimony of a proud slut, against our express and certain knowledge, I desire you would provide me with another Gentleman of the same coat, who may be fit to undertake the government of my son. This is all I have to offer at present to the honoured Congregation, besides my earnest desire of your good prayers, and repeated assurances of being to the utmost of my power,

Your humble servant,
JOHN SHELLEY.

The following is the answer :

SIR,

We are deeply sensible of the endeavours which have been used by sundry persons, upon several aims to create a disturbance in your honourable family : and we are no less edified at your more than ordinary prudence, in baffling all their petty designs, by preserving a good understanding with each other. The hand of Providence seems to have manifestly appeared in confirmation of its own edict : " Whom God has joined, let no man separate." Moreover, we humbly hope, it has made Mr. Fortescue particularly instrumental. Hence we are glad of the occasion you present us, of giving him the character, we in our consciences think he deserves. Wherefore we, whose names are underwritten, after upward of twenty years experience do declare, to the best of our judgments, we believe him a man of solid virtue and learning, ever truly obedient to his superiors, and truly beloved by his brethren, and as he was the first that appeared at the King's bench bar, since the late revolution, upon account of Religion ; so if any person or persons upon a pique, or hatred to the Catholic Faith, think fit to make a further trial of his Christian fortitude, we firmly believe, and hope, God by his grace will enable him to convince the thinking part of mankind (for the giddy will never be satisfied), that his vocation, from a plentiful estate to evangelical poverty, was real and unfeigned. So leaving him, with your Honoured Self and family, to the blessing and protection of the Almighty, we subscribe to all above said, and remain,

Your humble servants,

BR. P. PRICE.
BR. B. PARRY.
BR. F. MIDDLETON.

This occurred in 1701. He was immediately after appointed titular Guardian of London, 1701-1704; Custos, 1704-1707; titular Guardian of Canterbury and Procurator of the Province in 1708; elected Provincial in 1710. He died in 1718.

FORTESCUE, BONAVENTURE, was approved for preaching and hearing confessions in 1683 ; appointed confessor at Aire in 1687 ; Vicar of Douai in 1692 and again in 1695; titular Guardian of Norwich, 1707-1710. He died at Douai in 1720.

FRANCIS, LEO, was approved for preaching and hearing confessions in 1749; Preses of Hexham, 1752-1758. About this time he resided at Lee House in Lancashire. He was Preses of White Hill, 1758-1761; titular Guardian of York, 1764-1767; Preses of White Hill, 1767-1770; Vicar of Douai, 1770-1773. He died in England in the year 1774.

FRENCH, ANTHONY, was approved for preaching and hearing confessions in 1743.

FROST, PETER (baptismal name JAMES), was approved for preaching and hearing confessions in 1755, and appointed professor of philosophy. He came to England in 1756. Shortly after he was at Ugbrooke, Devonshire, of which mission he took charge for full ten years. He was titular Guardian of Cambridge, 1764-1767; Preses of the residence of Warwick, 1767-1770; Guardian of Douai, 1770-1773; Definitor, 1773-1776. In the latter year he was called away from Ugbrooke to the Edgbaston school. Titular Guardian of Coventry, 1776-1779; Definitor, 1779-1782; elected Provincial in 1782. He died at Wootten, October 3, 1785, aged fifty-four years.

FULLART, BONAVENTURE, A S. MARIA, was approved for preaching and hearing confessions, and also for the mission, in 1647. Titular Guardian of Greenwich and confessor at Aire in 1648 and 1649; Definitor and novice master in 1650. He died the same year.

GARTER, JOHN, A S. MARIA, was appointed titular

Guardian of Cambridge in 1656; and of Oxford, 1662-1665; again of Cambridge, 1668-1671. He died in London in 1675.

GAYLE, BENEDICT, a lay-brother who asked to become a cleric in 1698; but it was decided that he should remain in the state in which he had made profession.

GENNINGS, JOHN, was born at Lichfield in 1570, and was educated a rank Puritan. His conversion was little short of miraculous, and reminds us of that of St. Paul. Not long after the martyrdom of his brother Edmund, he left England, and went to Douai, where he became a Catholic. He studied at the English College, and was ordained priest in 1607. The following year he came on to the English mission. He received the Franciscan habit from Father William Staney, Commissary of the Order for England, and went afterwards to the friary of Ypres in Flanders for his religious training. A few years later he founded the College of St. Bonaventure at Douai, and became the restorer of the English Franciscan Province. It was probably in 1618 or shortly after that the General made him " Vicar of England; " nor could he well bestow on him another title, the Commissary, Father Staney, being still alive. He was appointed Custos in 1625; and by the decree of the General of the Order, promulgated in 1630, he was made the first Provincial of the restored Province; he was re-elected to this office in 1634, and again in 1643. Long before his death, the fathers put up in the cloister at Douai a marble slab to his memory, on which he was represented in the Franciscan habit, kneeling before the crucifix. His portrait in oil, which was formerly at St. Peter's Presbytery, Birmingham, has been for many years at St. Francis', West Gorton, Manchester.

Father Gennings closed his long and laborious career at Douai on November 12, 1660, and was buried in the sanctuary of the old church. After the completion of the new church, a marble slab was put up in the sanctuary, over the sacristy door, on the epistle side thus inscribed :

D. O. M.

IN HUJUS ECCLESIÆ MEDIO,

QUOD OLIM FUERAT ANTIQUI ORATORII SANCTUARIUM, SIMUL

IN DOMINO CONDORMIUNT

R. A. P. JOANNES GENNINGS

PROVINCIÆ MINORITICÆ ANGLICANÆ A SE RESTITUTÆ PRIMUS

MINISTER PROVINCIALIS.

DILATANDÆ ENIM APOSTOLICÆ VITÆ ET LABORIS ZELO

E PRESBYTERO SECULARI MISSIONI ANGLICANÆ INSUDANTI

REGULAM S. P. N. FRANCISCI PROFESSUS,

PRIMO HOCCE FUNDAVIT CŒNOBIUM, DEINDE IPSAM

ANGLIÆ PROVINCIAM, QUONDAM TOTO ORDINE SERAPHICO

CELEBERRIMAM, SED TEMPORUM

ILLORUM INIQUITATE EXTINCTAM, EX RUDERIBUS RESUSCITAVIT.

CUJUS MINISTERIUM CUM TERTIO GESSISSET

OBIIT A.D. MDCLX., NOV. XII., ÆTAT. XC., MISS. LX.

PROF. XLIV.

[*Then follows a mention of FF. Angelus Mason, John Cross and Nicholas Cross.*]

VIRI QUA PIETATE, QUA DOCTRINA, SCRIPTISQUE POTENTES,
IN GENERATIONE SUA,
QUORUM MEMORIA IN BENEDICTIONE SIT.
ORA, VIATOR, UT ÆTERNE REQUIESCANT IN PACE
ET HÆREDITAS SANCTA SINT NEPOTES EORUM.
AMEN.

GIBSON, JOHN BAPTIST, was approved for preaching and hearing confessions in 1704, and appointed professor of philosophy. He was sent on the mission in 1708; Preses of Hereford, 1719-1728; titular Guardian of Cambridge, 1722-1725, and of Worcester, 1728-1731; Preses of Hereford in 1731; titular Guardian of Oxford in 1732, and of Bristol in 1733; Guardian of Douai in 1734; Preses of Monmouth, 1737-1743; titular Guardian of Bristol, 1740-1741; elected Custos on the death of Father Jerome Winter in 1742, and re-elected the following year; Preses of Warwick in 1746; titular Guardian of Canterbury, 1746-1749, and of Newcastle, 1750-1753. He died, a jubilarian, at Douai in 1757.

GILES, GEORGE, a lay brother who acted as physician at Douai in 1749. Owing to some difficulties and abuses, he was forbidden to mix any drugs or give medicine to the people of the town. The regulation was renewed in 1753. He was incorporated in the French Province of St. Denis in 1757.

GOLDING, EDWARD, was approved for preaching and hearing confessions, and also for the mission in 1657. He was sent to the mission of Maryland in 1675. Having returned, he was appointed titular Guardian of

Norwich, 1686-1689, in which year he died in London.

GOLDING, GEORGE, A S. BARBARA, was approved for preaching and hearing confessions in 1657. He came on the mission in 1665. He was titular Guardian of Oxford, 1668-1671 ; confessor at Aire in 1681 ; titular Guardian of Newcastle, 1686-1689 ; Preses of Hexham, 1687-1695 ; titular Guardian of Newcastle, 1692-1695 and 1698-1701, in which year he died.

GOODYEAR, or GOODYER, GEORGE, was approved for preaching and hearing confessions in 1683, and for the mission in 1686. He was titular Guardian of Newcastle in 1689 ; Preses of Hexham, 1695-1698, in which year he died.

GOODYEAR, HUGH, A S. URSULA, was approved for preaching and hearing confessions in 1675, and sent on the mission in 1677. He died in England in 1680.

GORDON, PETER OF ALCANTARA, was approved for preaching and hearing confessions in 1704, and for the mission in 1708. He was engaged in missionary work in Scotland before the year 1722 ; Vicar of Douai and novice master, 1722-1725 ; titular Guardian of Newcastle in 1728 ; Preses of Hexham in 1729 ; titular Guardian of York, 1731-1734 ; Preses of Mount Grace, 1732-1738; Definitor, 1734-1737 ; titular Guardian of Newcastle in 1737 ; of York in 1738 ; of Newcastle in 1741 ; of York in 1743 ; appointed again Preses of Hexham in 1746. He was a jubilarian in the Order.

GOSSART, ELZEAR, a tertiary, died at Douai in 1726.

GRAFTON, STEPHEN (baptismal name THOMAS), was

born at Rowington in Warwickshire, May 31, 1764. He received the habit at Douai, October 10, 1780. He was approved for preaching and hearing confessions in 1788, and appointed professor of philosophy. In 1791 he became professor of theology at Douai, and continued in that capacity at Tongres, when the fathers formed a community there, after their expulsion from Douai. He was appointed titular Guardian of Newcastle in 1800, and confessor of the nuns of the Third Order at Winchester. He was novice master, 1803-1806, and also titular Guardian of Douai. He was elected Vice-Commissary in 1806, 1814 and 1824; Custos, 1806-1809; master of novices in 1806 and 1807, and Preses of Abergavenny; in 1808 Preses of Monmouth; Provincial, 1809-1812. He continued to fill the office of novice master until 1823; Preses of the community at Perthyr in 1815; titular Guardian of Douai in 1817; Custos in 1818; Vicar-Provincial on the resignation of Father Augustine Roberts in 1820; Custos in 1821; titular Guardian of Douai in 1823; of Greenwich in 1826; Custos in 1827; titular Guardian of London in 1829, when he was declared a jubilarian; Vicar-Provincial in 1830; Custos in 1832. He presided at the last Chapter meeting at Clifton in 1838, and was nominated a Discreet of the Province by the General in 1839. In 1840 he went to Abergavenny, where he died, December 23, 1847, in the eighty-third year of his age.

GRAY, PHILIP, A S. CLARA, was approved for preaching and hearing confessions in 1640, and also made instructor to the newly professed. Appointed titular,

Guardian of Greenwich and confessor at Aire in 1647; titular Guardian of Newcastle in 1650, and of Oxford in 1651; Definitor, 1653-1656; titular Guardian of York, 1656-1659; Definitor, 1659-1662; titular Guardian of London, 1662-1665; Definitor, 1665-1668; titular Guardian of Greenwich, 1668-1671; Definitor, 1671-1674; titular Guardian of Greenwich, 1674-1677; and of Coventry in 1677; again of Greenwich in 1681; Definitor, 1683-1686; titular Guardian of Greenwich, 1686-1689; Definitor, 1689-1692; titular Guardian of Greenwich, 1692-1695. He died the following year, a jubilarian in the Order.

GREENWOOD, GABRIEL, a young priest, who died in 1710.

GRESWOLD, ANDREW (baptismal name THOMAS), was approved for preaching and hearing confessions in 1734, and for the mission the following year, when he went to White Knights near Reading. He was titular Guardian of Norwich in 1741, and of London in 1747; Definitor, 1749-1752; titular Guardian of Norwich, 1752-1755; Definitor, 1755-1758. He resided then in London. Titular Guardian of Newcastle, 1758-1761; Definitor, 1761-1764; titular Guardian of Greenwich in 1764; of London in 1766. About this time he resided in Duke Street, Grosvenor Square. Definitor in 1767, in which office he died, June 19, 1770, on the English mission.

GRIFFIN, EDWARD, lay brother, died at Douai in 1716.

GRIMBALSTON, or GRIMBALSON, LEWIS, was approved

for preaching and hearing confessions in 1683, and appointed professor of philosophy the following year. Sent on the mission in 1687. He was imprisoned for the Faith in York Castle at the period of the Revolution, in 1689. Confessor at Bruges in 1691 ; Guardian of Douai, 1692-1695 ; Vicar of Douai and novice master in 1696. He was asked to explain the Franciscan Rule in English to the community on Fridays at collation, and continued novice master until 1700. Guardian of Douai in 1700 ; Definitor, and confessor at Bruges, 1701-1704 ; titular Guardian of Greenwich, 1704-1706, when he was elected Vicar-Provincial on the death of Father Pacificus Price. He remained confessor at Bruges until 1716 ; titular Guardian of Greenwich, 1707-1710; Procurator of the Province in 1710; titular Guardian of Cambridge in 1711 ; and of Coventry in 1714. He died a jubilarian at Douai in 1737.

GRIMSTON, MARTIN, A S. CAROLO, was approved for preaching and hearing confessions in 1683. Vicar of Douai, 1686-1692 ; novice master, 1686-1689, when he was appointed professor of philosophy ; titular Guardian of Norwich, 1689-1692 ; confessor at Bruges in 1692 ; sent on the mission in 1695 ; titular Guardian of Coventry in 1700 ; and of Newcastle, 1701-1704 ; Definitor, 1704-1707 ; elected Provincial in 1707 ; Guardian of Douai in 1711. Of all the great works he was instrumental in achieving for the greater glory of God, the most striking was the conversion to the Catholic Faith of Sir Henry Fletcher of Hutton, in Cumberland, Bart., who afterwards became very much attached to the Franciscan Order, and built, at his sole expense, the new Church of St. Bonaventure's College, Douai, where he also died. Seventeen years later he was followed to his reward by his spiritual father, who was laid to rest by his side in the sanctuary of the new church, as the following inscription shows : *

EI AD LATUS APPOSITUS EST, UT OPTAVERAT,
QUEM HABUIT AD ECCLESIAM CATHOLICAM
FACEM ET DUCTOREM,
R. A. P. MARTINUS GRIMSTON
JUBILARIUS, PROVINCLÆ ANGLIÆ FF. MM. RECOLLECTORUM
PATER
VIR FRANCISCANA SIMPLICITATE AC SALUTIS ANIMARUM
ZELO SPECTABILIS,
QUI DE SUIS BENE MERITUS
DECESSIT 2 APRILIS 1729,
ÆTAT. 72, PROF. 54, SACERD. 47.
R. I. P.

HADDOCK, JAMES, was approved for preaching and hearing confessions in 1700. Soon after he was sent on the Maryland mission, and died there in 1720.

HADDON, LEO, was approved for preaching and hearing confessions in 1779 ; Vicar of Douai in 1782 ; Preses of Hereford in 1787 ; titular Guardian of Bristol, 1788-1791. About this time he was at Sarnesfield Court, near Weobly in Herefordshire ; Preses of Hereford, 1791-1794 ; titular Guardian of Newcastle in 1794. He died before the year 1800.

HAGGERSTON, FRANCIS, was approved for preaching

* This is a continuation of the inscription over the sacristy door, for which see page 117.

and hearing confessions in 1693; appointed Procurator in 1695, and again in 1698. He died in 1703 or 1704.

HANCOCK, ALEXIUS, was approved for preaching and hearing confessions, and also for the mission in 1681. He was Preses of the residence of Hereford from 1686 until 1719; titular Guardian of Norwich, 1695-1698; and of Bristol, 1701-1704; of Worcester in 1714. He died in England in 1721 or 1722.

HARCOURT, FRANCIS, lay brother, was at Aire in 1790, as appears from the civil list. He resided some time with Father Juliaens at Sardinian House, Lincoln's Inn Fields, and died in 1828 or 1829.

HARDWICK, FRANCIS, A S. LUDOVICO (baptismal name WILLIAM), was approved for preaching and hearing confessions, and also for the mission, in 1677; appointed Preses of Mount Grace in 1680; confessor at Bruges in 1684. He became a member of the newly established community at Lincoln's Inn Fields in 1687, where he had the charge of visiting the sick. The following year he was appointed Vicar of that friary. In December of the same year, 1688, he was imprisoned at Newgate for the Faith. He was still in prison in 1689, when he was appointed titular Guardian of Canterbury. He was Procurator of the Province, 1695-1698; titular Guardian of London, 1698-1701; Definitor, 1701-1704; again appointed titular Guardian of London in 1704. He died the following year.

HARRISON, PASCHAL, was approved for preaching and hearing confessions in 1785; Preses of Hereford in 1790; of Abergavenny, 1791-1794; titular Guardian of Coventry in 1794; Preses of Hexham in 1800; titular Guardian of York in 1803; of Greenwich in 1805; Preses of Warwick in 1806; titular Guardian of Newcastle in 1808; Definitor, 1809-1812; from the year 1803 to this time, he had been confessor to the Poor Clares of Aire, who had come over to England, and was with them at Britwell, Nettlebed, Oxon; titular Guardian of Canterbury, 1812-1815; of Douai, 1815-1818; of York, 1818-1821; of Bristol in 1821 and 1822; of Coventry in 1823; of Greenwich in 1824 and 1825; of Bristol in 1826; of Newcastle in 1827 and 1828; of Coventry in 1829. He died a jubilarian in the Order in 1830.

HART, JOSEPH, was born in 1760; approved for preaching and hearing confessions in 1784. He was appointed professor of philosophy in 1785, and of theology in 1788; titular Guardian of Canterbury in 1800.

HAWARDEN or HOWARDEN, MICHAEL, was born in 1664. Still a cleric, he was sent to the new friary at Lincoln's Inn Fields in 1687; the following year he was ordained, and sent as assistant priest to Hereford. He was appointed novice master at Douai in 1689; confessor at Aire, 1695-1698; and at Bruges, 1698-1701; titular Guardian of Canterbury, 1701-1704; of Newcastle, 1710-1713; of Cambridge, 1716-1719. He was many years at Lower Hall, until 1717, when he became Vicar of Douai; titular Guardian of Bristol, 1722-1725; Preses of Hereford in 1728. The following year, on the death of the Custos, he was elected to that office. Titular Guardian of Cambridge in 1731; and the following year of Worcester; Preses of Hereford, 1732-1733. In 1734 he was declared a jubilarian; titular Guardian of Norwich, 1735-1736; Definitor in 1737. He died in 1738.

HAWLEY, LAWRENCE (baptismal name JAMES), was born in 1752; approved for preaching and hearing confessions in 1779; appointed Preses of Hereford in 1784; titular Guardian of Norwich in 1785; Vicar of Douai and novice master 1788-1791; Guardian at Douai in 1791; and at Tongres in 1793, when the community was formed there, after the expulsion from Douai; titular Guardian of Greenwich 1800-1803; Definitor, 1803-1806; titular Guardian of Bristol in 1806 and 1807; of Coventry in 1808; Custos, and also Preses of Hereford, 1809-1812; Provincial, 1812-1815; he was declared a jubilarian in 1817; elected Vice-Commissary General in 1818; Custos in 1820, when Father Grafton, till then Custos, became Provincial in succession to Father Roberts, who resigned that office; Definitor, 1824-1827; titular Guardian of London in 1826; of Norwich in 1827; of Greenwich in 1829. For many years he served the mission of St. Peter's, Birmingham. He died at Worcester, June 30, 1834, aged eighty years.

HEALY, BONAVENTURE (baptismal name RICHARD), was, when still a cleric, appointed professor of philosophy at Douai in 1749; then ordained, and in 1750 approved for preaching and hearing confessions; from 1762 until 1767 he was professor of theology; Guardian of Douai, 1766-1768, when he was sent on the mission;

Custos, 1770-1773 ; Provincial, 1773-1775. About this time he was at Sir Harry Englefield's, White Knights, near Reading. He died on the mission, September 25, 1777, aged 51. In the notice of his death he is described as " a man of truly Seraphic science and piety, who won all hearts by his affability and kindness."

HEATH, VENERABLE HENRY, MARTYR, in religion PAUL A S. MAGDALENA, was born at Peterborough about the year 1600, of Protestant parents. He studied at the university of Cambridge, and obtaining the degree of B.A. was appointed librarian to his college ; afterwards he went to London, where he was received into the Catholic Church. He entered the English College at Douai, but his stay there was short; for conceiving a strong desire of joining the English Franciscans in that town, the superiors of the College, satisfied that he had a true vocation for the Order, recommended him to the Franciscans, who admitted him to the habit in 1623. In 1630 he was appointed Vicar, and in 1632 Guardian of Douai. In 1634 he also began to teach theology. He was Custos, as well as Guardian of Douai, 1637-1640. Shortly after he was allowed to come on the English mission. Long and ardent had been his desire to give his life for Christ. His prayer was heard, and he obtained the martyr's crown on April 17, 1643. He wrote several works, among which the " Soliloquies " is the most remarkable.

HEATH, JOHN, lay brother, father of Venerable Henry Heath. He was a Protestant ; and, when almost four score years old, impelled by the desire of seeing his son before dying, he crossed the sea and went to Douai. He was instructed by his son in the Catholic Faith, and received into the Church. Whereupon the old man felt so happy that he did not wish to leave Douai again, but was admitted to the habit of St. Francis as a tertiary. At the moment when his son laid down his life for Christ, he had a vision, in which he saw a brilliant light ascending into heaven; and he told the bystanders that his son had that moment obtained the palm of martyrdom in England. When shortly afterwards the news came, the brethren believed in the truth of the vision. This aged brother died at Douai, December 29, 1652.

HENDREN, FRANCIS (baptismal names JOSEPH WILLIAM), was born in Birmingham on October 19, 1791, and baptized by Father Pacificus Nutt. On August 2, 1806, he received the Franciscan habit from Father Grafton, and made his profession on November 19, 1807, on which occasion Bishop Collingridge assisted and preached. He was afterwards sent to Baddesley to teach classics. On September 28, 1815, he was ordained priest. At the beginning of the following year he was sent to Perthyr to teach philosophy and theology; and when the small community was transferred to Aston, in October, 1818, he was continued in the same employment until the commencement of 1823, when it was resolved to try the education of Franciscans abroad. He had in the Order the honorary titles of Guardian of Coventry in 1817; of Oxford in 1820; of Cambridge in 1821; of York in 1823. He was Definitor in 1824; again in 1827 and 1832; Custos, 1835-1838; Definitor in 1838. In the following year the General appointed him Commissary for England. He had then served the mission of Abergavenny for thirteen years. On February 9, 1839, he went to Taunton. In 1847 Bishop Ullathorne selected him for his Vicar General and successor, and he was consecrated on September 10, 1848, Bishop of Uranopolis, as Vicar Apostolic of the Western District. Translated to Clifton in 1850; to Nottingham in 1851; to Martyropolis in 1853. He died suddenly at the Franciscan Convent, Taunton, November 14, 1866.

HENRION, CONSTANTIUS, was of French nationality. In 1773, when a cleric, he asked leave to go for twelve months to the Irish Franciscans at Louvain, in order to accelerate his ordination; but his request was not granted. He was approved for preaching and hearing confessions in 1779. In the civil list of 1790 he is said to be fifty-five years old. He was appointed Preses of Birmingham in 1803; titular Guardian of Canterbury, 1805-1808; Preses of Monmouth, 1809-1812; titular Guardian of York in 1811; of Bristol in 1812; of Newcastle in 1814; of Worcester in 1815; of Norwich in 1818; of Oxford in 1821; of York in 1824. He died a jubilarian in the Order, December 14, 1824, aged ninety-two years.

HICKINS, AUGUSTINE, was approved for preaching and hearing confessions in 1734; Vicar of Douai and novice master, 1740-1743; Guardian of Douai, 1743-1746; Definitor, 1746-1749, during which time he also filled the office of Vicar and novice master; titular Guardian of Newcastle in 1749; of Bristol in 1750; Definitor, 1752-1755, and also Preses of Hereford; titular Guardian of Bristol, 1755-1758; Preses of Hereford in 1756; and of Monmouth in 1758. He then resided at Perthyr. Titular Guardian of Bristol in 1759; Definitor, and also Preses of Abergavenny, 1761-1764; titular Guardian of Bristol, 1764-1767; Definitor, 1767-1770; titular Guardian of Bristol, 1770-1773; again appointed Preses of Abergavenny in 1773. He died on the mission the following year.

HICKINS, JOSEPH, was approved for preaching and hearing confessions in 1728. He was sent on the English mission in 1732; confessor of Aire in 1740; and at Bruges in 1741; titular Guardian of Bristol in 1746; of Newcastle in 1747; of Coventry in 1753. In 1758 he was at Shirefield, Hampshire. Titular Guardian of Greenwich, 1768-1771. In the latter year he was declared a jubilarian, and died in 1772 or 1773 at Douai.

HIGGEN, AUGUSTINE, A S. BARBARA, was approved for preaching and hearing confessions in 1686. He was told to prepare for teaching, and appointed professor of philosophy the following year. He was professor of theology, 1689-1702, with a short interruption in 1695; titular Guardian of Cambridge, 1704-1707; Definitor, 1707-1710, when he died.

HILL, AUGUSTINE, A S. MONICA, was approved for preaching and hearing confessions in 1657, and for the mission in 1660. Titular Guardian of Bristol, 1662-

1665; and again 1668-1671 ; Definitor, 1671-1674 ; titular Guardian of Oxford, 1674-1677. In 1680 he became Definitor, and Vicar and novice master at Douai.   Titular Guardian of Oxford, 1683-1686 ; Custos, 1686-1689 ; titular Guardian of Oxford, 1689-1692 ; Definitor, 1692-1695 ; titular Guardian of Greenwich, 1695-1698; and again 1701-1704, in which year he died.

HOBART, or HUBBARD, BASIL, A S. CATHARINA, was approved for preaching and hearing confessions, and also for the mission in 1668. He was sent to Maryland in 1674. He died in 1697.

HOLDEN, PASCHAL, lay brother, died at Douai in 1729.

HOLME, EDWARD, was a novice at Douai in 1757 ; and Father Felix Englefield, then Provincial, showed great solicitude for his success and perseverance. In 1766 he was at Aire as assistant chaplain.

HOLMES, GERMANUS, CONFESSOR OF THE FAITH, was a native of Goosnargh. In 1737 he was approved for preaching and hearing confessions, and appointed professor of philosophy. In the following year he came on the English mission. He went to White Hill, and from there served the mission at Lee House. After the Stuart rising of 1745, he was seized during the revival of persecution, and thrown into Lancaster Castle, where he died a prisoner, in 1746.

HOLMES, THOMAS, was approved for preaching and hearing confessions in 1713, and the following year for the mission. He was titular Guardian of Coventry,

1719-1722 ; Preses of Birmingham, 1719-1725 ; Definitor, 1722-1725 ; novice master and titular Guardian of Norwich, 1725-1728 ; Definitor, 1728-1731 ; Guardian of Douai, 1731-1734 ; Definitor, 1734-1737 ; titular Guardian of Oxford, 1737-1740 ; elected Provincial in 1740 ; and Vicar Provincial in 1748 on the death of Father John Pulton ; again elected Provincial in 1749 and 1758. About this time he resided at Idsworth in Hampshire. He died, a jubilarian, in 1772 or 1773.

HORNE, THOMAS, lay brother, died a jubilarian at Douai, in 1750.

HOWSE, JAMES (baptismal name JOSEPH), was approved for preaching and hearing confessions, and also for the mission in 1773. Appointed Preses of Birmingham, 1776-1779 ; titular Guardian of Worcester, 1779-1781 ; Preses of Birmingham in 1781 ; titular Guardian of Worcester, 1782-1785 ; Preses of Birmingham in 1785 and 1786 ; of White Hill in 1787 ; titular Guardian of Cambridge, 1788-1791 ; Definitor, 1791-1794 ; appointed titular Guardian of Bristol in 1794 ; Definitor, 1800-1803 ; Provincial in 1803 ; he was elected Vice-Commissary in 1809 ; Preses of Warwick in 1809 ; and of Mount Grace, 1809-1812. In the latter year he was declared a jubilarian. He died March 15, 1822, aged seventy-six years.

HUTCHINSON, BONAVENTURE, was approved for preaching and hearing confessions in 1716, and appointed professor of philosophy. In the following year he was sent on the mission. He was Preses of Hexham, 1725-

1729 ; confessor at Bruges in 1729 and 1730 ; and at Aire in 1731 ; Vicar of Douai and novice master in 1732 and 1733 ; titular Guardian of Newcastle, 1734-1737 ; and of Canterbury in 1740 ; Preses of Hexham, 1749-1752, in which year he died on the mission.

HYSLOP, CLEMENT, was approved for preaching and hearing confessions in 1704 ; and for the mission in 1708. He died at Douai in 1723, and is described as having been at one time missionary in England and Scotland.

INGRAM, ANGELUS, was approved for preaching and hearing confessions in 1767, and for the mission the following year. He was Preses of Abergavenny in 1774 and 1775 ; master of novices in 1776 ; Vicar of Douai, 1776-1779 ; confessor at Aire, 1779-1782 ; appointed Preses of Monmouth in 1790 ; titular Guardian of Coventry in 1791 ; Preses of Warwick in 1793. He died on the mission in 1793 or 1794.

INGRAM, JOACHIM (baptismal name GEORGE), was approved for preaching and hearing confessions in 1734, and at the same time appointed professor of philosophy, which office he filled till 1740, when he was made professor of theology till 1746 ; Guardian of Douai 1746-1749 ; Custos, and professor of theology, 1749-1752 ; titular Guardian of Canterbury, 1752-1755. He was then also Chronologist. Definitor, 1755-1758 ; titular Guardian of Cambridge, 1758-1761 ; Definitor, 1761-1764, and also Procurator, which office he held till 1767 ; titular Guardian of London in 1764 and 1765. He was elected Custos on the death of Father Philip

Loraine in 1766; Provincial in 1767. He died a jubilarian on the mission, in 1775.

INGRAM, JOACHIM, JUNIOR, was approved for preaching and hearing confessions in 1761; Professor of philosophy, 1762-1770; and of theology 1770-1779; titular Guardian of Cambridge in 1779; Confessor at Bruges, 1779-1782; Guardian of Douai, 1782-1785; Definitor, 1785-1788; titular Guardian of Greenwich, 1788-1791: Definitor, 1791-1794; titular Guardian of Cambridge in 1794; elected Definitor in 1800. He died in 1802 or 1803.

IRELAND, ANDREW, was approved for preaching and hearing confessions in 1710. He died in 1719.

JACKSON, BONAVENTURE, was called from the Franciscan friary of Mechlin or Malines in Belgium in 1618, to be the first Preses of the community at Douai. Not long after he came on the English mission, for in Gee's list of " priests resident about the city of London, 1623," we find him mentioned as " F. Jackson a Franciscan frier, brother to Nelson." This Nelson is described in the same list as " Jackson alias Nelson, a secular priest, a ancient man." * Father Jackson was appointed first Guardian of St. Bonaventure's at Douai in 1624. At the time of the erection of the Province, in 1630, he was made Definitor. He was also on that occasion appointed titular Guardian of London. Again Definitor in 1634. He is ranked among the authors, and also among the sufferers for the faith.

JACKSON, CONSTANTINE, was approved for preaching

* *Records of the English Province S.J.* This list was drawn up by Robert Gee, an apostate.

and hearing confessions, and also for the mission in 1686. From the year 1701 he was Preses of Hexham to the end of his life. He was titular Guardian of Newcastle, 1713-1716, and died the following year.

JACKSON, GREGORY, was approved for preaching and hearing confessions in 1691, and the following year for the mission. Titular Guardian of Norwich, 1704-1707, when he became Vicar of Douai and novice master; titular Guardian of Coventry, 1710-1713; Definitor, 1713-1716; titular Guardian of Oxford, 1716-1719; Definitor, 1719-1722: titular Guardian of Canterbury, 1722-1725; Custos, 1725-1728; he was appointed Commissary in 1728, during the Provincial's absence at the General Chapter; titular Guardian of Oxford, 1728-1731. He died at Douai in 1732.

JACKSON, MICHAEL, was approved for preaching and hearing confessions in 1677. Sent on the mission in 1686. He was appointed Preses of White Hill in 1687, and continued in that office until his death, which occurred about the year 1710.

JAMES, CHARLES, lay brother, died at Douai in 1708.

JENKS, CHRISTOPHER, A S. MARIA MAGDALENA, was a lay brother at Douai about the year 1635.

JENISON, AMBROSE (baptismal name THOMAS), was approved for preaching and hearing confessions in 1719. His name is mentioned in a deed of agreement between the English Franciscans and the Benedictines in the north, in 1731. He died at Douai in 1734.

JERNINGHAM, FELIX, lay brother, born in 1730. He

is mentioned as being at Douai in 1779, and also in 1790.

JOLLY, ALEXIUS, is mentioned as a cleric at Douai in 1702. He was approved for preaching and hearing confessions, and also appointed professor of philosophy, in 1704; in 1714 he was sent on the mission; Preses of Monmouth, 1719-1722; confessor at Bruges, 1722-1725; titular Guardian of Canterbury, 1725-1728; Confessor at Bruges in 1726; Guardian of Douai, 1728-1731; Definitor, 1731-1734; Confessor at Aire in 1732; titular Guardian of Greenwich, 1734-1737; Custos, and also Confessor at Aire, 1737-1740; titular Guardian of Greenwich in 1740; again 1743-1746 and 1747-1750. He died at Douai in 1757 or 1758.

JOLLY, ANDREW, was approved for preaching and hearing confessions in 1696; novice master, 1701-1703; Vicar of Douai, 1701-1706; appointed confessor at Aire in 1713; titular Guardian of Canterbury, 1719-1722; Definitor, 1722-1725; titular Guardian of London, 1725-1728; elected Custos in 1728, he died the following year in England.

JONES, ALBERT (baptismal name PETER), was approved for preaching and hearing confessions in 1776. He is mentioned in the civil list of 1790 as being then forty-three years old. He died at Bruges in 1793.

JONES, alias ANDREWS, GREGORY, was approved for preaching and hearing confessions in 1677, and for the mission the following year. He was titular Guardian of York, 1684-1687; Preses of York, 1689-1695; titular Guardian of York, 1689-1692; again 1695-1698; and again, 1701-1704 ; titular Guardian of Newcastle, 1707-1710; and again, 1716-1719; again titular Guardian of York in 1719 and 1722; he was Preses of Hexham from 1719 until 1725, when he died.

JONES, GREGORY, lay brother, died at Douai in 1668.

JONES, PETER, was approved for preaching and hearing confessions in 1800 ; appointed titular Guardian of Bristol in 1803; Preses of Abergavenny in 1805 ; titular Guardian of Douai, 1806-1815 ; of York in 1817; of Cambridge in 1818 ; of Douai in 1820 ; of Greenwich in 1823 ; of York in 1826 ; of Greenwich in 1827; of Douai in 1829 ; he was elected Definitor in 1815-1818, 1821 and 1824. He died in 1830.

JULIAENS, CHARLES, was approved for preaching and hearing confessions in 1764, and for the mission in 1766 ; Preses of Birmingham in 1767 ; titular Guardian of Worcester, 1770-1773; Preses of Hexham, 1773-1776 ; titular Guardian of Canterbury, 1776-1779; Preses of Birmingham in 1779 and 1780 ; titular Guardian of Bristol in 1781 ; appointed Chronologist in 1782 ; Definitor, 1782-1785; titular Guardian of London, 1785-1788; Definitor, 1788-1791 ; titular Guardian of London in 1791 and 1792; and of York in 1793 ; elected Definitor in 1794 ; Custos, 1800-1803 ; Definitor, 1803-1806, when he was declared a jubilarian. He was then at Sardinian House, Lincoln's Inn Fields, He died in 1807.

KEARNEY, FRANCIS, an Irish Franciscan, incorporated in the English Province in 1710 ; he was then also appointed professor of philosophy; professor of Holy

Scripture in 1716, and continued professor of theology from 1717-1722; titular Guardian of Norwich, 1722-1725 ; Definitor, 1725-1728 ; titular Guardian of Cambridge, 1728-1731 ; Custos, 1731-1734; titular Guardian of London, 1734-1737; Definitor, 1737-1740, in which year he was declared a jubilarian. He died at Douai in 1747.

KELLAM, JOACHIM, was approved for preaching and hearing confessions in 1700. He died three or four years later.

KELLERY, LEWIS, when a cleric, in 1773, asked leave to go for twelve months to the Irish Franciscans at Louvain, to accelerate his ordination : his request was not granted. He was approved for preaching and hearing confessions in 1779; in 1790 he was at Aire, as appears from the civil list; appointed Preses of Warwick, 1800-1803; titular Guardian of Coventry in 1803 ; of Newcastle in 1805 ; again of Coventry in 1806. He died in 1808.

KEMBLE, AUGUSTINE, was approved for preaching and hearing confessions in 1770 ; professor of philosophy, 1770-1773 ; Vicar of Douai and novice master, 1773-1776 ; confessor at Aire, 1776-1779 ; Guardian of Douai, 1779-1782 ; professor of theology, 1782-1785 ; Preses of Monmouth in 1785 and 1786; titular Guardian of Coventry in 1787,—he was then at Grove Park ; Preses of Monmouth in 1788 and 1789 ; titular Guardian of Norwich in 1790, about which time he was at Tusmore near Brackley ; Preses of Monmouth in 1791 and 1792 ; titular Guardian of Canterbury in

1793; elected Definitor in 1794 and again in 1800; appointed Preses of Birmingham in 1800. He died two or three years later.

KINGTON, PACIFICUS (baptismal name THOMAS), a native of Warwick, was approved for preaching and hearing confessions in 1779. He was at Bruges in 1790, as appears from the civil list. Vicar of Douai and novice master in 1791 and 1792; appointed confessor at Aire in 1793. Whilst he was ministering to the spiritual wants of the community in those dangerous days, the Poor Clares were confined and guarded as prisoners in their own convent. Father Kington was apprehended and thrown into a dungeon, and would have been guillotined on July 28, 1794, if the tyrant Robespierre had not been executed on the preceding day. * The nuns were kept in strict confinement for a lengthy period, and were denied permission to proceed to England until the autumn of 1799. Having thus almost miraculously escaped death, Father Kington was afterwards made Preses of White Hill in 1800; titular Guardian of Worcester in 1803; of Bristol in 1805; of Oxford in 1806; of Bristol in 1808; he was confessor of the nuns of the Third Order at Taunton from 1808 till 1812; elected Definitor in 1812 and again in 1815; titular Guardian of Norwich in 1815; of Bristol in 1817; of Oxford in 1818; of Bristol in 1820; of London in 1821; of Canterbury in 1823; of Oxford in 1826. He died a jubilarian, February 18, 1827, aged seventy-three years.

* In the Directory of 1794 (p. 14) he is reported to have been guillotined at Aire for having ventured to exercise his functions.

KNIGHT, NICHOLAS (baptismal name WILLIAM), was a native of Cannington, and had a brother a Jesuit. He was approved for preaching and hearing confessions in 1758. Vicar of Douai, 1759-1762, part of which time he was also novice master; Preses of Hereford, 1764-1767; titular Guardian of Cambridge, 1767-1770; Preses of Monmouth, 1770-1773; titular Guardian of Worcester, 1773-1776; Definitor, and also confessor at Bruges, 1776-1779; titular Guardian of Coventry, 1779-1782; Definitor, 1782-1785. For some years he was incumbent at Fawley, Berkshire. He was titular Guardian of York, 1785-1788; Definitor in 1788, and also Preses of White Hill; titular Guardian of Greenwich, 1791-1794; Custos in 1794; elected Vicar Provincial on the death of Father Pacificus Nutt in 1799; Provincial in 1800. In 1803 he was declared a jubilarian. He died at Osmotherley, April 1, 1806, aged seventy-six years.

LALOR, PETER, a lay brother at Douai, who was held in great esteem for his holiness of life and his strict observance of the Rule. He was sent to Lincoln's Inn Fields as a member of the newly formed community in 1687; but he had soon after to return to Douai. It is related of him that one day, as he was returning from the quest, together with a cart and driver, and torrents of rain were falling continuously for three hours, neither he nor the driver or cart got wet in the least, but came home as dry as if not a drop of rain had fallen. All the while the driver ceased not wondering, nor the saintly brother thanking God. This exemplary religious went to his reward on April 2, 1705.

LAMBERT, ALEXANDER, was approved for preaching and hearing confessions, and also for the mission, in 1687.   He died in England in 1707.

LAMBERT, ANTHONY, was approved for preaching and hearing confessions in 1701, and sent on the mission. He was titular Guardian of Oxford, 1707-1710 ; Preses of Birmingham, 1711-1714 ; titular Guardian of Coventry in 1713 and 1714.   In the latter year he died on the mission.

LAMBERT, JAMES, professed cleric, died at Douai in 1686.

LANCASTER, ANTHONY, was approved for preaching and hearing confessions in 1752.   Soon after he was sent on the mission.   Appointed Preses of Warwick, 1755-1758.   The following year he died in England.

LANCASTER, GEORGE, was approved for preaching and hearing confessions in 1722.   He was titular Guardian of Coventry in 1725 ; Preses of Birmingham, 1725-1728 ; again appointed titular Guardian of Coventry in 1729, when he resided at Grove Park ; Preses of Warwick in 1731, and of Birmingham in 1732 ; titular Guardian of Coventry, 1734-1737.   In the latter year he became Definitor and Preses of Birmingham until 1741. Titular Guardian of Coventry, 1740-1743 ; Definitor, 1743-1746 ; titular Guardian of Coventry, 1746-1749 ; Preses of Warwick, 1747-1755 ; titular Guardian of Coventry in 1750 and 1751 ; Definitor, 1752-1755 ; titular Guardian of Norwich in 1755 ; and of Coventry in 1756 and 1757.   In 1758 he was at Wootten Hall.   Definitor, 1758-1761 ;   titular Guardian of

Coventry, 1761-1764, when 'he was declared a jubilarian.   He died at Douai in 1766.

LANCASTER, GEORGE, was approved for preaching and hearing confessions in 1767, and sent on the mission the following year.   He was Preses of Warwick, 1770-1773; and of Hereford, 1773-1776; titular Guardian of Norwich, 1776-1779; Preses of Abergavenny in 1779 and 1780; titular Guardian of Newcastle in 1781. He died at Douai in 1783 or 1784.

LANGWORTH, BERNARDINE (baptismal name ANTHONY), was approved for preaching and hearing confessions in 1674, and appointed professor of philosophy.   The following year he was sent on the mission.   Appointed Rector of Mount Grace in 1677 and 1678.   He suffered imprisonment for the Faith the following year.   Appointed titular Guardian of York in 1680.   He was Rector and Preses of Mount Grace from 1681 till 1701, with a slight interruption in 1692 and 1693; titular Guardian of Coventry, 1686-1689; of York in 1692; of Canterbury, 1692-1695; in 1693 he was deputed to go to the General Chapter.   He died in 1704.

LAWRENCE, LAWRENCE, professed cleric, died in 1699.

LAW, JOSEPH, lay brother, died at Douai in 1778.

LAWSON, RICHARD, A S. MAGDALENA, was titular Guardian of Coventry, 1668-1671.   In the latter year he was appointed Secretary and Procurator of the Province.   Vicar of Douai in 1674; titular Guardian of Newcastle in 1677; Definitor, 1680-1683; titular Guardian of Cambridge, 1683-1686.   In 1689 he was appointed Commissary for England. Definitor, 1689-1692 ; titular Guardian of Cambridge, 1692-1695. He died the following year.

LE DIEU, PETER, was approved for preaching and hearing confessions in 1716. Vicar of Douai, 1725-1729. He died at Douai in 1731.

LE GRAND, ANTHONY, A S. JOSEPHO, was a native of Douai, but joined the English Franciscans at an early age. He was approved for preaching and hearing confessions in 1655, and also appointed professor of philosophy. Sent on the mission, and made Vicar of London in 1656 ; in this capacity he continued teaching philosophy. He was titular Guardian of London in 1671 ; Definitor, 1674-1677 ; titular Guardian of London, 1678-1681 ; Definitor, 1683-1686 ; titular Guardian of London, 1686-1692 ; Definitor, 1692-1695 ; titular Guardian of Oxford, 1695-1698 ; elected Provincial in 1698.

Dodd says that he resided chiefly in Oxfordshire. He led a very studious and retired life, and was the first philosopher of the age that reduced the Cartesian system to the method of the schools; an attempt so much admired that one of the Royal Society translated it into English from the original, which was published in elegant Latin. He had frequent contests towards the latter end of his days with Mr. John Sergeant concerning the nature of ideas and other metaphysical matters. He died in the office of Provincial on July 26, 1699.

LEMAN, MARTIALIS, was approved for preaching and

hearing confessions in 1746 ; and for the mission in 1749. Appointed confessor at Aire, 1755-1758 ; Vicar of Douai in 1758 ; titular Guardian of London, 1767-1770 ; and again from 1773 until his death, which occurred in England in 1775 or 1776.

LEONARD, LEONARD, was approved for preaching and hearing confessions in 1695. He died about the year 1700.

LEVESON, JOHN BAPTIST, A S. MARIA, was approved for preaching and hearing confessions in 1674. He was titular Guardian of Coventry, 1683-1686 ; confessor at Aire in 1686 ; Procurator of the Province, 1691-1700 ; Definitor, 1695-1698 ; titular Guardian of Greenwich, 1698-1701 ; and again in 1702 ; Definitor, 1704-1707 ; titular Guardian of London from 1707 till his death, which happened in 1709 or 1710.

LEVISON, or LEWSON, FRANCIS, in religion IGNATIUS A S. CLARA, VENERABLE, CONFESSOR OF THE FAITH, was approved for preaching and hearing confessions in 1674, and then sent on the mission. When he had laboured about four years in God's vineyard, he was thrown into prison ; and after fourteen months of close confinement, he died a Confessor of Christ, February 11, 1680, in the thirty-fourth year of his age, and the sixteenth of his religious profession.

LEWIS, LEWIS, was approved for preaching and hearing confessions in 1695, and for the mission in 1698. He was Preses of Monmouth from 1716 until 1732, with two interruptions, one 1719-1722, when he was titular Guardian of Norwich ; the other in 1725, when he was Preses of Abergavenny. He was also titular Guardian of Worcester, 1725-1728; and again in 1731. He died the following year on the mission.

LILLIE, BENVENUTUS, a professed cleric at Douai, mentioned in 1676.

LINGEN, ALEXIUS, professed cleric, died at Douai in 1684.

LINGEN, FRANCIS, twin brother of Alexius Lingen, came to England when still a cleric, as a member of the newly formed community at Lincoln's Inn Fields. He was afterwards ordained, and approved for preaching and hearing confessions in 1689. Though young, he appeared to his brethren an accomplished model of a perfect religious. He was innocent and humble, and seemed always absorbed in prayer. In return he received many special favours from God, but a few months before his death these were all withdrawn, and he suffered intensely from spiritual aridity. After that God visited him again with consolations, and made him understand how much he had merited by this trial. Once more he fell into great anxiety and dryness, but this time for a few days only ; for at the conclusion of the Gospel " Ante diem festum Paschæ," which was read to him, he peacefully breathed his last, October 19, 1693, aged twenty-eight.

LOCKIER, WILLIAM A S. FRANCISCO, was approved for preaching and hearing confessions, and also for the mission, in 1686. The following year he came to England as a member of the new friary at Lincoln's Inn Fields. He was imprisoned in Newgate

at the beginning of December, 1688, and was still
there in September, 1689. He was novice master at
Douai, 1691-1695, and also Vicar in 1693 and 1694;
confessor at Bruges, 1695-1698; at Aire, 1698-1700;
Vicar of Douai and novice master in 1700; Guardian
of Douai, 1701-1704; Definitor, 1704-1707; confessor
at Aire, 1707-1713; titular Guardian of Cambridge,
1710-1713; and of Greenwich, 1716-1719, and again
in 1720; Preses of Birmingham in 1716. He died
in England in 1721 or 1722.

LORAIN, or LORAINE, LAWRENCE, alias THOMAS
HALL, was approved for preaching and hearing confessions, and also for the mission in 1720. Appointed
Preses of Birmingham in 1731. When he had been
labouring on the mission with great zeal for some time,
he had to undergo a severe trial. He was reported to his
ecclesiastical superiors as neglecting his pastoral duties,
and constantly making excursions outside his district,
and in neighbouring counties, especially in Derbyshire.
But his brethren, as well as the Catholics of the locality,
were unanimous in defending his character. It was in
these circumstances that he showed the list of his
converts, with their places of abode, dated 1737. As
a sign that he never lost the confidence of his superiors
in the Order, he was made titular Guardian of Cambridge in 1738; Preses of Warwick, 1740-1744; titular
Guardian of Newcastle, 1753-1756. In 1758 he was
at Warkworth, Northamptonshire; titular Guardian of
Worcester in 1758; and of Coventry in 1759 and
1760; again titular Guardian of Worcester, 1764-1767;
Definitor, 1767-1770; titular Guardian of York, 1770-

1773; Preses of Monmouth in 1773; of Mount Grace, 1779-1782; and of Hexham in 1782. He died a jubilarian in England in 1783 or 1784.

LORAINE, LAWRENCE, was approved for preaching and hearing confessions in 1668; and for the mission in 1674; titular Guardian of Bristol in 1677; again 1683-1686; and again in 1689; titular Guardian of Cambridge, 1701-1704; and of Bristol, 1707-1710; Definitor, 1710-1713. He died a jubilarian in 1719.

LORAINE, PHILIP, was approved for preaching and hearing confessions in 1722, and at the same time appointed professor of philosophy, which office he filled until 1725; from that time he was professor of theology until 1735; Guardian of Douai in 1735 and 1736; in 1737 he was made Procurator, and came on the mission; Definitor, 1740-1743; titular Guardian of Cambridge, 1743-1746; Custos, 1746-1749; titular Guardian of London, 1749-1752; Definitor, 1752-1755; titular Guardian of London and Procurator, 1755-1758; Custos, 1758-1761, during which time he remained Procurator; titular Guardian of London, 1761-1764; elected Custos for the third time in 1764, he died in that office on the mission, in 1766.

LOVELADY, PETER, born in 1765, described in the civil list of Douai in 1790 as " not professed," lived at the residence of Tongres after the expulsion from Douai, and received the tonsure from the coadjutor Bishop of the diocese of Liége on December 20, 1793.

MADEW, EDWARD, was approved for preaching and hearing confessions in 1732, and for the mission the following year. He was titular Guardian of Bristol in 1742 ; of Norwich in 1743 ; of Bristol, 1747-1750 ; of Newcastle, 1756-1757 ; Definitor, 1758-1761 ; about this time he resided at Mapledurham. Titular Guardian of Newcastle, 1761-1764 ; of Canterbury, 1771-1772 ; Definitor, 1773-1776 ; titular Guardian of Oxford, 1776-1779 ; Preses of Monmouth, 1779-1782, in which year he died, a jubilarian, in England.

MAHEW, DIDACUS, lay brother, died at Douai in 1782.

MANTELL, DIDACUS, lay brother, died at Douai, in 1755.

MARKHAM, BERNARDINE, was, while still a cleric, made professor of philosophy in 1740, to which office he was reappointed the following year, when he was approved for preaching and hearing confessions. He died at Douai in 1743.

MARSHALL, JAMES, lay brother, died at Douai in 1755.

MARTIAL, ANDREW, lay brother at Douai. In 1684 he was allowed the use of a mule on the quest, on account of his age. He died at Douai in 1689, having been a faithful Questor for forty years.

MARTIN, ALEXIUS, was approved for preaching and hearing confessions in 1731, and at the same time appointed professor of philosophy. He came on the mission in 1734, and was Preses of Birmingham from that year until 1737 ; titular Guardian of Coventry, 1737-1740, when he was teaching at the Edgbaston

school.   Shortly after he was removed from there, and
made Preses of Hereford, which office he filled until
1752 ; titular Guardian of Bristol, 1752-1755 ; being
again appointed Preses of Hereford in 1755, he died
on the mission in the same year.

MARTIN, BONAVENTURE (baptismal name JOSEPH),
was ordained in London in the year 1800 by the
Bishop of Montpellier, who had been compelled to retire
from France on account of the Revolution.   In the
same year he was approved for preaching and hearing
confessions.   He was titular Guardian of Canterbury
in 1803 ; Preses of White Hill, 1805-1808; titular
Guardian of Cambridge in 1808 ; and of Worcester,
1809-1812; elected Definitor in 1812, 1815, and 1818 ;
titular Guardian of Greenwich in 1817, and again in
1820 ; Definitor, 1821-1824 ; titular Guardian of
Newcastle in 1823; of Worcester in 1824; again of
Newcastle in 1826.   He was again elected Definitor in
1827 and in 1832 ; titular Guardian of London in
1827 ; of York in 1829 ; again of London in 1832. He
died in 1833 or 1834.

MARTIN, GREGORY, was approved for preaching and
hearing confessions in 1725, and also appointed
professor of philosophy.   He came on the mission in
1729.   He was titular Guardian of Cambridge, 1735-
1738 ; of Canterbury in 1741 ; of Oxford in 1743 ;
again of Oxford, 1746-1749 ; Definitor, 1749-1752 ;
titular Guardian of Coventry in 1752 ; of Oxford in
1753 ; again of Oxford, 1758-1761, about which time
he was at Brambridge, Hampshire ; titular Guardian

of Canterbury, 1764-1767. He died a jubilarian at Douai in 1773.

Mason, Richard, in religion Angelus a S. Francisco, was born in Wiltshire in the year 1600, and was Dean of Emly before entering the Order. He was approved for the English mission in 1632; Vicar of Douai and novice master in 1634; in 1637 he was appointed Guardian at Douai and professor of theology. He was Commissary of the English Province for Belgium in 1640. On one occasion he was appointed Visitor of the Province of Lower Germany, or Brabant, and presided there at the Provincial Chapter. Afterwards he laboured with great zeal and fruit in England. He was elected Definitor in 1647, and again in 1653; Provincial in 1659; declared Doctor of Divinity in 1662. In the year 1675 he obtained leave, at his earnest request, to return to Douai from England, "that he might live for God in his old age," as he said. He died there on December 30, 1678, aged seventy-eight years, and was buried in the sanctuary of the old Church. Among his writings is the celebrated " Certamen."

Mason, James, professed cleric, died at Douai in 1680.

Massey, Masseus, a S. Barbara, was approved for preaching and hearing confessions in 1660; confessor of the nuns of the Third Order at Nieuport in 1662; at Bruges in 1663; at Aire, 1665-1668; Guardian of Douai, 1668-1671; appointed Preses of the Maryland mission in 1675, and again in 1680; titular Guardian of Canterbury in 1677, and of Greenwich in 1684; Guardian of Douai, 1686-1689; elected Custos in 1689, he became Vicar Provincial on the resignation of Father Nicholas Lacroix in 1691; Provincial, 1692-1695; again Vicar Provincial in 1699 on the death of Father Anthony Le Grand. He finished his mortal course in 1702.

MATTHEWS, BASIL, was approved for preaching and hearing confessions in 1731, and for the mission in 1743. He died in 1759.

MATTHEWS, PETER OF ALCANTARA, was appointed confessor to the Poor Clares of Gravelines, then at Aire, in 1630; titular Guardian of York, 1632-1635; Definitor, 1637-1640; titular Guardian of Greenwich in 1640; of Bristol, 1647-1650; of York in 1655; Definitor, 1656-1659. He resided about this time in Warwickshire, for in 1657 Sir Hercules Underhill made a bequest to him for his maintenance, and that of another Franciscan missioner in Warwickshire after his death. He was titular Guardian of Oxford, 1659-1662; subrogated Definitor at the death of Father Bernardine Wood in 1666. He died a jubilarian at Douai in 1676.

MCDONNELL, FRANCIS (baptismal name CHARLES), brother of Daniel McDonnell, Bishop of Olympus, and Vicar Apostolic of the Leeward Islands, who died in 1844, was born in the year 1770. In 1790 he was at St. Bonaventure's, Douai, and in the civil list of that year he is described as "not professed." He was approved for preaching and hearing confessions in

1800; titular Guardian of Oxford in 1803; of Cambridge in 1805; Definitor, 1806-1809; Procurator in 1809—his address was then Mill Street, Hanover Square; titular Guardian of London, 1809-1812; Custos, 1812-1815—he resided then at West Grinstead; Provincial, 1815-1818; titular Guardian of London in 1818; Vice-Commissary in 1821 and 1827. All this time he had continued Procurator. Again Provincial, 1821-1824; Custos and titular Guardian of Douai, 1824-1827; elected Vicar-Provincial on the death of Father Ignatius Richards in 1829; elected Provincial in 1832, and again in 1835; Definitor in 1838. Bishop Collingridge had desired to secure him for his coadjutor, and bulls had actually been expedited on December 10, 1812, and again on January 26, 1816, nominating him in that quality Bishop of Ionopolis. But he could not be prevailed upon to accept the proffered dignity. After 1820 he resided some time at Baddesley; then for many years at Witham in Essex; finally in London, where he lived in Upper King Street, Bloomsbury Square. From the year 1840 he contemplated retiring into a friary of the Order in Belgium; but the execution of this plan was cut short by his death, which occurred on November 5, 1842.

METCALFE, BERNARDINE, was approved for preaching and hearing confessions in 1695, and the following year for the mission; Preses of Hexham, 1698-1701; novice master at Douai in 1704; titular Guardian of Canterbury, 1705-1708; of York, 1710-1713, and again 1716-1719. In 1717 he was again Preses of

Hexham ; Definitor, 1719-1722 ; titular Guardian of Newcastle in 1722, and of York in 1723, Definitor, 1725-1728 ; Preses of Mount Grace in 1728 ; titular Guardian of York, 1728-1731 ; Definitor, 1731-1734, and also Preses of Hexham ; titular Guardian of York in 1734. He died on the mission in 1738.

MIDDLEMORE, LEWIS, was approved for preaching and hearing confessions in 1728, and for the mission the following year. He was Vicar of Douai and novice master, 1734-1737 ; confessor at Bruges in 1737 ; Guardian of Douai, 1738-1741 ; titular Guardian of Cambridge and confessor at Aire in 1741 and 1742 ; Definitor, 1743-1746, and also confessor at Bruges ; titular Guardian of Greenwich in 1746, when he was also re-appointed confessor at Bruges.

MILES, EDWARD, was approved for preaching and hearing confessions in 1746, and for the mission in 1747. He died in England in 1752.

MILLARD, MARTIN, lay brother, died a jubilarian in the Order at Douai in the year 1722.

MILLWARD, ANSELM, was appointed professor of philosophy, when still a cleric, in 1779, and filled that office until 1785. He was ordained in 1782 ; approved for preaching and hearing confessions in 1784. In 1785 he was appointed novice master, and in 1787 Vicar of Douai. In 1790 he was at Bruges, as appears from the civil list. Preses of Monmouth in 1793 ; titular Guardian of Worcester in 1794 ; of Oxford in 1800, when he was also appointed confessor to the Poor Clares of Aire. In 1803 he became confessor of the nuns of the Third Order, then at Winchester; titular Guardian of Norwich in 1803; of Worcester in 1805; of Norwich in 1806; of Worcester in 1808; Definitor, and Preses of White Hill, 1809-1812. In 1811 he was professor of theology; titular Guardian of Oxford in 1812. He died February 8, 1813.

MILLWARD, ANSELM (baptismal name JAMES), was approved for preaching and hearing confessions, and also for the mission in 1821; he was titular Guardian of Norwich in 1821 and 1822; of Cambridge, 1823-1826; of Coventry in 1826; of Bristol in 1827 and 1828; of Norwich in 1829; of Oxford, 1832-1835; of Cambridge, 1835-1838; he was one of the signatories at the last Chapter meeting held at Clifton in 1838; in that year and the following he resided at Aston Hall, Stone, and from 1839 until 1848 he was at Abergavenny; he then went to Wappenbury, Leamington, where he died, October 10, 1868.

MILLWARD, LAURENCE, lay brother, died in 1698.

MONSON, ANGELUS (baptismal name RICHARD), was approved for preaching and hearing confessions in 1696. He died at Douai in 1713.

MONSON, GEORGE, was approved for preaching and hearing confessions in 1713. He died at Aire in 1720.

MOORE, HENRY, lay brother, was sent to Lincoln's Inn Fields as a member of the new community in 1687. He died about the year 1690.

MORGAN, DAVID, A S. WINIFREDA, was approved

for preaching and hearing confessions, and also for the mission in 1668; he was titular Guardian of Worcester, 1680-1683. He died in 1701 or 1702.

NAPIER, BASIL, was approved for preaching and hearing confessions, and also for the mission in 1700; he was titular Guardian of Norwich, 1713-1716; and of Cambridge in 1720; afterwards he obtained leave to go to Ireland for a time, whence he returned in 1726; he was again titular Guardian of Norwich, 1728-1731; elected Definitor in 1731, he died the following year in England.

NAPIER, or NAPPER, FRANCIS, A S. ANNA, was approved for preaching and hearing confessions in 1660; confessor at Aire, 1662-1665; Guardian of Douai, 1665-1668; he became Definitor, and was sent on the mission in 1668; titular Guardian of Oxford, 1671-1674; Custos, 1674-1677; Definitor, 1677-1680, in which year he died on the English mission.

NAPIER, alias RUSSELL, MARIANUS, A S. FRANCISCO (baptismal name WILLIAM), a native of Oxford, was approved for preaching and hearing confessions in 1650; confessor at Aire, 1651-1656, when he was approved for the mission; titular Guardian of Coventry, 1674-1677; Preses of Mount Grace in 1675 and 1676; titular Guardian of Greenwich in 1683. He was tried and condemned to death for Oates's plot; but when he had been a long time in prison, his death sentence was commuted into one of exile in 1684. He then returned to Douai, where he passed the remainder of his life. He died on October 4, 1693, in the 74th year of his age and the 54th of his profession, and was buried in the cloister on the north side.

NAZARETH (A) LEWIS, was approved for preaching and hearing confessions in 1634; titular Guardian of York in 1640, and of Oxford in 1648. He was appointed to the residence of Bransford in 1665.

NECHELLS, FRANCIS, lay brother, mentioned as being at Douai in 1756.

NEEDHAM, BONAVENTURE, a young priest who died at Douai in 1743.

NEEDHAM, JOSEPH, was appointed professor of philosophy in 1740, and the following year approved for preaching and hearing confessions; professor of theology, 1746-1749; confessor at Aire, 1749; Guardian of Douai in 1750 and 1751; confessor at Bruges, 1752-1758, when he came on the mission; titular Guardian of Oxford, 1761-1764, and again, 1767-1770; Definitor, 1770-1773; titular Guardian of Oxford, 1773-1776; Provincial, 1776-1779. He was declared a jubilarian in 1784, and died in London March 24, 1791, in the 74th year of his age and the 58th of his profession.

NIFFO, AUGUSTINE, was incorporated in the English Province in 1663, and at the same time subrogated Custos; he had presided at our Chapter the preceding year, and was superior of missionaries in Flanders; titular Guardian, of London in 1665. He died in England in 1666.

NORTON, EDWARD, was admitted to the English Province in 1660, and incorporated in 1662. He died the following year.

NORTON, HENRY, was one of the fathers appointed to look after the temporal affairs of the Poor Clares at Aire in 1632. He was titular Guardian of Dorchester in 1634.

NOTTÉ, AUBERT, lay brother, died at Douai in 1773.

NOWELL, PHILIP, lay brother, born in 1736; he was at Douai in 1790.

NUTT, PACIFICUS, was approved for preaching and hearing confessions in 1761, and also appointed professor of philosophy; he was novice master, 1762-1767; Vicar of Douai, 1762-1768, when he was made Guardian there; approved for the mission, and appointed titular Guardian of Coventry in 1770; Preses of Birmingham in 1771; titular Guardian of Cambridge in 1773; of Bristol in 1776; Guardian of Douai in 1778; Definitor, 1779-1782; titular Guardian of Coventry, 1782-1785; Provincial, 1785-1788; Preses of Birmingham, 1787-1796. He was elected Provincial in 1794, and again in 1797; and died in that office at Birmingham, September 27, 1799.

O'BRIAN, FRANCIS, was professor of philosophy at Douai, 1707-1710; approved for preaching and hearing confessions in 1710. He died the following year.

O'FARRELL, PASCHAL (baptismal name PATRICK), born at Bristol on November 21, 1796, was approved for preaching and hearing confessions in 1820. For some years he taught at the Baddesley school. He was titular Guardian of York in 1821; of Bristol, 1823-1826; of Newcastle in 1826; of Coventry in 1827; of Bristol in 1829; Definitor, 1827-1830; at the end of this year he went to St. Joseph's Chapel, Bristol. He was one of the signatories at the last Chapter meeting held at Clifton in 1838. After that, he, as well as Father Edgeworth, continued to reside and labour in Bristol. In 1843 he purchased the Irvingite church, which was opened for Catholic worship the same year, under the title of St. Mary's; in 1858 his address was at St. Catherine's Convent, Park Place; in 1860 he lived at Greenfield Cottage, Weston-super-Mare. He died at the Convent of the Third Order at Taunton, November 18, 1877; he was the last survivor of the Second Province.

OGLE, AMBROSE, was approved for preaching and hearing confessions, and also for the mission in 1704; he was Preses of Mount Grace from 1707 until 1728; appointed titular Guardian of York in 1713; of Newcastle in 1719; of York in 1725; confessor at Bruges in 1728. He died the following year in England. *

OSBALDESTON, FRANCIS, A S. MAGDALENA, was approved for preaching and hearing confessions in 1648; titular Guardian of Newcastle in 1651; of York in 1653. In 1666 he was asked to recommend the convents of Aire and Bruges to young ladies who had a vocation for the religious life. He was again titular

---

* Father William O'Meara, O.S.F., who served the Cannington mission in 1826, was an Irish Franciscan.

Guardian of Newcastle in 1671; shortly afterwards he was appointed Preses of Mount Grace, but his health seems to have been failing, and he was sent to Bruges for a rest in 1675; afterwards he returned to England, and suffered imprisonment for the Faith. He died at Douai in 1685 or 1686.*

OUDART, WILLIAM, A S. BONAVENTURA, was approved for hearing confessions in 1650, and for the mission in 1656. He was Vicar of Douai, 1656-1662; titular Guardian of Worcester, 1662-1665.

OVERS, RICHARD, lay brother, died at Douai in 1764.

OWEN, GREGORY, lay brother, died about the year 1647.

PAINTER, ROBERT, was approved for preaching and hearing confessions in 1731, and the following year for the mission. He was Preses of Birmingham, 1741-1746; titular Guardian of Norwich in 1746; confessor at Bruges in 1747 and 1748; Guardian of Douai in 1749; titular Guardian of Norwich and confessor at Aire in 1750; Preses of White Hill in 1753; titular Guardian of York, 1755-1758. About this time he resided at Lower Hall, Lancashire. Preses of Mount Grace, 1758-1761; of Hexham, 1761-1764; of White Hill, 1764-1767. He died on the mission in 1769 or 1770.

PARKER, alias CROSS, BERNARD, was approved for preaching and hearing confessions, and also for the

* Father Henry O'Shea, O.S.F., who was at Taunton in 1848, belonged to the Irish Franciscan Province.

mission in 1725 ; Preses of Birmingham in 1728 and 1729. In 1730 he taught at the Edgbaston school.

PARKER, GILBERT, a novice, mentioned in 1686.

PARKINSON, ANTHONY, was appointed professor of philosophy at Douai in 1692. The following year he was approved for preaching and hearing confessions. He came on the mission in 1695. He was Preses of Warwick, 1698-1701 ; of Birmingham, 1701-1710 ; titular Guardian of Worcester, 1704-1707 ; Definitor, 1707-1710 ; titular Guardian of Oxford, 1710-1713 ; elected Provincial in 1713, and again in 1722. He assisted at the General Chapter in Rome in May, 1723. He was titular Guardian of Coventry in 1726, when he resided at Mr. Eyston's, East Hendred. He died January 30, 1728, on the English mission. His work " Collectanea : or, Antiquities of the English Franciscans " is much esteemed.

PARKINSON, ANTHONY, JUNIOR, was approved for preaching and hearing confessions in 1729, and soon afterwards sent on the mission ; appointed Preses of Monmouth in 1735 ; titular Guardian of Newcastle in 1738 ; of Norwich in 1740 ; of Newcastle, 1744-1747 ; of Coventry in 1749. He died in England the following year.

PARKINSON, ANTHONY, was appointed Vicar of Douai and novice master in 1750, and again in 1753. He came on the mission in 1762. He died in England in 1767.

PARKINSON, BERNARDINE, was approved for preaching and hearing confessions in 1722, and for the mission in

1725. He was titular Guardian of Norwich, 1731-1734. He died in England in 1736 or 1737.

PARLER, LEO, was approved for preaching and hearing confessions in 1692, and the following year for the mission.   He died in 1693.

PARRY, BONAVENTURE, A S. ANNA, was approved for preaching and hearing confessions in 1671 ; appointed professor of philosophy in 1672, and of theology 1674-1677 ; Guardian of Douai, 1677-1680.   Elected Custos in 1680, he resigned that office the following year, when he was made Commissary ; titular Guardian of Cambridge in 1681 ; again professor of theology in 1683 ; declared Doctor of Divinity in 1684 ; Preses and Guardian of York in 1687 ; Definitor, and Guardian of Douai, 1689-1692 ; Preses of Mount Grace in 1692 ; titular Guardian of Norwich in 1693 ; Custos, 1698-1701 ; Provincial, 1701-1704.   It is said in his praise that he was animated with great zeal for the beauty of God's house.   The character of this remarkable man is well illustrated by the following instructions which he handed to Father John Capistran Eyston, together with his faculties :

" Be very cautious how you put your sickle into another's harvest.   Be courteous, civil and obliging to all ; familiar with few, and with none of the other sex. Compassionate the poor, helping them when you can. Be tender and careful of the sick.   Relate not, nor report the defects, abuses, or liberties of your own or other families, either regular or secular, but rather vindicate them if you can, or waive the discourse.   Beware of idleness, taverns, inns, ale-houses and clubs, which I earnestly beg you to forbear as much as possible. Omit not daily mental prayer, nor an annual recollection. Be punctual and exact in observing the rubrics of both Mass and Office. Be very wary what obligations of Masses and prayers you take, and none of any moment or long duration without the Superior's, or some prudent grave Father's approbation.   Extol virtue, cry down vice. Ground your flock in solid piety and devotion ; more particularly insisting on matters relating to frequenting the Sacraments, for which catechistical discourse upon the Commandments and the dispositions required for the Sacrament of Penance and the Holy Communion are, in my judgment, the most proper. Let not your manners contradict your doctrine, nor life and actions belie your words. Be zealous for the conversion of souls, but temper zeal with prudence and discretion. Meddle as little as may be with the temporal concerns of your flock, or economy of families ; and be not forward in recommending servants or making matches. Remember, perfect expropriation is our great treasure, which we must endeavour to preserve by renouncing all dominion : in the case of money we ought to be very moderate ; and in all matters of moment have recourse, if possible, to the Superior."

Broken down by the mission work, Father Parry sought rest at Douai ; and at length, after two years illness, he reached the end of his course on August 7, 1720, aged seventy-three years, and professed fiftyeight.   He was buried in the cloister on the west side.

PARRY, JEROME, was approved for preaching and hearing confessions in 1678, and for the mission in 1681. He was Preses of Monmouth from 1705 till 1714; titular Guardian of Cambridge, 1707-1710; of Worcester in 1713. He died on the mission in 1714.

PAYNE, AMBROSE, was approved for preaching and hearing confessions in 1743, and for the mission in 1749. He was Preses of Mount Grace in 1770. He died at Douai in 1772 or 1773.

PAYNE, ANSELM, was approved for preaching and hearing confessions in 1761. He spent most of his life in retirement at Douai. In 1776 he was appointed professor of philosophy. He died at Douai in 1782.

PAYNE, PLACID, was approved for the mission in 1755, and sent to West Grinstead, in Sussex, where he furnished the residence. In 1758 he was at Highden in the same neighbourhood. He remained at West Grinstead until 1763. From 1764 to 1767 he was Preses of Warwick; titular Guardian of Newcastle, 1767-1770. He died the following year on the mission.

PEACHE, JUNIPER, lay brother, died in 1711.

PEDLEY, HENRY, A S. MARIA, was approved for preaching and hearing confessions in 1657, and also for the mission. In 1668 he was appointed confessor of seculars at Douai. Not long afterwards he was sent on the English mission, but recalled about 1677. He died at Douai in 1695.

PEDLEY, JOSEPH, was approved for preaching and

hearing confessions in 1691, and for the mission the following year.

PENNY, FRANCIS, A S. MARIA, was approved for preaching and hearing confessions in 1668. He was professor of philosophy at Douai from 1668 to 1672, and professor of theology from that year until his death, which happened a couple of years later.

PENNY, ROBERT, was approved for preaching and hearing confessions, and also for the mission, in 1681. Although he did not neglect his spiritual duties, he is said to have indulged somewhat too much in harmless but worldly pastimes, such as driving, hunting and playing loud musical instruments. In consequence, his superiors thought it expedient to give him a gentle reprimand, to which he readily submitted. He died in England in 1721 or 1722.

PERROT, GEORGE, A S. GULIELMO, entered the Order at Douai in 1618. He was appointed titular Guardian of Berkshire at the first Chapter in 1630; titular Guardian of Greenwich in 1634, and confessor of the nuns of the Third Order at Brussels; Definitor, 1637-1640; elected Provincial in 1640; Commissary in England, 1647-1650; Definitor, 1650-1653; Provincial, 1656-1659. He died in England in 1670 or 1671. In the record of his death it is added that " his memory is in benediction, for he was a lover of the brethren."

PETIT, PAUL, lay brother, died at Douai in 1782.

PETRE, FRANCIS, was approved for preaching and hearing confessions in 1684. He died at Douai in 1695.

PICKFORD, JEROME, A S. BONAVENTURA, a learned priest, who received the habit at Douai in 1618. He was Preses of Douai before the erection of the Province. He became Definitor in 1630 ; in 1632 he was selected to go instead of the Provincial to the General Chapter ; Custos in 1634 ; titular Guardian of Reading, 1637-1640 ; Definitor in 1640 ; Provincial in 1647. He died in 1664 or 1665.

PIERRE, BONAVENTURE, lay brother, died at Douai in 1743.

PILLING, BONAVENTURE (baptismal name JOHN), was appointed professor of philosophy when still a cleric in 1758 ; afterwards ordained and approved for preaching and hearing confessions in 1759 ; professor of theology, 1761-1773 ; Guardian of Douai, 1773-1776 ; sent on the mission, and elected Definitor in 1776, when he took up his residence at West Grinstead ; titular Guardian of London, 1779-1782 ; Preses of Birmingham in 1782 and 1783 ; titular Guardian of York in 1784 ; Definitor, 1785-1788 ; titular Guardian of Coventry, where he also resided, 1788-1791 ; he was elected Provincial in 1791. He died at Osmotherley, January 12, 1800, aged sixty-six years.

PILLING, LEO (baptismal name WILLIAM), younger brother of Bonaventure, was appointed professor of philosophy when still a cleric in 1770 ; then ordained, and approved for preaching and hearing confessions in 1773. He continued teaching philosophy until 1776 ; professor of theology, 1776-1782 ; titular Guardian of Canterbury, 1782-1785 ; Preses of Hereford in 1785 and 1786; titular Guardian of Oxford in 1787; Definitor, 1788-1791; titular Guardian of Oxford in 1793; Definitor in 1794; from 1788 until 1800 he was Procurator; titular Guardian of York in 1800. He died at Lower Hall, December 4, 1801, aged 60.*

PORA, CHARLES, a novice, who died about the year 1647.

PORA, CHARLES, was approved for hearing confessions and for the mission in 1655; for preaching the following year. He was confessor at Aire, 1671-1674; titular Guardian of Newcastle, 1674-1677; in 1677 he was again confessor at Bruges, but, getting into bad health, he was sent to England for change of air in 1678; in 1680 he was made Procurator, and filled that office for many years; Definitor, 1683-1686; titular Guardian of Cambridge, 1686-1689; Preses of London, 1689-1692; titular Guardian of London, 1692-1695, when he died on the mission. He published a work in French on true charity.

POTIER, LEWIS, tertiary, described in 1680 as having been a long time in the Order. He died in 1719.

POWELL, GREGORY (baptismal name DAVID), was approved for preaching and hearing confessions, and also for the mission, in 1740. He was Preses of Abergavenny from that year until 1767, with two slight interruptions, one in 1755, the other in 1761 and 1762; titular Guardian of Worcester, 1749-1752;

* Father James Platt, O.S.F., who served the Cannington mission towards the middle of the nineteenth century, was not connected with the English Province. He was professed at Pisa.

again, 1755-1758; of Bristol, 1761-1764; again, 1767-1770; Definitor, 1770-1773; titular Guardian of Bristol, 1773-1776; Definitor, 1776-1779; titular Guardian of Cambridge in 1781. He died at Abergavenny, October 12, of the same year.

PRESCOT, THOMAS, lay brother, died at Douai in 1671.

PRICE, BERNARD, was approved for preaching and hearing confessions in 1693, and for the mission in 1698. He was Preses of Mount Grace, 1701-1704; titular Guardian of Bristol, 1716-1719; of Worcester, 1722-1725; of Bristol, 1728-1731, in which year he died in England.

PRICE, FELIX, was approved for preaching and hearing confessions, and also for the mission in 1678. He came to England in 1681. He was Preses of Leominster, 1687-1695; titular Guardian of Bristol, 1695-1698. He died about the year 1700.

PRICE, PACIFICUS, A S. ALBANO (baptismal name PHILIP), was approved for preaching and hearing confessions in 1671, when he was also appointed professor of philosophy. With a slight interruption he was professor of theology from 1674 until 1686, when he received the title of Doctor of Divinity. In 1686 he came on the mission and went to East Hendred. He was Custos, 1692-1695; elected Provincial in 1695; again in 1704. He died in May, 1706. He is described as "truly peaceable, and beloved by all."

PRITCHARD, MATTHEW, of the family of the

Pritchards of Graig, about half way between Monmouth and Abergavenny, received the Franciscan habit at Douai in 1686. He was appointed professor of philosophy in 1692, and the following year approved for preaching and hearing confessions. He was professor of theology from 1695-1710. In 1705 he was deputed to go to the General Chapter. In 1710 he came to England, and was sent to the Perthyr mission in his native county. He was titular Guardian of Bristol, 1710-1713; Definitor, and Preses of Abergavenny, in 1713. Pope Clement XI. having preferred the first Vicar Apostolic of the Western District, Bishop Ellis, to the See of Segni, issued his bull, dated Rome, September 20, 1713, appointing Father Pritchard titular Bishop of Myrina, and three days later instituted him Vicar Apostolic. Owing to the renewed persecution of Catholics on the accession of King George I., and the unusual delay in the receipt of the bulls, his consecration at Cologne did not take place until Whitsuntide, 1715. It may be mentioned as an illustration of his genuine piety that, when he had been promoted to the episcopal dignity, he promised the fathers that he would continue to say the usual number of Masses for the Religious who died, asking them to do the like for him at his death.

This prudent and zealous prelate went to his eternal reward at Perthyr in 1750, and was buried at St. Kenelm's Church, Rockfield, deanery of Abergavenny. The following epitaph is inscribed on the slab which covers his remains : *

* Dr. Oliver's Collections.

✠

Hic jacent Exuviæ R^{mi} et Ill^{mi} in
Christo P. D. MATTHÆI PRITCHARD, Epⁱ
Myrinensis, V. Ap. Ord. FF. MM.
Recoll. Angl. Conventus Duaceni
Alumni, S. T. L. Jub.
Vir erat
Eruditionis summæ,
Doctrinæ approbatæ,
Famæ integræ et plusquam vulgaris :
Vixit omnibus charus,
Pauperum et afflictorum columen.
Flent ejus obitum orphanus et vidua ;
Collachrymantur universim omnes,
Nobilis et ignobilis,
Dives et pauper,
Quibus æquale Pastoralis officii Ministerium
Semper exhibuit.
In Perthyre multis annis vixit, et ibidem
Animam Creatori reddidit anno
Ætatis suæ 81, Rel. 63, Sacer. 57,
Ep. 35, Jub. 13, Die 22 Maii, 1750.
R. I. P.

PULTON, JOSEPH (baptismal name JOHN), was
approved for preaching and hearing confessions in
1710 ; Vicar of Douai and novice master, 1710-1716 ;
Guardian of Douai, 1716-1719 ; titular Guardian of
York, and confessor at Bruges, 1719-1722 ; Guardian
of Douai, 1722-1725 ; he then came on the mission,
and was Definitor, 1725-1728. He was many years
Procurator, and resided first in Henrietta Street,
Covent Garden, later in Holborn. He was elected

Provincial three times—in 1728, 1733 and 1746, and assisted at the General Chapter held at Bologna in 1728. He did not see the end of his last term of office, but died on the mission, May 29, 1748.

PURCELL, or PURSELL, JOSEPH (baptismal name WILLIAM), was approved for preaching and hearing confessions in 1788; Preses of Monmouth in 1800; titular Guardian of London in 1803; Preses of Mount Grace in 1805; titular Guardian of Newcastle in 1806; of York in 1808; of Norwich in 1811; Definitor, 1812-1815; titular Guardian of Canterbury in 1815; of Norwich in 1820. In this year he accepted the mission of Tor Abbey, where he arrived with a broken constitution, on September 23. On July 29 following, he saw the end of his labours. In Tor Mohun church-yard his patron erected a tombstone, thus inscribed:*

✠

CINERIBUS ET MEMORIÆ
GULIELMI PURCELL, O.S.F.
SACERDOTIS INTEGERRIMI, PIENTISSIMI.
VIXIT ANNOS 57, MENS. 2.
DECESSIT 4 KAL. AUGUSTI, 1821.
H. M. P.
GEORGIUS CARY
PIETATIS CAUSA.

RAMSEY, DOMINIC, A S. CLARA, was professor of philosophy at Douai, 1666-1669. He was approved for preaching and hearing confessions in 1668, and was sent on the mission in 1669.

* Dr. Oliver's *Collections.*

RANDOLPH, LEO, A S. MAGDALENA, was approved for preaching and hearing confessions and also for the mission in 1657, and on September 12 of that year he entered on his missionary labours. He was titular Guardian of Worcester, 1665-1668. He was requested by the Chapter to look for postulants for the English Convents of Aire and Bruges. From 1668 to 1671 he was Definitor; titular Guardian of Coventry, 1671-1674; again elected Definitor in 1674, and again in 1680; titular Guardian of Worcester, 1683-1686; Definitor, 1686-1689. In 1687 he was appointed Preses of Birmingham, and began the building of the Chapel dedicated to St. Mary Magdalene. He continued Preses of Birmingham during the remainder of his life. He was titular Guardian of Worcester, 1689-1692; Definitor, 1692-1695; titular Guardian of Coventry, 1695, until his death which occurred in the year 1698.

RAVENHILL, ANGELUS, was approved for preaching and hearing confessions in 1752, and for the mission the following year. In 1758 he was at Tichborne in Hampshire. He was Preses of Monmouth, 1761-1764; titular Guardian of Newcastle, 1764-1767; of Oxford, 1770-1773; Definitor, 1773-1776; titular Guardian of Cambridge, 1776-1779; Definitor, 1779-1782; titular Guardian of Cambridge, 1782-1785; Definitor, 1785-1788; titular Guardian of Newcastle, 1788-1791; appointed Preses of Hexham in 1791, he died a year or two later in England.

RAVENHILL, DIDACUS, a tertiary, died at Douai in 1695

RAVENHILL, THOMAS, alias ANTHONY A S. JOSEPHO,

admitted at Douai as a tertiary in 1666. His father gave an alms of one hundred pounds at his profession. Afterwards he went to Ireland, where he was ordained priest. A long time afterwards he came on the English mission.

REEVES, LEWIS, A S. MARIA MAGDALENA, born in 1647. At a very early age he entered the Order at Douai. Though young he was a model of mortification to his brethren. At the age of nineteen he became dangerously ill, and was in a few days reduced to the last extremity. As death was approaching, he sang the " Veni Creator " and " Te Deum," which being ended he gave up his soul to God. The religious were greatly astonished and edified, and related that the room was filled with a very sweet odour at the time of his death, which occurred on January 23, 1666. He was buried near the door leading to the garden.

RENSHAW, JUNIPER, lay brother, died at Douai in 1668.

RICHARDS, IGNATIUS (baptismal name EDWARD), was approved for preaching and hearing confessions in 1812, and at the same time appointed professor of philosophy and theology. He was titular Guardian of Norwich, 1812-1815; of Newcastle, 1815-1820; of York in 1820; Definitor, 1821-1824. About this time he resided at Abergavenny. He was elected Provincial in 1824 and re-elected in 1827. In that year he went to Rome on business of the Order, and Father McDonnell, who was then at Witham, wrote to him as follows, on September 1:

Hon^d Dear Sir,

With my best wishes of a good journey to you, and for your safe and speedy return, I send you the letters of Father General, as you directed . . .

But Father Richards was not to see England again: he died in Rome on December 19, 1828. Bishop Baines, O.S.B., Vicar Apostolic of the Western District, who was then in the Eternal City, attended him, and gave in a letter this account to Father McDonnell: " He died making the sign of the Cross, and embracing the Crucifix. I can truly say that I never beheld a more edifying or saintly death."

The same Prelate ordered the following epitaph, which he himself composed, to be put upon Father Richards' monument in St. Isidore's Church :

A ☧ Ω

IGNATIO RICHARDS Presbytero Brittanno
In Districtu Occidentali Brittanniæ
Missionario Apostolico
Fratrum Franciscalium Provinciæ suæ
Rectori,
Qui pius, mansuetus, eruditus,
Dei et proximorum charitate flagrans,
Bonus Pastor, laboribus attritus,
Vitam sanctam Justorum morte clausit
xiv. Kal. Januar. Ann. MDCCCXXVIII.
Natus annos XXXIX.
P. A. Baines Præsul Amicus mærens
P. C.

ROBERTS, AUGUSTINE (baptismal name WILLIAM), was born in 1763. He was ordained priest in 1789, but had already from the previous year been appointed professor of philosophy ; and he also continued to teach afterwards at Tongres, when the community of Douai was transferred to that town. In 1800 he was appointed chronologist, and also titular Guardian of Worcester; Definitor, 1803-1806 ; he was confessor of the nuns of the Third Order, then at Winchester, 1803-1807; Preses of Mount Grace in 1806 ; elected Vicar Provincial on the elevation of Father Bernardine Collingridge, then Provincial, to the episcopal dignity, July 7, 1807. He then resided at Baddesley. He was Preses of Birmingham, 1809-1812; he was elected Vice-Commissary in 1812 ; appointed titular Guardian of London in 1814 ; Custos, 1815-1818 ; elected Provincial in 1818, he resigned in 1820 on account of failing health. He became confessor to the Poor Clares of Aire, then at Plymouth. Afterwards he was again made Definitor, but resigned that office also owing to ill-health. He died at St. Omers, May 10, 1827, aged 64 years.

ROBERTS, GREGORY, began his noviceship in 1700. At the beginning he was very exact and edifying ; afterwards, however, he failed in obtaining the requisite number of votes for his profession, and it was decided to dismiss him. But he begged so hard and so humbly to be allowed another trial, that his request was granted. This time he gave general satisfaction, and made his profession. He was approved for preaching and hearing confessions and also for the mission in 1710.   He died the following year.

Robes, Gabriel, a S. Maria, was approved for preaching and hearing confessions and also for the mission in 1647 ; titular Guardian of Cambridge, 1650-1653 ; confessor at Aire, 1656-1659 ; of the English nuns of the Third Order, then at Paris, in 1659 ; Definitor, 1662-1665 ; Guardian of Douai in 1663; titular Guardian of Bristol, 1665-1668 ; and of London in 1669 ; confessor at Bruges in 1672.   He died in England in 1679 or 1680.

Robinson, Lawrence, was approved for preaching and hearing confessions in 1734.   He came afterwards on the mission, and was Preses of Hexham from 1737 until 1743 ; titular Guardian of Coventry, 1743-1746 ; of Bristol in 1758, when he resided at Beckford in Gloucestershire ; titular Guardian of Worcester in 1759.   He died in England one or two years later.

Rogerson, James, was approved for preaching and hearing confessions in 1746, and professor of philosophy from that year till 1749 ; Vicar of Douai and novice master in 1749 ; professor of theology in 1750 ; sent on the mission in 1753 ; titular Guardian of Canterbury, 1755-1758 ; again 1761-1764 ; professor of theology, 1767-1770 ; novice master, 1770-1773 ; he again taught philosophy in 1778, and theology from 1779 almost until his death ; titular Guardian of Oxford in 1785, and again in 1788.   He died a jubilarian, in England, in 1790.

Rookwood, John, or Robert Rose, was approved for preaching and hearing confessions in 1695, and for the mission in 1698 ; titular Guardian of Canterbury, 1713-1716 ; Definitor, 1716-1719 ; titular Guardian of Worcester, 1719-1722 ; Definitor, 1722-1725 ; titular Guardian of Greenwich, 1725-1728. He died on the mission, a jubilarian, in 1746.

ROUSSEAU, THEODORE, lay brother, died at Douai in 1738.

RUSSELL, MICHAEL, was appointed Preses of Holywell in the year 1687.

SADLER, PHILIP, was approved for preaching and hearing confessions in 1691, and the following year for the mission. He was Preses of Birmingham, 1698-1701 ; titular Guardian of Coventry, 1701-1704, again 1707-1710 ; Definitor, and Preses of Birmingham, 1710-1713 ; titular Guardian of Greenwich, 1713-1716 ; Definitor, and confessor at Bruges, 1716-1719 ; titular Guardian of London, 1719-1722 ; Definitor, 1722-1725. He was made Commissary in 1723 during the Provincial's absence at the General Chapter. Provincial, 1725-1728. He was elected Vicar Provincial on the death of Father John Capistran Eyston in 1732, and died in that office on August 27 the following year, " having," as the record says, " deserved well of the Province."

S. (A) AUGUSTINO, WILLIAM, was appointed professor of theology at Douai in 1630. He died before the year 1634.

S. (A) BARBARA, GEORGE, JUNIOR, was sent on the mission in 1671. He died in England in 1674.

S. (A) BERNARDO, PAUL, was appointed Vicar at Douai in 1671; approved for preaching in 1674; confessor at Aire, 1674-1677; professor of philosophy at Douai in 1677. He died at Douai in 1680.

S. (A) BLASIO, VINCENT, was approved for preaching and hearing confessions in 1634, and at the same time appointed secretary of the Province. In 1637 he was elected Definitor.

S. (A) BONAVENTURA, FELIX, was approved for preaching and hearing confessions in 1663, and also appointed novice master, in which office he was continued in 1665, when he became Vicar at Douai. He was confessor at Bruges, 1668-1671; appointed Guardian of Douai in 1671. He died in that office in 1674.

S. (A) BONAVENTURA, FRANCIS, was approved for preaching and hearing confessions in 1634; appointed novice master in 1637, and in addition professor of philosophy in 1638; approved for the mission in 1640, and appointed titular Guardian of London. He died before the year 1647 at Dunkirk, where the Poor Clares had a Convent.

S. (A) EDMUNDO, LAWRENCE (presumably EDMONDS, who was on the mission in London in 1623), * was appointed professor of philosophy in 1630, and of theology in 1634. He was Definitor, 1634-1637; titular Guardian of Greenwich, 1637-1640; elected Custos in 1640; titular Guardian of Oxford in 1647, and again in 1650; Definitor, 1653-1656; titular

* *Records of the English Province S.J.*

Guardian of Oxford, 1656-1659 ; Definitor, 1659-1662 ; titular Guardian of Canterbury, 1662-1665 ; Definitor, 1665-1668 ; titular Guardian of Canterbury, 1668-1671. He died on the English mission either in that year or the next.

S. (A) Francisco, Ambrose, was approved to hear confessions of seculars in 1650, and at the same time appointed confessor at Aire.

S. (A) Francisco, Robert, was approved for preaching and hearing confessions in 1647 ; Vicar of Douai in 1648 ; confessor of the nuns of the Third Order at Nieuport, 1650-1653 ; Guardian of Douai, 1653-1656 ; Definitor, 1656-1659. He died either in that or the following year.

S. (A) Ludovico, Bernard, was approved for preaching and hearing confessions in 1640, and at the same time appointed confessor at Nieuport. He died before the year 1647.

S. (A) Magdalena, Angelus, was approved for hearing the confessions of seculars in 1650. He was at the same time sent on the mission, and signed the usual mission oath. He was titular Guardian of Bristol in 1660. He died in 1663.

S. (A) Maria, Didacus, was approved for preaching and hearing confessions about the year 1643. He died before 1647.

S. (A) Maria, Didacus, lay brother, died at Douai in 1680.

S. (A) MARIA, EDWARD, lay brother, died at the Convent of the Third Order at Bruges in 1668.

S. (A) MARIA, LEWIS, returned to his own Province, presumably Spain, in 1632.

S. (A) MARIA, PETER, was approved for preaching and hearing confessions in 1647. Appointed titular Guardian of Greenwich, 1650-1653. He died probably not long after, for about 1660 we meet with another Peter a S. Maria.

S. (A) PETRO, FRANCIS, was approved for preaching and hearing confessions in 1632, and at the same time appointed confessor at Aire. He was titular Guardian of York, 1637-1640, and of Newcastle, 1647-1650; Commissary for the parts of the Province where the Provincial did not reside, 1650-1653; titular Guardian of Newcastle, 1653-1656; novice master in 1656; Custos, 1656-1659; titular Guardian of Greenwich in 1660. He died in 1661 or 1662.

S. (A) THOMA, BONAVENTURE, was appointed manager of the printing press which was set up at Douai in 1632; approved for preaching and hearing confessions in 1634. He was appointed titular Guardian of Bristol in 1656.

SCANDRET, PAUL, was approved for preaching and hearing confessions in 1713, and at the same time appointed professor of philosophy at Douai. In 1722 he was made professor of theology.

SCUDAMORE, GEORGE, was approved for preaching and hearing confessions in 1695, and for the mission in 1698. He was titular Guardian of Worcester, 1710-1713; Vicar of Douai and novice master in 1716; titular Guardian of Oxford in 1722. He died the following year.

SELBY, DANIEL, A S. FRANCISCO, was approved for preaching and hearing confessions, and also appointed professor of philosophy at Douai in 1677. Being in bad health the following year, he was sent as second chaplain to Bruges for a rest. He came on the mission in 1681. In 1689 he was imprisoned in York Castle for the Faith. He was titular Guardian of Newcastle in 1695; appointed Preses of the residence of York in 1696; titular Guardian of York, 1707-1710; Definitor, 1710-1713. He died on the mission in 1715 or 1716.

SENIS (DE), BERNARDINE, was approved for preaching and hearing confessions, and also for the mission in 1632. Appointed titular Guardian of Reading in 1634; of Leicester, 1637-1640; Definitor in 1640; again in 1647, when he was also made novice master and professor of philosophy. He was elected Custos in 1650, and appointed professor of theology. In the same year he assisted at the National Congregation of the Order at Brussels. In 1653 he was confessor of the nuns of the Third Order, then at Nieuport.

SIMPSON, BENEDICT, was approved for preaching and hearing confessions in 1776. He died at Douai in 1783 or 1784.

SIMPSON, BONIFACE (baptismal name JOSEPH), was approved for preaching and hearing confessions in

1743; novice master, 1758-1761; confessor at Aire in 1768, and again in 1774.

SHARPLES, PHILIP, a professed cleric at Douai, mentioned in 1767.

SHARROCK, BERNARDINE, lay brother, died at Douai in 1773.

SHEPHEARD, WILLIAM, was approved for preaching and hearing confessions in 1665. The following year he was sent on the mission, and appointed to the residence of Mount Grace. He died in England in 1679 or 1680.

SHEPPEY, NICHOLAS, A S. CLARA, was professor of classics at Douai in 1666. He was approved for the mission in 1671. Titular Guardian of Norwich in 1677. His name occurs again in 1680.

SIMON, FRANCIS, was approved for preaching and hearing confessions in 1725. He was declared a jubilarian in 1766. He died at Douai in 1772 or 1773.

SIMONS, WILLIAM, professed cleric, died at Douai in 1695.

SINGLETON, SILVESTER, lay brother, received the habit on October 3, 1677. A doubt afterwards arose concerning the validity of his profession, and the case was referred to the Commissary General in 1687. The decision was for the validity. He died at Douai in 1695.

SMALLWOOD, ALEXIUS, was approved for preaching and hearing confessions in 1722, and for the mission in 1725. He was Procurator of the Province, 1728-1732;

titular Guardian of Canterbury, 1732-1735 ; of London, 1737-1740 ; Definitor, 1740-1743 ; titular Guardian of London, 1743-1746 ; Definitor, 1746-1749 ; titular Guardian of Canterbury, 1749-1752 ; elected Provincial in 1752.   He died in England in 1756.

SMITHSON, ALPHONSUS, A S. CLARA, was approved for preaching and hearing confessions in 1653, and sent on the mission in 1655.   In 1668 he was recalled from the mission.   He died at Douai in 1671 or 1672.

SMYTH, or SMITH, BERNARDINE, was approved for preaching and hearing confessions in 1683, and for the mission in 1686.   He was titular Guardian of Coventry in 1692; of York, 1698-1701 ; Definitor, 1701-1704; titular Guardian of York, 1704-1707 ; Custos, 1707-1710 ; titular Guardian of London in 1710.   The following year he was deputed to go to the General Chapter.   Custos, 1713-1716 ; Provincial, 1716-1719; titular Guardian of Oxford, 1725-1728; of Newcastle in 1729.   He was declared a jubilarian in 1734.   He died at Douai in 1742.

SPENCER, DANIEL (baptismal name JOHN), lay brother, died at Aire in 1790.

SPENCER, JOHN, lay brother, born in 1714.   He was at Douai in 1790.   He died before the year 1800.

STEINBACH, NORBERT, professed cleric, died at Douai in 1726.

STORY, EGIDIUS, lay brother, died at Douai in 1677.

STREET, JOSEPH, lay brother, born in 1752.   He was at Douai in 1790.   Afterwards his address was at

Mr. Kenyon's, Catholic Chapel, Manchester. He died probably about 1810. .

STROTTER, LEWIS, professed cleric, died at Douai in 1675.

STUART, alias STEVENS, CHARLES, was approved for preaching and hearing confessions in 1752, and for the mission in 1755. He was titular Guardian of Norwich, 1770-1773; Definitor, 1773-1776; titular Guardian of Greenwich, 1776-1779; Definitor, 1779-1782; titular Guardian of Greenwich, 1782-1785; Definitor, 1785-1788; titular Guardian of London, 1788-1791; Definitor, 1791-1794. He died before the year 1800.

He does not rank among the authors, as he did not properly compose a work. But we have from him a neat manuscript volume inscribed " Cæremoniale ad usum Diffinitorii Almæ Provinciæ Angliæ FF. Minorum Recollectorum, transcriptum ac tandem completum per F. Carolum Stuart, A.D. 1765. Orate pro eo." *

SUMNER, ANTHONY (baptismal name RICHARD), born at Chipping in Lancashire in 1775, was approved for preaching and hearing confessions in 1800, and for the mission in 1803. He resided some time at Whatcombe House, Lambourne, Berkshire. He was made titular Guardian of Cambridge in 1811 ; of London in 1812 ; of Greenwich in 1814 ; of Oxford in 1815; of Canterbury in 1818. He became confessor to the Poor Clares at Plymouth in August, 1821, and died on July 16 in

* It was presented to our friary at Glasgow by the Rev. Henry Gall in 1884.

W

the following year. He was interred in the nuns' burial ground at Coxside.

SUMNER, LEO (baptismal name JAMES), twin brother to Anthony, was approved for preaching and hearing confessions at the same time as his brother in the year 1800. He was Preses of Hereford in 1803; titular Guardian of Norwich in 1805; of Worcester in 1806; of London in 1808; of Coventry, 1809-1815; of Oxford in 1817; Definitor, 1818-1821; titular Guardian of Bristol in 1818; of Worcester in 1820; of Newcastle in 1821. He resided many years at Baddesley. In 1821 he was appointed confessor to the Poor Clares, then at Plymouth. He died a few days before his brother, on July 10, 1822, at Taunton, and was buried in the convent grounds.

SUTTON, THOMAS, was approved for preaching and hearing confessions in 1677, and sent to Bruges as assistant chaplain. He returned to Douai from Bruges the following year, to make room for Father Daniel Selby, who was sent there to recruit his health. He was approved for the mission in 1686; titular Guardian of Newcastle, 1704-1707; of London, 1713-1716; in 1713 he was surrogated Custos; titular Guardian of Greenwich in 1719. He died at Douai in 1722 or 1723.

TALBOT, JOHN, a secular priest, admitted to the habit of probation in England by virtue of special faculties granted to the English Province in 1638. It is not improbable that he was afterwards known as THOMAS A S. BONAVENTURA, and died on the mission in 1668.

TANNER, ANDREW (baptismal name JAMES), was approved for preaching and hearing confessions, and also for the mission, in 1814, and was at the same time appointed titular Guardian of Bristol; of York in 1815; of Worcester, 1817-1820; of Newcastle in 1820; of Greenwich in 1821. In this year his address was Sardinian House, London. He was titular Guardian of Norwich from 1823 until his death, which occurred February 11, 1826. He was but 39 years of age.

TATE, JOSEPH, was approved for preaching and hearing confessions in 1779. Novice master at Douai, 1782-1785; Vicar at Douai, 1784-1787; confessor at Aire, 1787-1793; approved for the mission in 1793. He became Guardian of Tongres when the Community of Douai was transferred to that town at the time of the French Revolution. Afterwards he came to England, and resided for some time at Cheeseburn Grange, Newcastle. He was titular Guardian of Cambridge in 1800; Preses of White Hill in 1803; titular Guardian of Oxford in 1805; Definitor in 1806, and also Preses of Monmouth; Preses of White Hill in 1808, when he resided at Lee House; titular Guardian of Canterbury, 1809-1812; confessor of the Poor Clares, then at Britwell, in 1812; titular Guardian of York in 1814. He died the following year.

TAYLOR, BERNARDINE, subdeacon, died at Douai in 1725.

TAYLOR, BRUNO, was appointed professor of philosophy when still a cleric in 1695. He was afterwards ordained and approved for preaching and hearing confessions in 1696 ; sent on the mission of Maryland in 1700 ; Preses of Mount Grace in 1704.

TEMPEST, BARTHOLOMEW, a young priest who died in 1648.

TERWHIT, JOHN, lay brother, died at Bruges in 1680.

THOROLD, ANTHONY, a native of Lincolnshire, whose mother was of the celebrated Roper family, studied at the English colleges of St. Omers and Rome, and entered the Society of Jesus, in Flanders, in the year 1652. He left after some months, to join the English Franciscans at Douai, where he died in the novitiate.*

TOOTELL, CHARLES, was approved for preaching and hearing confessions in 1734, and came on the mission in 1737. He was Preses of White Hill from 1738 until 1752 ; titular Guardian of Worcester, 1752-1755 ; Preses of White Hill, 1755-1758 ; titular Guardian of Norwich, 1758-1761 ; Preses of White Hill, 1761-1764 ; titular Guardian of York, 1767-1770. He died in England in 1771.

TOOTELL, JOHN EVANGELIST, was approved for preaching and hearing confessions in 1704 ; confessor at Aire, 1714-1719 ; Vicar of Douai and novice master, 1719-1722 ; confessor at Aire, 1722-1725, when he was approved for the mission ; confessor at Aire in 1726 ; titular Guardian of Canterbury, 1728-1731, and again in 1735 ; Definitor, 1737-1740 ; titular Guardian of Newcastle in 1740 ; of Greenwich in 1741 ; declared a

* *Records of the English Province S.J.*

jubilarian in 1747; Preses of White Hill in 1752. He died at Douai in 1759.

TOTTY, FRANCIS, tertiary, died in 1711.

TOWNSENDE, THEODORE, was approved for preaching and hearing confessions in 1640, and also appointed Vicar of Douai. He died in 1647 or 1648.

TRAPPES, JOSEPH, A S. TERESIA, was approved for preaching and hearing confessions in 1671, and for the mission in 1674, when he was also appointed titular Guardian of York. In 1687 he lived at Douai, and asked leave to go to another Province of the Order; the case was left in the hands of the Provincial, who decided that he should go on the English mission. He was accordingly sent to White Hill in 1688. Titular Guardian of London, 1695-1698. He died about this year.

TRAPPES, alias BRAITHWAITE, RICHARD, was approved for preaching and hearing confessions in 1681. He was professor of philosophy at Douai, 1680-1684, when he began to teach theology. At the end of the year 1686, he lost one eye through illness, and as he was in danger of losing the other also, he had to give up teaching, and came on the mission in 1687. In the same year he was appointed titular Guardian of Worcester; of Bristol in 1691; of Norwich in 1692. He died in England in 1694 or 1695.

TRESHAM, FRANCIS, a Benedictine father of Douai, who joined the English Franciscans in 1650. He was sent on the mission in the same year. He died in 1660.

TYAS, PETER OF ALCANTARA, was a lay brother at Douai in 1750. He died in 1756.

TYLDESLEY, ANTHONY, was approved for preaching and hearing confessions in 1713, and the following year for the mission. He died in England in 1720.

TYRAR, ANTHONY, lay brother, declared a jubilarian in 1779. He died at Douai in 1787.

VAUGHAN, DOMINIC, A S. FRANCISCO, was approved for preaching and hearing confessions, and also for the mission, in 1653. He was titular Guardian of Bristol, 1653-1656. He died in 1661 or 1662.

WACASINE, MODESTUS, lay brother, died at St. Germain-en-Laye,* a small town not far from Paris, in 1689.

WAKELEY, THOMAS, professed cleric, died at Douai in 1668.

WALL, alias WEBB or JOHNSON, JOHN, in religion JOACHIM A S. ANNA, VENERABLE, MARTYR, was born of a distinguished family in Norfolk, and cheerfully relinquished an estate of five hundred pounds per annum to become a Franciscan. He studied first at the English College, Douai; then in Rome, where he was ordained priest on December 3, 1645. About three years later, May 12, 1648, he was sent on the mission. In 1651 he received the Franciscan habit at St. Bona-

* There was in this town a friary of Recollects, of which King Louis XIII. had laid the foundation stone. (R. P. Hélyot.)

venture's, Douai.   He was appointed novice master and Vicar there in 1653.   After three years he came to England.   He was titular Guardian of Worcester, 1659-1662, and again in 1671 ; Definitor, 1674-1677. In the latter year he was appointed confessor of the Poor Clares at Aire.

There is an interesting description of an interview he had with the Jesuit Father Claude de la Colombière, the apostle of the Sacred Heart, who was then residing at St. James's Palace.   As it is but little known, we shall insert it here.

" The apostle of the Sacred Heart of Jesus had been sent over by his superiors to visit the Court of the Duchess of York, in order to impart spiritual instruction to the numerous foreigners who had gathered around her in London.   He came fresh from Paray-le-Monial, and was full of ardent zeal to propagate the beautiful devotion so lately revealed by our Blessed Lord himself to the saintly nun of the Visitation. During two years he had preached those lessons of Divine love in the Chapel of St. James's, and had kindled the sacred flame in many a breast amid the obloquy and persecution which overshadowed the Faith in England.   Some few of our countrymen had contrived to slip in and hearken to his consolatory discourses.   They may have imbibed such fervour from the revelations which he disclosed, as to have enabled them to bear the terrible trials in store for them.   The love of the Sacred Heart was no new doctrine.   It had been revealed to the beloved disciple as he lay upon his Master's breast in the Cœnaculum, and was well known to St. Augustine, St. Bernard and St. Gertrude; but it had recently been manifested with renewed lustre to the Blessed Margaret Mary in the chapel and the garden of the Convent at Paray. The flame then kindled smouldered imperceptibly, and was often seemingly extinct, until two centuries later it burst forth again among our Catholic countrymen, when a pilgrimage departed from our shores to suspend the banners of England over the shrine where the mystery was revealed.

"Father Wall had heard of the famous young Jesuit, and was prepared to meet with one deeply versed in the science of Divine love; but when he found himself in the presence of the holy priest, it seemed to him as if the apostle St. John had reappeared on earth to rekindle those flames from the Heart of Jesus with which his writings abound. His calm and beautiful countenance was precisely such as one may picture that of the beloved disciple who stood beside the Cross when the lance pierced his Master's side, and revealed the material tabernacle of His ardent charity.

"'Father,' he said, 'I am a poor Minorite of St. Francis, come to seek strength and counsel of the Sacred Heart of Jesus, of which you are known far and wide among us as the apostle. Among the friends I longed to see in London is one of your own Society, Father Turner, now a prisoner in Newgate, looking forward to the blessed crown of martyrdom. Had I not been called away by my superiors, I should ere this have been in prison, with the certain prospect of a similar reward, if God but granted me the grace to merit it by my constancy.'

"'My friend,' said the holy man, 'you have indeed come to the fount of graces for the strength you need, and yet none can probe the mysteries of His Heart without tasting of the cup of bitterness which He drained in the Garden of Gethsemani. Whosoever taketh up His Cross and followeth in His wake, though he gain an hundredfold even in this life in the way of consolations, must yet feel the sharp edge of persecution. Oh, that I were granted this great grace which your English priests are reaping in this land of crosses ; but God may yet have something in store for me !' *

"' Our Lord will not let you go hence, may be, without much suffering,' said Father Joachim of St. Ann ; 'but I foresee that your life will be spared to propagate this sweet devotion, and rekindle the flagging zeal in many hearts.'

"Thus communing they spent together that day, which was the Vigil of All Saints, in sweet converse on the love of Jesus ; and it was not until after Father Wall had said Mass at the little Altar of the Sacred Heart, which Father de la Colombière had erected in his oratory, that they finally parted at dawn on the feast. The former proceeded in the direction of Charing Cross with a view of returning to his friend's

* He was apprehended and imprisoned, but finally shipped off to France in January, 1679.

house near to Clerkenwell, where he had left his horse." *

Not long afterwards we find Father Wall again in Worcestershire, which seems to have been the scene of his missionary labours. And there, at the breaking out of Oates's plot, he was apprehended, and after five months' confinement in the county gaol, he was arraigned on April 15, 1679. He suffered death at Worcester on August 22 of the same year, in the 59th year of his age, and the 29th of his religious profession. His head was privately conveyed to Father Leo Randolph, to be sent to St. Bonaventure's at Douai, where it was respectfully kept in the cloister until the time of the French Revolution.

The following note is taken from a paper called "A true relation of some judgments of God against those who accused the priests and other Catholics after the pretended conspiracy in England."

"Before Mr. Johnson the priest was executed in the city of Worcester, Pakington, the justice of the peace who had imprisoned him, as he sat at table at his meal, fell to the ground senseless, and died the next day without having ever been able to utter a word; and his sister-in-law went altogether out of her mind, no one knowing why. A man called Rogers, who betrayed the priest and got him put in prison, going home immediately after the false oath taken in court, when passing a bridge was knocked down by an ox and grievously hurt; and his two companions who had

---

* *Records of the English Province S.J.*—Theodore Galton, Esq.

taken a like oath against the said priest, both of them died in a boiling cauldron, where one was trying to help the other who had fallen in ; and the mistress of these two servants, who had advised them to commit the crime, had her own brother imprisoned in Newgate, and, before the priest was put to death, executed for having killed his own illegitimate child." *

WARING, BRUNO, was approved for preaching and hearing confessions in 1755.   He died at Douai in 1779.

WARING, HENRY (baptismal name JOHN), was approved for preaching and hearing confessions in 1770, and the following year for the mission.   He was Preses of Hereford in 1778 ; titular Guardian of Oxford in 1779 ; Preses of Hereford in 1781 ; titular Guardian of Newcastle, 1782-1785 ; Preses of Abergavenny in 1785 ; titular Guardian of Newcastle in 1787 ; Preses of Mount Grace in 1790 ; titular Guardian of Newcastle, 1791-1794 ; Preses of White Hill in 1794 ; appointed Guardian of Osmotherley in 1800 ; Definitor in 1803 ; titular Guardian of Oxford, 1808.   About this time he resided at Lower Hall, Salmesbury.   Definitor and Preses of Warwick, 1809-1812 ; titular Guardian of Worcester, 1812-1815 ; and of Bristol in 1815.   He died, a jubilarian in the Order, in 1816 or 1817.

WATKINS, alias VAUGHAN, CHARLES, was approved for preaching and hearing confessions in 1691, and the following year for the mission.   He was Preses of Abergavenny from 1701 till 1713 ; titular Guardian of

* *Records of the English Province S.J.*—Stonyhurst MSS.

Norwich, 1710-1713; Guardian of Douai, 1713-1716. From this year till 1725 he was again Preses of Abergavenny. Definitor, 1716-1719; titular Guardian of Bristol, 1719-1722, and of Cambridge, 1725-1728; confessor at Bruges in 1725. The following year he became again Preses of Abergavenny, and continued in that office until his death. He was titular Guardian of Cambridge in 1726; Definitor, 1728-1731; titular Guardian of Bristol, 1731-1734; surrogated Definitor in 1733; Definitor, 1734-1737; titular Guardian of Bristol in 1737. He died the following year in England, a jubilarian in the Order.

WATKINS, GREGORY (baptismal name WALTER), was approved for preaching and hearing confessions in 1770; appointed Preses of Abergavenny, 1776-1779; titular Guardian of Norwich, 1779-1782; Preses of Abergavenny, 1782-1785; titular Guardian of Bristol, 1785-1788; Preses of Abergavenny, 1788-1791; titular Guardian of Norwich, 1791-1794; Preses of Abergavenny in 1794; titular Guardian of Bristol in 1800; Preses of Abergavenny in 1803; titular Guardian of Coventry in 1805; Preses of Hereford in 1806; of Abergavenny in 1808 and 1809. From 1806-1809 he was Definitor.

WATSON, CUTHBERT, tertiary, an upright, humble and God-fearing man, who zealously collected alms among the Catholics in England for our fathers who were imprisoned at the time of the persecution. He died at Douai on February 7, 1729, in the 81st year of his age and the 40th of his profession.

WEBB, CHARLES, lay brother, born in 1724.   He was at Douai in 1790, and died there in 1805.

WEETMAN, ANDREW (baptismal name FRANCIS), was approved for preaching and hearing confessions in 1767, and appointed novice master.   He was sent on the mission in 1768 ; Preses of Abergavenny, 1770-1773 ; titular Guardian of Norwich, 1773-1776 ; Preses of Hereford in 1776 ; titular Guardian of Bristol, 1778-1781 ; Preses of Abergavenny in 1781 ; titular Guardian of Bristol, 1782-1785 ; Guardian of Douai, 1785-1788 ; Definitor, 1788-1791 ; Preses of Hereford in 1788 ; titular Guardian of Bristol, 1791-1794.   In 1794 he was appointed Preses of Monmouth.

WEETMAN, ANDREW, JUNIOR, (baptismal name EDWARD), born at Rowington in Warwickshire, May 2, 1765.   He he is described in the civil list of 1790 as " Deacon."   He was approved for preaching and hearing confessions in 1791.   He came on the mission in 1793, and was sent to Lower Hall.   After a stay of five years there, he went to Wootten, then to Perthyr. He had in the Order the honourable titles of Preses of Hexham in 1794; of Hereford in 1800; titular Guardian of Cambridge in 1803 ; of York in 1805 ; Definitor, 1806-1809 ; Preses of Hereford in 1808 ; titular Guardian of Newcastle, 1809-1812.   He became confessor of the Poor Clares of Aire in 1811, and the following year of the nuns of the Third Order at Taunton, which office he continued to fill during the thirty-one remaining years of his life.   He was

Definitor from 1812 till 1835; titular Guardian of Coventry in 1815; of London in 1817; of Greenwich in 1818; of London in 1820; of Cambridge in 1826; of Worcester in 1827; of Cambridge in 1829; of Douai in 1832. In that year he was declared a jubilarian. He was one of the signatories at the last Chapter meeting in 1838. He died at Taunton, January 14, 1843, and was buried in the conventual cemetery.

WESTBY, ANTHONY, was approved for preaching and hearing confessions in 1704. He died on the English mission in 1714.

WESTON, JOHN BAPTIST (baptismal name WILLIAM), was approved for preaching and hearing confessions, and also for the mission, in 1686. He was appointed professor of philosophy at Douai in 1691; Guardian of Douai, 1704-1707; Definitor, 1707-1710; Vicar of Douai and novice master in 1708; titular Guardian of Greenwich in 1711; Custos, 1716-1719; titular Guardian of Cambridge in 1719. For many years he was a zealous labourer on the English mission. He had some trouble with his work on the Rule of the Friars Minor, for in 1716 the fathers assembled in Chapter passed a resolution that he should not proceed with the printing of his book until he had obtained leave in writing from the Provincial. Later, however, when the work was printed, it earned great and well-deserved praise. To his brethren he was ever a model of regularity, mortification and humility. He died rather suddenly at Douai, April 11, 1729, in the 74th year of his age, the 56th of profession, the 50th of priesthood, and was buried in the cloister on the north side.

WHALLEY, ALEXIUS, was approved for preaching and hearing confessions in 1764; Preses of Abergavenny, 1767-1770; of Hexham in 1771; of Monmouth in 1774; of White Hill in 1778; titular Guardian of Canterbury, 1779-1782; Preses of Hereford in 1782; titular Guardian of Norwich in 1784; confessor at Aire in 1785; Preses of Mount Grace in 1803; of Hexham in 1805; titular Guardian of Cambridge in 1806; Preses of Hexham in 1808, he was then residing at Wooller, in Northumberland; titular Guardian of York in 1809. He died, a jubilarian, in 1812, aged 73 years.

WHEELER, JOHN, was approved for preaching and hearing confessions in 1740, and for the mission in 1743. He was titular Guardian of Norwich, 1747-1750; of Cambridge, 1755-1758; of Norwich, 1761-1764; of Greenwich, 1766-1769; of London in 1770. The following year he resided at Beoley. He died in 1772 or 1773.

WHITE, ANSELM, was approved for preaching and hearing confessions in 1746. The following year he was appointed professor of philosophy; approved for the mission in 1749; Preses of Birmingham, 1752-1755; titular Guardian of Coventry in 1755; of Norwich in 1756; Preses of Birmingham, 1758-1761, when he resided at Edgbaston. Not long after, he was recalled from the mission, and resided some years at Douai. He died in England in 1777 or 1778.

WICKET, HUBERT, not long after his ordination, in 1686, obtained leave to say all his Masses, with a few exceptions, for his mother. He was approved for preaching and hearing confessions, and also for the mission, in 1687. He died in Germany in 1720.

WICKSTED, POLYCARP, was approved for preaching and hearing confessions in 1674, and in the same year sent on the mission of Maryland. He died at Douai in 1725.

WIDDRINGTON, PAUL, A S. MAGDALENA, was approved for preaching and hearing confessions, and also for the mission, in 1653; titular Guardian of Newcastle, 1656-1659; confessor at Nieuport, 1659-1662; titular Guardian of Newcastle, 1662-1665; and again 1668-1671; of London, 1675-1678; again 1681-1684. He died in England in 1685 or 1686.

WILKINSON, PASCHAL, lay brother, died at Douai in 1767.

WILLAYS, JOHN, was approved for preaching and hearing confessions in 1640. He was Definitor, and Vicar of Douai in 1647. He died in that or the following year.

WILLCOX or WILLCOCK, PETER, was approved for preaching and hearing confessions, and also appointed professor of philosophy at Douai, in 1773. He was Preses of Monmouth, 1776-1779; of White Hill in 1779; titular Guardian of York in 1782; Preses of White Hill in 1784; titular Guardian of Worcester in 1785; Preses of Mount Grace in 1787; titular Guardian of Worcester in 1788; of Canterbury in 1790 ; Preses of White Hill, 1791-1794 ; titular Guardian of Canterbury in 1794; of Norwich in 1800. He died in 1802 or 1803.

WILLIAMS, FELIX, professed cleric, died at Douai in 1689.

WILLIAMS, JOHN, a youth whose profession was declared invalid in 1672 : he left accordingly.

WILLIAMS, PACIFICUS, SENIOR, A S. FRANCISCO, was approved for the mission in 1648. Titular Guardian of Bristol, 1650-1653; again 1657-1660; Guardian of Douai in 1662; confessor at Bruges in 1665. He was, with a few other fathers, asked to recommend the Convents of Aire and Bruges to young ladies who showed signs of a religious vocation. Titular Guardian of Worcester, 1668-1671; Definitor, 1671-1674; titular Guardian of Bristol, 1674-1677; again 1680-1683; Definitor, 1683-1686; Preses of Hereford in 1684; titular Guardian of Bristol, 1686-1689; first Preses of Monmouth from 1687 until his death; titular Guardian of Bristol, 1692-1695; he was then declared a jubilarian. Definitor, 1695-1698; titular Guardian of Bristol, 1698-1701. He died in 1705.

WILLIAMS, PACIFICUS, JUNIOR, was approved for preaching and hearing confessions in 1684. He was Preses of Abergavenny from 1687-1701 ; titular Guardian of Worcester in 1701 ; Procurator and Secretary, 1701-1705. He died in 1707.

WILLIAMS, PACIFICUS, A S. JOANNE BAPTISTA, was

X

born in Glamorganshire, and entered the Order at the early age of fifteen. He showed such alacrity in serving and in hearing Mass, that it seemed as if he could find no pleasure in anything else. In his application to study and regularity of life, he was an example to all. He appeared not to lack a single virtue, and never relented from the first fervour of his noviceship. He was looked upon as a saint, not only in the friary, but also in the town of Douai. To the great regret of his brethren God called him out of this vale of tears in 1718, being but in the 21st year of his age, and the 6th of religious life. He was buried in the long cloister on the south side near the door.

WILLIAMSON, AMBROSE, was professor of philosophy at Douai, 1689-1692. In 1691 he was approved for preaching and hearing confessions; professor of theology from 1692 until his death; Guardian of Douai, 1698-1701. In 1699 he was deputed to go to the General Chapter. He died in 1701.

WILLOUGHBY, EGIDIUS, A S. AMBROSIO, was appointed confessor of the nuns of the Third Order at Brussels in 1630. Titular Guardian of London in 1634, Definitor, 1637-1640; titular Guardian of Chichester in 1640; and of London, 1647-1650; Definitor, 1650-1653; titular Guardian of London, 1653-1656; Definitor, 1656-1659; titular Guardian of Greenwich in 1659. He translated into English the treatise of St. Peter of Alcantara on Mental Prayer. He died in 1660.

WILSON, LEWIS, lay brother, died in 1790.

WINTER, JEROME, was approved for preaching and

hearing confessions in 1704, and for the mission in 1708. He was titular Guardian of Oxford, 1713-1716; and 1719-1722; and again in 1723; confessor at Aire, 1725-1731; titular Guardian of Greenwich and confessor at Bruges, 1731-1734; Definitor, 1734-1737; titular Guardian of Greenwich in 1737; of Worcester in 1738; elected Custos in 1740. He died in England in 1742.

WITHY, DIDACUS, lay brother, died about the year 1790.

WOOD, BERNARDINE, A S. CLARA, was approved for preaching and hearing confessions, and also for the mission in 1647. He was titular Guardian of Cambridge, 1647-1650; of Oxford, 1653-1656; of Cambridge in 1657; Definitor, and also Commissary, 1659-1662; titular Guardian of York, 1662-1665; again elected Definitor in 1665, he died in that office the following year, in England.

WOODCOCK, or OADCOCK, JOHN, alias FRANCIS FARRINGTON, in religion, MARTIN A S. FELICE, VENERABLE, MARTYR, was born at Leyland in Lancashire in 1603. His father was a Protestant, his mother a good Catholic. He was nearly twenty years old when he was received into the Catholic Church. He first studied at St. Omers; afterwards, at the age of twenty-six, he went to the English College, Rome, where he afforded a remarkable example of the mildest disposition.* But he felt an irresistible attraction to a penitential life, and applied for admission

* *Records of the English Province S.J.*

among the Capuchins at Paris, where he was received in 1630. It was, however, not God's will that he should remain there. After a few months he was, without any fault of his own, dismissed, chiefly for these reasons: no answer had been obtained to letters of enquiry addressed to his mother and friends in England; his mother and elder brother were opposed to his embracing the religious life; lastly, his health was not good. The youth thereupon went to Douai, and applied for admission among the English Franciscans; and they, judging that he had been unfairly dismissed by the Capuchins, received him into the Order in 1631, when he was clothed with the habit of St. Francis by Father Heath; and at the expiration of his noviceship he made his profession in the hands of Father Bel. He was approved for preaching and hearing confessions, as well as for the mission, in 1637; confessor of the nuns of the Third Order at Nieuport in 1638. After that he came on the mission, and was imprisoned in Lancaster gaol in 1644. He obtained the palm of martyrdom on August 7, 1646, in the forty-fourth year of his age, and the fifteenth of his religious profession.

WOODWARD, ANTHONY, a native of Lancashire, entered the Order at the age of sixteen. All admired his singular devotion to our Blessed Lady; and before her altar he was soon to be laid to rest, for God would not have this pure and innocent soul to be long on earth. He died regretted by all, not fully twenty years old, on April 14, 1686, at Douai, and was buried on the south side of the cloister, right in front of our Lady's altar.

WOODWARD, JOSEPH, was approved for preaching and hearing confessions in 1683, and appointed Vicar of Douai, and the following year also novice master; confessor at Bruges in 1686. He came on the mission in 1687. He was titular Guardian of Coventry, 1691-1694. Love for regular discipline induced him to ask leave to return to Douai. His request was granted. He was appointed Guardian of Douai, 1695-1698; Definitor in 1698, in which office he died about the year 1700.

WOODWARD, MATHIAS, was approved for preaching and hearing confessions in 1704. He died at Douai in 1720.

WOOLMER, JOSEPH, was approved for preaching and hearing confessions in 1657, and for the mission in 1660. He died in 1664 or 1665.

WOOLMER, MASSEUS, was approved for preaching and hearing confessions, and also for the mission, in 1681. He was assistant priest at Mount Grace in 1688. The Spanish ambassador asked to have him for his second chaplain, but it was thought inconvenient to let him go. He was titular Guardian of Canterbury, 1695-1698; of Norwich, 1701-1704; of London in 1705; Definitor, 1707-1710; titular Guardian of Greenwich in 1710; of London in 1711; Definitor, 1713-1716; titular Guardian of London, 1716-1719, in which year he died.

WREST, THOMAS, in religion LEWIS A S. AUGUSTINO, a native of Kent, was approved for preaching and hearing confessions in 1634, and for the mission in 1650. He came to England in 1655. He was titular Guardian of Worcester, 1656-1659 ; Procurator of the Province, 1659-1665. He worked for many years with great fruit on the mission ; then he suffered a long incarceration in Lancaster Castle. On his release he retired to St. Bonaventure's, Douai, where he died, "full of days and good works," on May 8, 1669, in the 73rd year of his age and the 38th of his profession.

WYART, GREGORY, A S. MARIA, was approved for preaching and hearing confessions in 1656, and for the mission in 1660. He was Vicar of Douai, 1668-1671. At his request leave was granted him to go to another Province of our Order in 1672. It seems he did not go, or soon returned, for two years later he was appointed director of the choir at Douai. In 1676 he went as representative of the English Province to the National Congregation of the Order at Antwerp. He was titular Guardian of Norwich, 1680-1683. He died in 1691 or 1692.

YARDLY, LAWRENCE, professed cleric, died at Douai in 1747.

YATES, BERNARD, was approved for preaching and hearing confessions in 1737. He came on the mission, and was appointed Preses of Mount Grace in 1738 ; of Hexham, 1743-1746 ; of Birmingham, 1746-1749 ; of Mount Grace, 1749-1752 ; titular Guardian of York, 1752-1755 ; Guardian of Douai, 1755-1758 ; Definitor, 1758-1761 ; titular Guardian of Cambridge, 1761-1764 ; Preses of Hexham in 1764 ; Definitor, 1764-

1767 ; titular Guardian of Canterbury, 1767-1770 ; Definitor, 1770-1773; titular Guardian of Newcastle, 1773-1776; Preses of White Hill in 1776, when he was declared a jubilarian. He died in England in 1777 or 1778.

YATES, DANIEL, A S. JOANNE, was approved for preaching and hearing confessions in 1637, and also appointed confessor of the nuns of the Third Order, then at Brussels. The following year he was approved for the mission. He was titular Guardian of Leicester in 1640 ; and of Worcester, 1647-1650 ; Definitor, 1650-1653; elected Provincial in 1653. He died in 1659 or 1660.

YOUNG, ANTHONY, A S. FRANCISCO, was approved for preaching and hearing confessions, and also for the mission, in 1674. He was titular Guardian of Canterbury, 1683-1686; and again 1698-1701 ; titular Guardian of Worcester in 1702; and of Oxford, 1704-1707. He died on the English mission in 1712 or 1713.

———

The following are the real names or aliases of some of the Religious described above; but there are not sufficient indications to show who they are.

HOUGHTON, MR., was at West Grinstead in 1758, when Father Placid Payne was at Highden. (*Father Felix Englefield's list.*)

MIDDLETON, F. This name only occurs once, in the year 1701. It may have been an alias for Francis Hardwick.

RIGBY, JAMES, born in 1705, was admitted at the English College, Rome, in 1724, and ordained priest in 1730. Shortly afterwards he went to Douai, where he entered the Franciscan Order, on November 20 of the same year. (*Records of the English Province S.J.*)

. SEYES, alias LAMBERT, ROGER, a native of Glamorgan, brought up a Protestant, became a convert to the Catholic Church in his youth. He was admitted at the English College, Rome, in 1617, and ordained priest on May 16, 1622. He entered the Franciscan Order at the friary of St. Peter in Montorio, Rome, on the feast of the Stigmata, 1622, and after some months left for (Douai) Belgium. (*Records of the English Province S.J.*)

It seems not improbable that he is the same as BERNARDINE DE SENIS.

VAVASOUR, FRANCIS, of an old Catholic family, son of Thomas Vavasour, who was created a baronet in 1628, and had thirteen children. Francis became a Franciscan at Douai, and had died a holy death before the year 1672. (*Records of the English Province S.J.; Troubles*, p. 459.)

We meet sometimes with other names in the seventeenth century to which is added " Franciscan," or " Grey Friar : " we may safely assume that, except in case of an alias, it is a mistake.

PROVINCIAL SUPERIORS, FROM THE YEAR 1600

1601. William Staney, Commissary for England.
1618. John Gennings, Vicar of England.
1625. John Gennings, Custos.
1630. John Gennings, Provincial.
1637. Francis a S. Clara (Davenport), Provincial.
1640. George Perrot, Provincial.
1643. John Gennings, Provincial.
1647. Jerome Pickford, Provincial.
1650. Francis a S. Clara, Provincial.
1653. Daniel Yates, Provincial.
1656. George Perrot, Provincial.
1659. Angelus a S. Francisco (Mason), Provincial.
1662. Nicholas Cross, Provincial.
1665. Francis a S. Clara, Provincial.
1668. Daniel Clay, Provincial.
1671. Nicholas Cross, Provincial.
1674. John Cross, Provincial.
1677. Daniel Clay, Provincial.
1680. Nicholas Cross, Provincial.
1683. Gervase Cartwright, Provincial.
1686. John Cross, Provincial.
1689. Nicholas Cross, Provincial.
1691. Masseus Massey, Vicar Provincial.
1692. Masseus Massey, Provincial.
1695. Pacificus Price, Provincial.
1698. Anthony Le Grand, Provincial.
1699. Masseus Massey, Vicar Provincial.
1701. Bonaventure Parry, Provincial.

1704.   Pacificus Price, Provincial.
1706.   Lewis Grimbalson, Vicar Provincial.
1707.   Martin Grimston, Provincial.
1710.   Angelus Fortescue, Provincial.
1713.   Anthony Parkinson, Provincial.
1716.   Bernardine Smith, Provincial.
1719.   Bernard Baskerville, Provincial.
1722.   Anthony Parkinson, Provincial.
1725.   Philip Sadler, Provincial.
1728.   Joseph Pulton, Provincial.
1731.   John Capistran Eyston, Provincial.
1732.   Philip Sadler, Vicar Provincial.
1733.   Bruno Cantrill, Vicar Provincial.
1734.   Bruno Cantrill, Provincial.
1737.   Joseph Pulton, Provincial.
1740.   Thomas Holmes, Provincial.
1743.   Bruno Cantrill, Provincial.
1746.   Joseph Pulton, Provincial.
1748.   Thomas Holmes, Vicar Provincial.
1749.   Thomas Holmes, Provincial.
1752.   Alexius Smallwood, Provincial.
1755.   Felix Englefield, Provincial.
1758.   Thomas Holmes, Provincial.
1761.   Pacificus Baker, Provincial.
1764.   Philip André, Provincial.
1767.   Joachim Ingram, Provincial.
1770.   Pacificus Baker, Provincial.
1773.   Bonaventure Healy, Provincial.
1776.   Joseph Needham, Provincial.
1779.   Romanus Chapman, Provincial.
1782.   Peter Frost, Provincial.
1785.   Pacificus Nutt, Provincial.
1788.   Romanus Chapman, Provincial.
1791.   Bonaventure Pilling, Provincial.

1794. Pacificus Nutt, Provincial.
1799. Nicholas Knight, Vicar Provincial.
1800. Nicholas Knight, Provincial.
1803. James Howse, Provincial.
1806. Bernardine Collingridge, Provincial.
1807. Augustine Roberts, Vicar Provincial.
1809. Stephen Grafton, Provincial.
1812. Lawrence Hawley, Provincial.
1815. Francis McDonnell, Provincial.
1818. Augustine Roberts, Provincial.
1820. Stephen Grafton, Vicar Provincial.
1821. Francis McDonnell, Provincial.
1824. Ignatius Richards, Provincial.
1827. Francis McDonnell, Vicar Provincial.
1830. Stephen Grafton, Vicar Provincial.
1832. Francis McDonnell, Provincial.
1838. Leo Edgeworth, Provincial (minus canonice).
1839. Francis Hendren, Commissary.
1841. The Vicar Apostolic of the Welsh District, Bishop Brown, appointed Visitor Apostolic of the English Recollects.

EPILOGUE.

It was a fine summer evening in 1848. A carriage drove smartly through the dusty streets of Taunton, towards the Franciscan Convent, at the far end of the town.

The visitor was evidently expected, for the Sisters, with the children arranged in due order, had held themselves in readiness for some time. "There he is!" they whispered at last; the door of the carriage was thrown open, and the aged and saintly Bishop of Liége, Cornelius van Bommel, stepped out. When the blessing had been given and received in respectful silence, the air rang with joyous peals of welcome.

"My Lord," said the Mother Abbess, "it is extremely kind of you to come to see us, after the long journey you had undertaken to assist at the opening of St. George's Cathedral."

The Bishop replied: "I could not well decline coming to the inauguration of what was once 'the Belgian Chapel.' * And, after that, I could not forego the pleasure of coming a little further, to see the nuns of the Third Order of the great St. Francis, for whom I have always cherished a special veneration."

"Half a century has passed, my Lord," explained Mother Abbess, "since we had to leave your country, where we, as well as our Fathers, had been so hospitably received, and spent many a happy and peaceful day. And now we are doubly glad to welcome you, as the Pastor of the diocese

* See early numbers of the English Catholic Directory.

where our fathers found a shelter, when they were expelled from Douai."

"They would have found a lasting home with us," said the bishop, "had not the French come to continue in Catholic Belgium also their disgraceful work of profanation and destruction."

"Alas!" exclaimed the Abbess, "we have lost nearly all our fathers. Scarce half-a-dozen remain: they are getting old, scattered over the country, and there is no hope of their recruiting new members. I wish our Holy Father St. Francis would come to our assistance. But, my Lord, have you any Franciscans in your diocese?"

"Oh yes!" answered the Prelate, "there are in my diocese three Franciscan friaries, which the Fathers have recovered since the French Revolution.* The Franciscans are multiplying rapidly in Belgium, and considering that it is not much more than a dozen years since they were allowed by the law to live in community, their increase is most wonderful."

"Will your Lordship excuse me," pleaded the Abbess, for making so free as to ask what kind of men they are?"

"They are very exemplary," the Bishop explained, "and a source of edification to the faithful, and among them many learned and holy men. But, Mother Abbess, you ought to know them, for they are the very Fathers that lived side by side with the English Franciscans before the Revolution. When religious Houses were allowed to be reopened, a handful of veterans, who had survived the storms of fifty years, returned to their old homes. I have been told of one of those good old Franciscans,† that he was often seen kissing the steps that lead to the choir."

* St. Trond, founded A.D. 1220; Hasselt, A.D. 1634; Reckheim, A.D. 1707.

† Father James Vergauwen.

"My Lord!" exclaimed the Abbess, "send us a few of those men!"

"Now, Mother Abbess," said the Bishop, "you know that you are asking something which is beyond my power. But for the love of dear St. Francis I promise you that I shall do what I can in the matter. And if I fail to succeed, it will not be my fault." *

The Bishop was as good as his word. On his return to Belgium he went straight to the Provincial, and succeeded so well in persuading him, that he lost no time in calling his Definitory together, and laying the matter before them. And they, as zealous children of St. Francis, consented to undertake the arduous task. Ten years, however, were still to elapse before all the arrangements were completed, and the fathers came.

But the record of their labours and vicissitudes must be left to another chronicler.

* Bishop Hendren, O.S.F., also took a great interest in the project.

THE END.

INDEX.

—

Note.—The headings of Residences, pp. 135-189, and of Members of the Second English Franciscan Province pp. 191-328, are not inserted here, as they are arranged alphabetically. The numbers indicate the pages.

www.ingramcontent.com/pod-product-compliance
Lightning Source LLC
Chambersburg PA
CBHW021709110726
47902CB00005B/1123